The
Black
1 0 0

The
Black
1 0 0

A Ranking of the
Most Influential
African-Americans,
Past and Present

REVISED AND UPDATED

Columbus Salley

A Citadel Press Book
Published by Carol Publishing Group

A Citadel Press Book
Published by Carol Publishing Group
Citadel Press is a registered trademark of Carol Communications,
Inc.

Editorial, sales and distribution, and rights and permissions
inquiries should be addressed to Carol Publishing Group, 120
Enterprise Avenue, Secaucus, N.J. 07094.

In Canada: Canadian Manda Group, One Atlantic Avenue, Suite
105, Toronto, Ontario M6K 3E7

Carol Publishing Group books may be purchased in bulk at special
discounts for sales promotion, fund-raising, or educational
purposes. Special editions can be created to specifications. For
details, contact Special Sales Department, Carol Publishing
Group, 120 Enterprise Avenue, Secaucus, N.J. 07094.

Manufactured in the United States of America
10 9 8 7 6 5 4 3 2 1

Library of Congress Cataloging-in-Publication Data

Salley, Columbus.
    The Black 100 : a ranking of the most influential African-
Americans, past and present / Columbus Salley.—Rev. and
updated.
        p.   cm.
    "A Citadel Press book."
    Includes bibliographical references (p.   ) and index.
    ISBN 0–8065–2048–5 (pbk.)
    1. Afro-Americans—Biography.   2. Afro-Americans—History.
I. Title.
E185.96.S225   1998
973'.0496073—dc21   94–47713
                                                              CIP

To Vurnetha Redd Salley Donley and Richard Paul Proctor Sr., who were a strong black woman and a strong black man, respectively, in our continuous struggle *to be*.

And to Zachary Alexander C. Salley, who, it is hoped, will help lead a generation of those who will tear aside the veil of color-conscious racism for all Americans in the next millenium: The problem of the twenty-first century is the color-line!

A STRUGGLE TO BE

a collective contribution
to a singular focus:
FREEDOM...
no shuffling here
just traveling forward
on a well-traveled road
of deferred dreams and conscious nightmares
of "new day" gains and "jim crow" losses

no half-stepping here
just making strides
milestone after milestone
heading toward EQUALITY...

with all deliberate speed

—*Marvin W. Wyche, Jr.*

CONTENTS

CONTENTS

ACKNOWLEDGMENTS

I would like to thank the following colleagues, who helped me flesh out the original concept of *The Black 100* through stimulating dialogue and often heated debate: Robert Taylor, Marvin Wyche, and Hubert Williams, who also acted as a battering ram for disparate opinions and ideas.

This book would not have been possible without the contributions of the following, who acted as project associates by providing source documents and singular perspectives (of course, if discrepant data and errors exist, they are mine alone): Resa Proctor-Lassiter, who critiqued the different versions of the vignettes throughout the editorial process; Robert A. Gumbs, who did the main photographic research and served as my conceptual alter ego; Virginia Salas, who typed the many drafts of the original manuscript; Christopher W. C. Salley, who provided invaluable historical perspectives that were often like a two-edged sword; and Jennifer Lynn Salley, who provided support and encouragement from the beginning of this project.

Gil Noble and Carmen J. Smith of WABC-TV's *Like It Is* were extremely helpful in making one of the most valuable video archives extant on the African-American experience available to me.

John Russell Houston of Nippy, Inc., is appreciated as a sage and as an example of the persistence of strong black men *to be*.

I would like to thank the staff of the Newark, New Jersey, Public Library and Jim Huffman and the staff of the Schomburg Center for Research in Black Culture in Harlem for documents and materials that have helped "to restore what slavery took away...."

I would especially like to thank Gary Fitzgerald of Carol Publishing for his assistance and encouragement throughout the many drafts of this manuscript and for becoming my editorial alter ego during this project, and Donald J. Davidson for his helpful insights.

This edition of *The Black 100* includes OPRAH WINFREY [89], AUGUST WILSON [96], and ARTHUR ASHE [98]. Each meets the criteria of influence in the continuous struggle of African Americans *to be*, as detailed in the Introduction.

Like its previous edition, it's my hope that this updated edition of *The Black 100* will get us Americans—black and nonblack—to dialogue with one another about the singular struggle of African Americans *to be* in a color-conscious global village.

Columbus Salley
Newark, New Jersey

INTRODUCTION

> When the history books are written in future generations, the
> historians will have to pause and say, "There lived a great
> people—a black people—who injected new meaning and
> dignity into the veins of civilization."
>
> Dr. Martin Luther King, Jr.

The Black 100 is not a history book per se nor am I an historian or
historiographer per se. Notwithstanding, *The Black 100* is offered as a
set of confirmable historical perspectives on the lives of influential
Americans of African descent who have "injected new meaning and
dignity into the veins of civilization" and America. They have accomplished this through their ongoing struggle to realize full citizenship in a
society made racist by its declaration of the equal rights of all
Americans, yet its simultaneous denial of those rights to people of
African descent.

The Premise of the Black 100

Although the history of blacks in the so-called New World began
arguably centuries before John Rolfe's report in 1620 of "twenty and odd
Negroes" being sold as indentured servants in Jamestown, Virginia, in
August, 1619,* the timeline utilized in *The Black 100* for looking at the
continuous struggle of African-Americans for full freedom and equality
is roughly from 1619 to 1992.

The eighty-one men and twenty-one women listed and ranked in

---

*See Jackson's *Man, God and Civilization*, Ben-Jochannan's *Africa: Mother of
Western Civilization*, Davis's *Slavery and Human Progress*, and Toppin's *A Biog-
raphical History of Blacks in America Since 1528* for further discussion on the
African past and presence in the New World, i.e., North, South, and Central
Americas and the Caribbean before Columbus and the English-speaking colonists at
Jamestown.

*The Black 100** have met the following definition and criteria of influence on the black struggle: Black influentials are those who by their individual or institutional personas and efforts have had the greatest influence on Americans of African descent in their struggle for full economic, political, and social equality in American life; and who have influenced nonblack people to alter their institutions or practices toward blacks, so as to accept their demands for equality.

Although the author is not unfamiliar with scientific methods and quantitative procedures,† the rankings of these influentials are not to be taken as scientific or quantitative. The rankings reflect the author's evaluation of the above criteria when looking at the ongoing struggle of blacks *to be* and my judgments of the relative impact of each of *The Black 100* on that struggle. Further, the rankings are intended to provide a more expansive set of insights into the interrelationships of *The Black 100*—and millions of others—to the struggle of blacks *to be whatever they choose*, i.e., Democrat or Republican, separatist or integrationist, conservative or liberal, radical or moderate, or whatever combination of these and other ideologies or lifestyles one cares to identify.

The Black 100 is *not* a debate on the most talented, most famous, or most popular black Americans, past and present, but is rather a listing and ranking of those Americans of African descent who in the view of the author have had the most impact on the lives of generations— millions upon millions—of blacks in their singular struggle for full equality and participation in American life and ultimately their struggle *to be*.

A biographical sketch or vignette is provided for each of *The Black 100*, justifying and supporting his or her listing and ranking. A given ranking is not meant to diminish or slight the contributions of others, below or above. To better understand a given influential, the reader is encouraged to read each of the epigraphs that accompanies the sketch or vignette; they are integral to the understanding of that listing and ranking.

---

*A total of 102 black influentials results from three pairs being listed and ranked as one: Richard Allen and Absalom Jones [6], Samuel Cornish and John Russwurm [8] and Ruby Dee and Ossie Davis [91]. Black Power [99] is a concept or assertion, not, obviously, a person.

†See my research on the school principalship and the school superintendency: "What Principals Do: A Preliminary Occupational Analysis" [with others] (Berkeley, 1978) and "Superintendents' Job Priorities" (Chicago, 1980).

The reader is discouraged from concluding that a given influential ranked higher is qualitatively better than someone ranked below them. For example, DR. MARTIN LUTHER KING, JR., [1] is not to be viewed as 100 times better than ROSA PARKS [100], who midwifed the very civil rights revolution led by King. Indisputably, King had *more influence* on the ongoing black struggle than Parks and, in my view, had more influence than all of the others listed and ranked in this volume.

These listings and rankings attempt to show the interrelatedness of *The Black 100* as the collective giant on whose shoulders African-Americans stand in their unending quest for full economic, political, and social equality. This view will demonstrate the insight of the words spoken by A. PHILIP RANDOLPH [31] about the initiatives and courage of those listed in *The Black 100*: "The task of realizing full citizenship for the Negro people is largely in the hands of the Negro people themselves. . . . Freedom is never given; it is won. And the Negro people must win their freedom. They must achieve justice. This involves struggle, continuous struggle."

After reading *The Black 100*, the reader is encouraged to identify his or her own list of black influentials and to rank them according to his or her own criteria of influence on the continuous struggle of blacks *to be*; the result of such a process might just corroborate more similarities with *The Black 100* than not. When all is discussed and debated about *The Black 100*, the author's ultimate goal will have been served if we as a people—blacks and nonblacks—start talking to one another again about "a great people—a black people—who injected new meaning and dignity into the veins of civilization" and America.

To Americans of African descent, in particular, *The Black 100* is offered as a compendium of our history for helping to get our consciousness—often ahistoric, "Kente cloth" dominated, "X"–T-shirted and -capped—refocused on a struggle that can and must be won, only by rediscovering our past. JOHN HOPE FRANKLIN [74] has said on this point, "If the house is to be set in order, one cannot begin with the present, [we] must begin with the past."

The
Black
1 0 0

1

Rev. Dr. Martin Luther King, Jr.

1929–1968

I do not oppose the efforts of those who endeavor to instill into the Negro a genuine belief in the brotherhood of man and the superiority of moral force. But suppose there should arise a Gandhi to lead Negroes without hate in their hearts to stop tilling the fields of the South under the peonage system; to cease paying taxes to States that keep their children in ignorance; and to ignore the iniquitous disenfranchisement and Jim Crow laws. I fear we would witness an unprecedented massacre of defenseless black men and women in the name of Law and Order and there would scarcely be enough Christian sentiment in America to stay the flood of blood.

E. Franklin Frazier

But when the fulness of the time was come, God sent forth...

Galatians 4:4

The quintessential leader of the African-American unending quest for full economic, political, and social equality was Martin Luther King, Jr. "He became the symbol not only of the civil rights movement but of America itself," said James H. Cone, "a symbol of the land of freedom where people of all races, creeds, and nationalities could live together as a 'beloved community.'" Martin Luther King, Jr., became E. Franklin Frazier's prophesied "Gandhi," with a "belief in the brotherhood of man and the superiority of moral force."

Born on January 15, 1929, in Atlanta, Georgia, Michael (later changed to Martin) Luther King, Jr., was heir to a tradition—through his grandfather and father—of the black church as a source of leadership and as a tool of protest for the equal rights and justice for African-Americans. It was Dr. Martin Luther King, Jr.'s vision of "the brother-

3

hood of man," his ability to link or fuse the black church to the historic struggle of blacks for freedom and equality in America, and his skills in using and manipulating "the fulness of time"—media technology—that make him the most influential African-American, past and present.

Lerone Bennett's perceptive observations on this fusion during the Montgomery bus boycott that began on December 5, 1955, are instructive:

> By superimposing the image of the black preacher on the image of Gandhi, by adding songs and symbols with concrete significance to black America, King transformed a spontaneous local protest into a national passive resistance movement with a method and ideology. "Love your enemies," he said, and tens of thousands of blacks straightened their backs and sustained a yearlong bus boycott which was, as King pointed out, "one of the greatest [movements] in the history of the nation." The movement brought together laborers, professionals and students. More importantly perhaps, it fired the imagination of blacks all over America. . . . Skillfully utilizing the resources of television and mass journalism, King made Montgomery an international way station.

After the Montgomery bus boycott, and for nearly seven years thereafter, King and other civil rights leaders led boycotts, sit-ins and marches throughout the North and South. Also during this time, in 1957, Dr. King and his associates organized the Southern Christian Leadership Conference (SCLC). On April 3, 1963—in the year of the centennial of the Emancipation Proclamation—Dr. King carried his "gospel of freedom" and nonviolence to Birmingham, Alabama, a bastion of segregation in the South and a symbol of America's resistance to blacks' "constitutional and God-given rights." A little more than a week later, in defiance of an injunction barring protest marches, Dr. King led a mass march in which he confronted the archetype of segregation, Police Commissioner Eugene "Bull" Connor. He was arrested with about fifty demonstrators. From his jail cell, he issued his famous "Letter From a Birmingham Jail," which pricked forever the conscience of America. Detailing his moral mission and the urgency for "justice now," Dr. King's letter also speaks to the need to create crisis and "creative tension" in America until it accepted black demands for equality:

Just as Socrates felt that it was necessary to create a tension in the mind so that individuals could rise from the bondage of myths and half-truths to the unfettered realm of creative analysis and objective appraisal, we must see the need of having non-violent gadflies to create the kind of tension in society that will help men rise from the dark depths of prejudice and racism to the majestic heights of understanding and brotherhood. So the purpose of direct action is to create a situation so crisis-packed that it will inevitably open the doors to negotiations.

Later in the Birmingham campaign, Dr. King once again showed himself master tactician and media manipulator by strategically committing schoolchildren and youths to the struggle against "Bull" Connor, policemen with man-eating dogs, and firemen with hoses poised to wash them away like debris. In full view of the media (electronic and print), the sights and sounds of boys and girls being attacked by dogs and white policemen, and being swept away by high-powered hoses, made Birmingham "an international way station" to millions upon millions of television viewers and newspaper readers. "He got his dogs but it wasn't long before 'Bull' Connor discovered," Dr. King would say, reflecting on this aspect of the campaign, "that we had something within that dogs couldn't bite. . . . He got his firehoses. But it wasn't long after that that he discovered that we had a fire shut up in our bones that water couldn't put out. . . . He got his paddy-wagons but it wasn't long after that he discovered that we had numbers that paddy-wagons couldn't hold. . . . He took us to his jails and it wasn't long after that before he called the City Jail of Birmingham, the County Jail, the Fairfield Jail, the Bessamer Jail and the Bessamer fair grounds and they were filled up with Negroes and there were 2,000 more ready to go to jail."

The zenith of Dr. King's influence on the civil rights movement and America came during a speech at the March on Washington on August 28, 1963, when more than 250,000 persons, whites and blacks, poor and rich, laborers and managers, students and professionals, assembled (with millions upon millions watching on television) for the largest civil rights demonstration in the history of the republic.

Dr. King's "I Have a Dream" speech pointed to the primeval dream and affirmation of America and its original sin and contradiction—chattel slavery and racial intolerance:

I have a dream that one day this nation will rise up and live out the true meaning of its creed: "We hold these truths to be self-evident; that all men are created equal." I have a dream that one day on the red hills of Georgia the sons of former slaves and the sons of former slaveholders will be able to sit down together at the table of brotherhood. . . .

This will be the day when all of God's children will be able to sing with new meaning, "My country 'tis of thee, sweet land of liberty of thee I sing. Land where my fathers died, land of the pilgrims' pride, from every mountainside, let freedom ring. . . .

When we let freedom ring, when we let it ring from every village and hamlet, from every state and every city, we will be able to speed up the day when all of God's children, black men and white men, Jews and Gentiles, Protestants and Catholics, will be able to join hands and sing in the words of the old Negro spiritual: "Free at last! Free at last! Thank God Almighty, we are free at last."

Dr. Martin Luther King at the March on Washington, 1963.

The March on Washington and the "I Have a Dream" speech marked the crossing of the Rubicon in the African-American quest for equality in America. The impact of Dr. King as "a symbol of the civil rights movement and America itself" can be seen in the ratification of the Twenty-Fourth Amendment to the U.S. Constitution, which removed poll tax requirements for voting in federal elections; the 1964 Civil Rights Act, which acknowledged blacks' rights in public accommodations and to fair employment conditions; the 1965 Voting Rights Act, which did away with literacy tests and other arbitrary barriers to voting; and the conferring of the Nobel Peace Prize on Dr. King in December 1964. The latter not only gave recognition to Dr. King as *the* influential figure of the civil rights movement in America but also brought legitimacy to the human rights struggle throughout the world, a world fast becoming a "global village." Dr. King, reflecting on the Nobel Peace Prize in 1967, provided a sobering perspective on its meaning: "Another burden of responsibility was placed upon me in 1964, and I cannot forget that the Nobel Peace Prize was not just something taking place, but it was a commission—a commission to work harder than I had ever worked before for the brotherhood of man."

This commitment to the "brotherhood of man" obliged King to condemn America's role in the Vietnam War:

> I speak out against this war not in anger, but with anxiety and sorrow in my heart and, above all, with a passionate desire to see our beloved country stand as a moral example to the world. I speak out against this war because I am disappointed with America. There can be no great disappointment where there is no great love. I am disappointed with our failure to deal positively and forthrightly with the triple evils of racism, economic exploitation and militarism.

"When Dr. King denounces unjust and aggressive wars," Herbert Aptheker observed, "he is acting in the grand tradition of this nation's noblest souls and in the tradition of the finest Negro men and women of the past. . . . When Dr. King affirms that the present war in Vietnam threatens all democratic and progressive advances in the United States and does so for economic, political, ethical and psychological reasons, again he is saying what every fact and every day's events confirm. Hence Dr. King, precisely as a leader in the struggle against Jim Crow and against the ghetto, must be—and is—a leader in the struggle against war."

Dr. King's "struggle against war" took him on the global stage. Yet it was his persistent struggle against one of the triple evils—economic exploitation—that brought him and his movement to Memphis, Tennessee, in March 1968 to support striking sanitation workers. On April 4, 1968, he was shot down by a white assassin's bullet on a balcony at the Lorraine Motel.

Dr. King's last sermon, played at his funeral, is not only a fitting tribute to his life, but also a declaration of his influence on the African-American struggle and experience in America and, thus, the struggle of humankind against injustice:

> If any of you are around when I have to meet my death, I don't want a long speech. And if you get somebody to deliver the eulogy, tell him not to talk long. Every now and then I wonder what I want him to say. Tell him not to mention that I have the Nobel Peace Prize, that isn't important.
>
> Tell him not to mention that I have 300 or 400 other awards. That's not important. Tell him not to mention where I went to school. I'd like somebody to mention that day that Martin Luther King, Jr., tried to get his life further up. I'd like for somebody to say that day that Martin Luther King, Jr., tried to love somebody....
>
> I want you to be able to say that day that I did try to feed the hungry. I want you to be able to say that day that I did try in my life to clothe those who were naked. I want you to say on that day that I did try in my life to visit those who were imprisoned.
>
> I want you to say that I tried to love and serve humanity. Yes, if you want to say that I was a drum major, say that I was a drum major for justice. Say that I was a drum major for peace, I was a drum major for righteousness, and all of the other shallow things will not matter. I won't have any money to leave behind. I won't have the fine and luxurious things of life to leave behind. But I just want to leave a committed life behind. And that's all I want to say. If I can help somebody as I pass along, if I can cure somebody with a love song, if I can show somebody he's traveling wrong, then my living will not be in vain. If I can do my duty as a Christian, if I can bring salvation to a world enslaved, if I can spread the message of the master, then my living will not be in vain.

2

Frederick Douglass

1817–1895

Slavery, in whatever point of light it is considered, is repugnant
to the feelings of nature, and inconsistent with the original
rights of man. It ought, therefore, to be stigmatized for being
unnatural; and detested for being unjust.
"OTHELLO"
ANONYMOUS BLACK ORATOR/WRITER

An aspect of the repugnancy of slavery is visualized through the words
of Frederick Augustus Washington Bailey (changed to Frederick Douglass in 1841) in his uncertainty about when he was born:

The reader must not expect me to say much of my family. Genealogical trees did not flourish among slaves. A person of some consequence in civilized society, sometimes designated as father, was literally unknown to slave law and slave practice. I never met with a slave in that part of the country who could tell me with any certainty how old he was. Few at that time knew anything of the months of the year or of the days of the month. They measured the ages of their children by spring-time, winter-time, harvest-time, planting-time, and the like. Masters allowed no questions to be put to them by slaves concerning their ages. Such questions were regarded by the masters as evidence of an impudent curiosity. From certain events, however, the dates of which I have since learned, I suppose myself to have been born in February, 1817.

Douglass's mother was an African slave and his father was an unknown white man. He was born in Tuckahoe, Talbot County, Maryland, within a month of the most significant meeting held by blacks in Philadelphia under the leadership of JAMES FORTEN [11] to protest the attempts of the American Colonization Society to remove blacks from America.

Douglass escaped from slavery in 1838, and in the summer of 1841, in Nantucket, Massachusetts, he was introduced to a convention of the American Anti-Slavery Society and to William Lloyd Garrison—the most prominent white abolitionist of his time—by abolitionist John A. Collins as a "graduate from the peculiar institution, with his diploma written on his back." Douglass would later characterize the society as "the Garrison School of reformers, a school through which I have passed, a school which has many good qualities, but a school too narrow in its philosophy and too bigoted in spirit to do justice to any who venture to differ from it."

With the "diploma written on his back," Frederick Douglass became the most influential and eloquent advocate-protester-agitator of his time. He became the emblem of a generation of African-Americans who continued to protest, resist, and struggle against slavery—and its mutant social and political evils in America—as their ancestors had done from slavery's inception in both America and Africa. It was "a struggle that Africans had waged in Africa," as Leonard Jeffries described the continuum of African resistance, "a struggle waged in the slave ships, a struggle they waged as they crossed in the Middle Passage." Douglass for over fifty years struggled against slavery and the slave trade in America, with brilliant "oratory of defiance," as in his July 5, 1852, speech at Rochester, New York:

There is not a nation on the face of the Earth guilty of practices more shocking and bloody than the people of the United States at this very hour. Take the American slave trade,which we are told by the paper is especially prosperous just now. We are told the price of men was never higher than now. In several of our states this trade is a chief source of wealth. It is called the "internal slave trade." It is probably called so, too, in order to divert from it the horrors with which the foreign slave trade is contemplated. Now that trade has long since been denounced by this government as piracy, but it is a notable fact that, while so much execration is poured out upon all those engaged in the foreign slave trade, those others engaged in the slave trade between the states pass without condemnation and their business is deemed honorable.

Behold the practical operation of this internal slave trade—the American slave trade, sustained by American politics and American religion. Here you will see men, women and children reared like swine for the market. Do you know what is a swine drive? I will show you a man driver. You will see one of these human flesh jabbers armed with pistol whip and, boy, lash-driving a company of 100 men, women and children from the Potomac to the slave market of New Orleans. These wretched people are to be sold singly or in lots to suit purposes. They are food for the cotton field and the deadly sugar mill. Mark the sad procession as it moves wearily along and that inhuman wretch who drives them. . . .

Tell me citizens, where on Earth can you witness a spectacle more fiendish and shocking?! And this is but a glance at the American slave trade as it exists at this very moment in the ruling part of the United States.

Douglass identified the parameters of the struggle for equality of African-Americans in a famous speech in Canandaigua, New York, on August 4, 1857:

If there is no struggle there is no progress. . . . This struggle
may be a moral one, or it may be a physical one, and it may
be both moral and physical, but it must be a struggle. Power
concedes nothing without demand. It never did and it never
will. Find out just what any people will quietly submit to and
you have found out the exact measure of injustice and wrong
which will be imposed upon them, and these will continue
till they are resisted with either words or blows, or with both.
The limits of tyrants are prescribed by the endurance of those
whom they oppress.

"I say at once, in peace and in war," Frederick Douglass asserted,
"I am content with nothing for the black man short of equal and exact
justice." During the abolitionist period, the Civil War, Reconstruction,
and until his death on February 20, 1895, no single black American
before Dr. Martin Luther King, Jr., had more influence or impact on
bringing about "equal and exact justice" for African-Americans than
Frederick Douglass.

PROSPECTUS

FOR AN ANTI-SLAVERY PAPER, TO BE ENTITLED

NORTH STAR.

FREDERICK DOUGLASS

Proposes to publish, in ROCHESTER, N. Y., a **WEEKLY ANTI-SLAVERY
PAPER**, with the above title.

The object of the NORTH STAR will be to attack SLAVERY in all its forms and
aspects; advocate UNIVERSAL EMANCIPATION; exalt the standard of PUBLIC MORALITY; promote the Moral and Intellectual Improvement of the COLORED PEOPLE; and hasten
the day of FREEDOM to the Three Millions of our ENSLAVED FELLOW COUNTRYMEN.

The Paper will be printed upon a double medium sheet, at $2,00 per annum, if paid
in advance, or $2,50, if payment be delayed over six months.

The names of Subscribers may be sent to the following named persons, and should be
forwarded, as far as practicable, by the first of November, proximo.

FREDERICK DOUGLASS, Lynn, Mass.   JOEL P. DAVIS, Economy, Wayne County, Ind.
SAMUEL BROOKE, Salem, Ohio.   CHRISTIAN DONALDSON, Cincinnati, Ohio.
M. R. DELANY, Pittsburgh, Pa.   J. M M'KIM, Philadelphia, Pa.
VALENTINE NICHOLSON, Harveysburgh, Warren Co. O.   AMARANCY PAINE, Providence, R. I.
Mr. WALCOTT, 21 Cornhill, Boston.   Mr. GAY, 142 Nassau Street, New York.

| SUBSCRIBERS' NAMES. | RESIDENCE. | NO. OF COPIES. |

Douglass's ranking here further highlights the difficulties of "weighting" his "influence" to that of Dr. King or others who lived during different periods or eras of the black struggle in America. Admittedly, a good deal of Dr. King's impact was due to the development of media technologies which were nonexistent during Douglass's time; however, when one attempts to "equalize" for these differences, Dr. King's ranking over Douglass is still warranted because of his direct link, as a preacher, to an institution that affected the vast majority of black lives in America: the black church.

Frederick Douglass was the first "African-American to meet with a President of the United States," Herbert Aptheker said, "welcomed as a person and asked for his advice." The President was Abraham Lincoln. Douglass also assisted Lincoln in recruiting the 54th and 55th Massachusetts Negro Regiments.

"Measures" of his influence on black America and America were evinced by the popularity of his news publication, the *North Star*; during the Reconstruction period, his election as president of a national convention of African-American leaders in Washington, D.C., and being named president of the Freedmen's Bank; his being named by President Rutherford B. Hayes marshal of the District of Columbia (later he was appointed recorder of deeds); and his being named minister to Haiti and chargé d'affaires for Santo Domingo.

This matchless orator for "equal and exact justice" for African-Americans saw, in almost prophetic terms, the "Negro Question" as a larger issue of the condition of humankind:

One ground of hope is found and that is that discussion concerning the Negro still goes on. What Abraham Lincoln said of the United States is as true of the black people as of the relations of the states. They cannot remain half slaves and half free. You must give us all or take from us all. And until the half-and-half condition is ended, you will have an aggrieved class. And this discussion will go on until the public schools shall cease to be caste schools in every part of the country. This discussion will go on until the American people shall make character and not color the criterion of respectability. This discussion will go on. I want the whole American people to unite with the sentiment of their greatest captain, Ulysses S. Grant, and say with him on this subject, Lord, let us have peace. That it is idle—utterly idle—to dream of peace anywhere in this world while any part of the human family are the victims of marked injustice and oppression.

Douglass, also, throughout his life, championed and supported the cause of women's rights. He saw this cause, like the "Negro Question" as being linked to the "dream of peace anywhere." Thus, he devoted a good deal of his time to the cause of women's suffrage.

Douglass died at home in Washington, D.C., uttering to a young supporter and follower: "Agitate.... Agitate.... Agitate...."

3

Booker T. Washington

1856–1915

The wisest among my race understands that the agitation of
questions of social equality is the extremist folly, and that
progress in the enjoyment of all the privileges that will come to
us must be the result of severe and constant struggle rather than
of artificial forcing.

BOOKER T. WASHINGTON

The above words were spoken by Booker T. Washington approximately seven months after the death of Frederick Douglass. Part of his
"Atlanta Compromise" address on September 18, 1895, at the Cotton
States Exposition in Atlanta, they signaled a counterpoint in philosophy,
attitudes, and approaches to the black struggle and quest for equality in

America to that of Douglass and, later, to that of W. E. B. DU BOIS [4] over the next twenty years.

Biographer Genna Rae McNeil describes America during this period and the emergence of Booker T. Washington:

> In 1895—as in other years since Reconstruction—the months came and went with increasing pain to the spirits of Black Americans. Slavery had been replaced with tenancy, peonage, occupational ceilings for race and employment. Where once there had been promises and expressions of lofty ideals, the rhetoric of white supremacy rang, lynch mobs became self-appointed juries, disenfranchisement spread, the color line assumed greater national importance, and Booker T. Washington, white-ordained spokesman for the race emerged, preaching accommodation as the solutions to the "Negro Problem."

Booker Taliaferro Washington was born a slave on a plantation in Franklin County, Virginia. "As nearly as I have been able to learn, it was near a cross-road post-office called Hale's Ford," Washington said. "The year was 1858 or 1859. I do not know the month or the day." (Later research indicates that he was born April 5, 1856.)

In the fall of 1872, Washington started to attend Hampton Normal and Agricultural Institute in Virginia (Hampton Institute, founded in 1868). He finished his regular studies at Hampton in June 1875 and was hired in the fall of 1879 to teach Native American youths and later to direct a night school for young black men and women who worked during the day and attended school for two hours at night. In 1881, he became the president of Tuskegee Institute, which he and his associates built from a little shanty and church to a major educational institution for blacks to the "Tuskegee Movement": a set of policies, views, and tactics that projected Booker T. Washington as "the race leader" in dealing with the "Negro Problem," as his predominately white sponsors and supporters—North and South—saw it.

No matter what one might think of Washington as an accommodationist or "Uncle Tom" to white fears and interests regarding blacks or about the nobility or wisdom of his views and tactics regarding "industrial education," voting rights, civil rights, and equal educational opportunities, he was undeniably the most influential African-American leader of his day and is ranked here accordingly.

Beginning with his "Atlanta Compromise" address, and for the next twenty years until his death on November 14, 1915 (and even to this present day), Washington became a powerful symbol and interpreter of the black experience vis-à-vis blacks and nonblacks in America. His "cast down your bucket where you are" simile is both an often cited and misunderstood charge among black and white Americans. Disputes about the merits of this charge and its tactics aside, the facts are that Booker T. Washington met with and influenced presidents (Theodore Roosevelt and Grover Cleveland); he marshaled considerable finances from white backers of his day (Andrew Carnegie, William H. Baldwin, Julius Rosenwald, and others); he founded the influential National Negro Business League; and he outmaneuvered and outinfluenced— among the masses of blacks—the most eloquent and formidable of his contemporary opposition, W. E. B. Du Bois.

Washington's values, tactics, and motives were—and are—questioned and challenged, but he indisputably had a vision of a "free and united country." In his address at Harvard University in 1896, at which he received an honorary master of arts degree, Washington provided an epitaph to his own life and his views on the "struggle" for black equality in America:

> Tell them that the sacrifice was not in vain. Tell them that by habits of thrift and economy, by way of the industrial school and college, we are coming. We are crawling up, working up, yea, bursting up: often through oppression, unjust discrimination and prejudice, but through them all we are coming up, and with proper habits, intelligence and property, there is no power on earth that can permanently stay our progress.

4

W.E.B. Du Bois

1868 –1963

Du Bois was an agitator-prophet. He tore at the Veil; at the same time, behind that Veil, he had a particular perspective from which he saw this country and world, past, present and future.

HERBERT APTHEKER

This "agitator-prophet" was born William Edward Burghardt Du Bois, February 23, 1868, in Great Barrington, Massachusetts, during a vortex of change for African-Americans: approximately one month after constitutional conventions in Mississippi, Arkansas, North Carolina, and Florida that included blacks for the first time; five years after the

Emancipation Proclamation; five months before the ratification of the Fourteenth Amendment (the "due process" amendment); and six months before the death of Thaddeus Stevens, radical reconstruction Congressman from Pennsylvania.

After graduating from high school in Great Barrington—where he was the only African-American—Du Bois attended Fisk University (founded in 1866). In 1895, he became the first black person to receive a Ph.D. in the social sciences at Harvard University. His doctoral dissertation, *The Suppression of the African Slave Trade*, later became his first book—in 1896, the same year the U.S. Supreme Court ruled on *Plessy* v. *Ferguson*, which established the "separate but equal" treatment of blacks, ushering in the Jim Crow laws that would remain for the next sixty years.

In 1897 Du Bois became a professor of history and economics at Atlanta University (founded 1865) and taught there until 1910. During this period, he helped with the founding of the American Negro Academy (the first formal black intelligentsia group in America); wrote *The Souls of Black Folk* (seminal essays on the black experience, including his views on Booker T. Washington's tactics of accommodation and conciliation to whites); organized with WILLIAM M. TROTTER [28] and others the Niagara Movement (which later became the National Association for the Advancement of Colored People, the NAACP) as a counterpoint to the philosophy and practices of Booker T. Washington and the Tuskegee Movement; and published the first issue of *Crisis* (a monthly magazine addressing black issues and often featuring black writers and artists).

From 1910 to 1934, Du Bois was the most prominent and visible leader of the NAACP, as its director of research and publicity and as editor of *Crisis*. His effectiveness in these two roles alone would justify his ranking here among the most influential blacks of all time. As major spokesperson for the NAACP during this period, he directly confronted Booker T. Washington and his followers: "As to Mr. Washington, the people who think I am one of those who oppose many of his ideas are perfectly correct," Du Bois would say:

> I have no personal opposition to him—I honor much of his work. But his platform has done the race infinite harm and I'm working against it with all my might. Mr. Washington is today the chief instrument in the hands of the N.Y. clique who are seeking to syndicate the Negro and settle the

problem on the trust basis. They have bought and bribed
newspapers and men.

The much publicized and characterized observations of the polar-
ity between Washington and Du Bois don't begin to reveal the
substance of their differences as advocates of black equality or the
influence either had on black America or America and the world in
general. African-Americans, like all major ethnic groups, have had their
good leaders and bad leaders, their accommodators and radicals, their
"house niggers" and "field niggers" and their "Uncle Toms" and
"militants"; Du Bois and Washington were not the first to be characterized in these simplistic terms, for example, the radical Frederick
Douglass vs. a contemporary accommodator, Charles Lenox Redmond,
or, in modern times, the militant Malcolm X vs. the dreamer Dr. King.
Lerone Bennett insightfully describes the struggle between the Washington wing or faction and that of Du Bois:

W. E. B. Du Bois (second row, center) with some cofounders of the
Niagara Movement

The antagonism between the two wings is generally and inaccurately described as a struggle over industrial vs. higher education. But the core of the problem lay deeper than this. The whole controversy turned on leadership, not trade: on power, not education. To Washington's program of accommodation, Du Bois proposed a strategy of ceaseless agitation and insistent demand for equality [involving] the use of force of every sort: moral suasion, propaganda and where possible even physical resistance! He favored immediate social and political integration and higher education for a Talented Tenth of the black population. His main interest was in the education of the group leader, the man who sets the ideals of the community where he lives, directs its thoughts and heads its social movement. He therefore opposed Washington's exclusive stress on education of the hand and heart because without a "knowledge of modern culture, black Americans would have to accept white leadership, and...such leadership could not always be trusted to guide the Negro group into self-realization and to its highest cultural possibilities."

Although it can be concluded that Washington's views and tactics apparently prevailed over black and nonblack institutions in his day, it is equally true that Du Bois's views and tactics created a black intelligentsia that would "guide the Negro group into self-realization and its highest cultural possibilities."

This fact is the singular influence of Du Bois vis-à-vis African-Americans. Through *Crisis*, Du Bois helped and supported artists like Arna Bontemps, Langston Hughes, Countee Cullen, Marian Anderson, Jean Toomer, Claude McKay, and Alain Locke. It's not an exaggeration to say that Du Bois, Locke, and James Weldon Johnson were responsible for the flowering of black culture and art during the twenties and early thirties. Mislabeled the "Harlem Renaissance," it should more properly be called the "Negro or cultural Renaissance" because it occurred nationally (in Chicago, St. Louis, New York, Detroit, and other places).

Other "measures" of Du Bois's influence and impact on African-Americans, America, and the world are his numerous scholarly books, including two classics, *Black Reconstruction* and *The World and Africa*; his cofounding of the Pan-African Congress (1919) "for the future emancipation of the Africans in their own country"; his cochairing with PAUL ROBESON [24] the Council of African Affairs; and his chairing the

THE CRISIS

A RECORD OF THE DARKER RACES

Volume One   NOVEMBER, 1910   Number One

Edited by W. E. BURGHARDT DU BOIS, with the co-operation of Oswald Garrison Villard, J. Max Barber, Charles Edward Russell, Kelly Miller, W. S. Braithwaite and M. D. Maclean.

CONTENTS

Along the Color Line   3

Opinion   7

Editorial   10

The N. A. A. C. P.   12

Athens and Browns-
ville   13
By MOORFIELD STOREY

The Burden   .   .   .   14

What to Read   .   .   15

PUBLISHED MONTHLY BY THE
National Association for the Advancement of Colored People
AT TWENTY VESEY STREET   NEW YORK CITY

ONE DOLLAR A YEAR   TEN CENTS A COPY

Peace Information Center, an anti-atomic-bomb proliferation group. These later two associations in the early fifties made him the target of "Red baiting" and "witch hunting," which later were called "McCarthyism" (after U.S. Senator Joseph McCarthy, the fanatical anti-Communist during the cold war that began at the end of the second world war). Accused and acquitted, during the Truman administration, of being an unregistered foreign agent because of his peace activities, Du Bois decided in 1961 to go to Ghana at the behest of its president, Kwame Nkrumah, to edit the *Encyclopedia Africana*. Du Bois died in Ghana on August 27, 1963, on the eve of the momentous March on Washington. The torch had been passed to King!

5

Charles H. Houston

1895–1950

You have a large number of people who never heard of Charlie Houston. But you're going to hear about him, because he left us such important items.... When Brown against the Board of Education was being argued in the Supreme Court...[t]here were some dozen lawyers on the side of Negroes fighting for their schools.... [O]f those...lawyers...only two hadn't been touched by Charlie Houston.... [T]hat man was the engineer of all of it.... I can tell you this...if you do it legally, Charlie Houston made it possible.... This is what I think...Charlie Houston means to us.

THURGOOD MARSHALL

The legal engineer of the African-American quest for justice and equality in post-Reconstruction America, Charles Hamilton Houston was born September 3, 1895, in Washington D.C., fifteen days before Booker T. Washington's "Atlantic Compromise" address, nearly seven months after the death of Frederick Douglass and approximately eight months before *Plessy v. Ferguson*. These events and two personas would act as portents for the preoccupation of Houston's life: the struggle for justice and equality for black Americans—and all Americans—and his legacy as the architect of the modern civil rights legal attacks on the national policies of the United States that supported racial segregation and discrimination. Houston would become linked with the likes of Douglass and Du Bois, not with that of Washington; his life would be in the tradition of some of the earliest black petitioners for freedom who resisted the principles and practices of *Plessy v. Ferguson*, like those who pleaded to the governor and legislators of Massachusetts in 1774:

> That your Petitioners apprehind we have in common with all other men a Naturel right to our freedoms without Being depriv'd of them by our fellow men as we are a freeborn Pepel and have never forfeited this Blessing by aney compact or agreement whatever.... We therfor Bage your Excellency and Honours will give this its deer weight and consideration and that you will accordingly cause an act of the legislative to be pessed that we may obtain our Natural right our freedoms and our children be set a lebety....

Charles Hamilton Houston's grandparents were born to runaway slaves. His grandfather, Thomas Jefferson Houston, was a "conductor" on the Underground Railroad between Missouri and Illinois. His father, William Lepre Houston, was one of seven children. In 1890, after becoming a school principal for blacks in Paducah, Kentucky, William Houston moved to Washington, D.C., and became a clerk in the War Department Record and Pension Office and began legal studies at Howard University Evening Law Department. On July 16, 1891, William married Mary Ethel Hamilton, whom he had met while in Paducah.

Charles Hamilton Houston attended segregated elementary and secondary schools in Washington. He graduated from M Street High School (the first black high school in the United States, its name later changed to Paul Laurence Dunbar High School, which became a noted academic citadel for black youths). In June 1911, at the age of fifteen, Houston was admitted to Amherst College and, during his senior year, was elected to Phi Beta Kappa. He graduated in 1915—the year Booker T. Washington died—and delivered a commencement address on PAUL LAURENCE DUNBAR [18].

Houston began teaching at Howard University (established in 1867) as an English instructor in 1915. In 1917, he entered World War I as a commissioned first lieutenant in the segregated Seventeenth Provisional Training Regiment (Infantry) and later became a second lieutenant field artillery officer. "As a second lieutenant overseas, Charles Houston encountered racism, more virulent than he had ever known before," biographer Genna Rae McNeil said, "practiced by Red Cross workers, white enlisted men, and his fellow white officers.... Charles, like all the other black men in the American Expeditionary Forces, personally, suffered daily, arbitrary indignities and exposure to mortal danger. Talent, ability and character were of little significance; race set men apart from one another...."

In September 1919, during a year of extensive race riots and lynching of blacks, Houston entered Harvard Law School. While in his third year there, he became an editor of the distinguished *Harvard Law Review*. He received a doctor of juridical science degree from Harvard in 1923 and did post-doctoral work in civil law at the University of Madrid. He was admitted to the D.C. Bar in June 1924.

All of Charles Hamilton Houston's life, up to his appointment in 1924 as a faculty member of the Howard University Law School, could be considered a prologue to his struggle for justice and equality for blacks and all Americans. His influence and impact were to be felt when, in 1929, as vice dean, "he attempted to create a program that would demonstrate Howard Law School's societal significance and establish its excellence in education" (Howard was producing nearly 25 percent of the black law students in America during this time). Thurgood Marshall's "engineer" revolutionized the way black lawyers were thought of and taught. Houston would say, "[The] Negro lawyer must be trained as a social engineer and group interpreter. Due to the Negro's social and political condition...the Negro lawyer must be prepared to anticipate, guide and interpret his advancement.... [Moreover, he must act as] business adviser.... For the protection of the scattered resources possessed or controlled by the group...he must provide more ways and means for holding with the group the income now flowing through it."

With this vision and his skills as an institution builder, Houston transformed the Howard Law School from a part-time evening school into the major legal training center for black lawyers in the world. While transforming the Howard Law School, Houston in 1934 accepted the directorship of the Joint Committee of the NAACP and the American Fund for Public Service, a legal campaign against segregation and discrimination in America. In this role as director of the NAACP legal campaign (as it would be formally called) Houston would provide the template for challenging and eradicating the "separate but equal" doctrine of *Plessy* v. *Ferguson*, culminating in the landmark *Brown* v. *Board of Education* decision which declared segregation in public schools unconstitutional.

The impact and influence of Charles Hamilton Houston on black America and America—thus his ranking here—are summarized by the brilliant biographer Genna Rae McNeil:

> Charles Houston held a respected position of leadership among blacks during the 1930s and 1940s. His ability to educate and inspire lawyers and lay people, respectively, to work as social engineers and to pool their resources to seek enforcement of rights through the courts was of particular historical significance. His legal successes, especially in the U.S. Supreme Court, were key collective victories that laid the groundwork for subsequent civil right laws supporting equality of educational opportunity, fair housing and fair representation. These court victories had far-reaching significance for the future progress of blacks.... His work was also instrumental in creating a climate for more militant direct action.

Charles Hamilton Houston died April 22, 1950, nearly four years before the *Brown* v. *Board of Education* decision was handed down by the U.S. Supreme Court.

6

Richard Allen
1760–1831

Absalom Jones
1746–1818

Whereas Absalom Jones and Richard Allen, two men of the African race, who, for their religious life and conversation have obtained a good report among men, these persons, from a love to the people of their complexion whom they beheld with sorrow, because of their irreligious and uncivilized state, often communed together upon this painful and important subject in order to form some kind of religious society, but there being too few to be found under the like concern, and those who were, differed in their religious sentiments; with these circumstances they labored for some time, till it was proposed, after a serious communication of sentiments, that a society should be formed, without regard to religious tenets, provided, the persons lived an orderly and sober life, in order to support one another in sickness, and for the benefit of their widows and fatherless children.

PREAMBLE OF PHILADELPHIA
FREE AFRICAN SOCIETY

With these words, on April 12, 1787, Richard Allen and Absalom Jones and six other African-Americans formed the first black organization in English-speaking America—nearly eleven years after the Declaration of Independence and five months before the adoption of the U.S. Constitution.

The founding of a society "to support one another" had ripple effects for the next forty years or so among black organizers of such societies in the Northeast (Boston, New York, Newport), among black church organizers in the South and Northeast (Savannah and Philadelphia), and among black lodge organizers in the Northeast (Boston, Philadelphia, and Providence, Rhode Island).

As the principal leaders and pioneers of black "institution building"—for the organized assertions of the interests and rights of black people—in America, Richard Allen and Absalom Jones warrant their ranking here. Although each distinguished himself in his own right, it was their vision and courage in forming the Free African Society that will forever link them as influential to the black struggle and quest for equality and full participation in America.

Richard Allen was born a slave in Philadelphia, sixteen years before Thomas Jefferson wrote that "all men are created equal and are endowed by their Creator with certain unalienable rights"; Absalom Jones was born a slave in Sussex, Delaware, thirty years before the Declaration of Independence.

To be sure, the contradictions between what the white founders said and what defined the black experience—in these two cases, slavery—had an impact on both Allen and Jones. It was the institutionalization of these contradictions in the white Christian church, in November of the same year of the founding of the Free African Society, that provided cause for Allen and Jones to "form some kind of religious society" consistent with black meanings and definitions of their humanity. Leon Litwack describes the precipitating incident:

> Richard Allen and Absalom Jones—and several of their friends entered the St. George Methodist Episcopal Church for a regular Sunday service. Large numbers of Negroes had been drawn to this church and had been permitted to occupy comfortable seats on the main floor, but the increasing popularity of St. George's finally prompted church officials to announce that henceforth Negroes would be expected to sit in the gallery. Aware of this new seating arrangement, Allen, Jones, and other Negroes took seats in the front of the gallery, overlooking the places which they had previously occupied. But the church authorities had actually reserved an even less conspicuous place for their Negro worshipers in the rear of the gallery, and they soon made this quite apparent. "We had not been long upon our knees," Allen later recalled, "before I heard considerable scuffling and low talking. I raised my head up and saw one of the trustees...having hold of the Reverend Absalom Jones, pulling him off his knees, and saying, 'You must get up—you must not kneel here.'" Jones thereupon requested that the officials wait until the prayers had been completed. When the trustees persisted, however, and threatened forcible removal, "we all went out of the church in a body and they were no more plagued with us." In fact, "we were filled with fresh vigor to get a house to worship God in."

This event led eventually to the formation of two separate black denominations in 1794: Absalom Jones organized the African Protestant Episcopal Church of St. Thomas in Philadelphia with affiliations to the white Protestant Episcopal Church, and Richard Allen organized the Bethel African Methodist Episcopal Church in Philadelphia, a distinctively separate black denomination and the first black national organization of which he became the head as bishop in 1816.

Absalom Jones died February 13, 1818, two months before the founding of the Pennsylvania Augustine Society, one of the early societies for the education of blacks. Richard Allen died on March 26, 1831, nearly five months before Nat Turner's slave rebellion in Southampton County, Virginia.

7

Prince Hall
1748(?)–1807

To the Honorable the Senate and House of Representatives of the Commonwealth of Massachusetts Bay, in General Court assembled.

The petition of a great number of blacks, freemen of this Commonwealth, humbly sheweth, that your petitioners are held in common with other freemen of this town and Commonwealth and have never been backward in paying our proportionate part of the burdens under which they have, or may labor under; and as we are willing to pay our equal part of these burdens, we are of the humble opinion that we have the right to enjoy the privileges of free men. But that we do not will appear in many instances, and we beg leave to mention one out of many, and that is of the education of our children which now receive no benefit from the free schools in the town of Boston, which we think is a great grievance, as by woeful experience we now feel that the want of a common education. We, therefore, must fear for our rising offspring to see them in ignorance in a land of gospel light when there is provision made for them as well as others and yet can't enjoy them, and for not other reason can be given this they are black. . . . We therefore pray your Honors that you would in your wisdom some provision may be made for the education of our dear children. And in duty bound shall ever pray.

PRINCE HALL

As the leader of the petition to the Massachusetts State Legislature in October 1787, Prince Hall was continuing the black institution-building legacy of Richard Allen and Absalom Jones by pleading for the establishment of equal educational facilities for black children. His petition was denied; he would later in 1800 establish a school for black children at his home in Boston.

Several scholars reject the view that Prince Hall was born in Barbados in 1748, that he came to the United States in 1765, and that he fought in the Continental Army. The best evidence is inconclusive about his birthplace, parentage, and early life. However, it is indisputable that Hall later became an influential spokesperson against slavery and the slave trade (he led a mass petition to the Massachusetts Legislature against these twin evils in 1788). Out of the groundswell of institution building in the late eighteenth century, Hall's most important accomplishment came with his founding in Boston of the Negro Masonic Order in the United States—African Lodge No. 459—on May 6, 1787, less than one month after the founding of the Free African Society. Thus, "Master" Hall pioneered the first black self-help fraternal institution in America, chartered by the Grand Lodge of England. In 1797, Hall and his associates would create the first black interstate institution by forming Masonic Lodges in Philadelphia and Providence, Rhode Island.

The influence and impact of Prince Hall as an institution builder justify his ranking here. Further, it could be argued that Hall's advocacy of a "common education" for black children had reinforcing effects on the founding of a black school in Philadelphia by Quakers and the first African Free School in New York, in 1787.

Hall's influence can also be measured by his being the first advocate (as early as 1787 and before Paul Cuffe, MARTIN DELANY [13], and HENRY GARNET [14]) of the colonization of blacks in Africa.

Hall died in Boston on December 4, 1807.

8

Samuel E. Cornish

1795–1858

John Russwurm

1799–1851

The Negro was taken before a Justice of the Peace, who, after serious deliberation, waived his authority—perhaps through fear, as the crowd of persons from the above counties had collected to the number of seventy or eighty, near Mr. People's (the justice) house. He acted as President of the mob, and put the vote, when it was decided he should be immediately executed by being burnt to death—then the sable culprit was led to a tree and tied to it, and a large quality of pine knots collected and placed around him, and the fatal torch was applied to the pile, even against the remonstrance of several gentlemen who were present; and the miserable being was in a short time consumed to ashes.... This is the second Negro who had been thus put to death, without Judge or Jury in that county.

FREEDOM'S JOURNAL,
AUGUST 3, 1827

Almost forty years after the founding of the Free African Society, the above account—the first—of the lynching of a black man appeared in *Freedom's Journal*, the first black newspaper in America, founded by Samuel E. Cornish and John B. Russwurm on March 16, 1827. This seminal publication would prove to be yet another effective tool in communicating, from a black perspective, the African-American resistance to and protest against slavery, the slave trade, and white racism in general.

More specifically, the establishment of *Freedom's Journal* became another black assertion of the prerogatives and obligations of blacks to define and strategize their own struggle for the abolition of slavery. Cornish and Russwurm (both prominent abolitionists) were resolute in these regards in their first editorial:

The publication of this Journal; the expediency of its appearance at this time, when so many schemes are in action concerning our people—encourage us to come boldly before an enlightened publick. For we believe, that a paper devoted to the dissemination of useful knowledge among our brethren, and to their moral and religious improvement, must meet with the cordial approbation of every friend of humanity.

The peculiarities of this Journal, renders it important that we should advertise to the world our motives by which we are actuated, and the objects which we contemplate.

We wish to plead our own cause. Too long have others spoken for us. Too long has the publick been deceived by misrepresentations, in things which concern us dearly, though in the estimation of some mere trifles; for though there are many in society who exercise towards us benevolent feelings; still (with sorrow we confess it) there are others who make it their business to enlarge upon the least trifle, which tends to the discredit of any person of colour; and pronounce anathemas and denounce our whole body for the misconduct of this guilty one. . . .

Cornish and Russwurm also viewed the *Journal* as a medium for facilitating interstate dialogue among blacks about blacks and Africa:

> It is our earnest wish to make our Journal a medium of intercourse between our brethren in the different states of this great confederacy: that through its columns an expression of our sentiments, on many interesting subjects which concern us, may be offered to the publick. . . .
>
> Useful knowledge of every kind, and everything that relates to Africa, shall find a ready admission into our columns; and as that vast continent becomes daily more known, we trust that many things will come to light, proving that the natives of it are neither so ignorant nor stupid as they have generally been supposed to be.

The *Journal's* targeted population of free blacks (because it was against the law in slaveholding states to encourage literacy and thought of any kind among slaves) reveals Cornish and Russwurm's intended influence among this critical segment of antebellum blacks:

> The interesting fact that there are FIVE HUNDRED THOUSAND free person of colour, one half of whom might peruse, and the whole be benefitted by the publication of the Journal; that no publication, as yet, has been devoted exclusively to their improvement—that many selections from approved standard authors, which are within the reach of few, may occasionally be made—and more important still, that this large body of our citizens have no public channel—all serve to prove the real necessity, at present, for the appearance of the FREEDOM'S JOURNAL.

This "medium of intercourse between our brethren in the different states" encouraged other blacks to do likewise: *Colored American* (newspaper, 1837); *Mirror of Liberty* (magazine, 1838); *African Methodist Episcopal Church Magazine* (1841); and *North Star* (newspaper, 1847). The *North Star* was published by FREDERICK DOUGLASS [2], whose influence and contributions have been previously cited. (It should be noted that *Freedom's Journal* predates *Liberator*, the white abolitionist journal published by William Lloyd Garrison, by nearly four years, and thus shows again blacks leading their own cause for freedom and equality through the print medium.)

The ranking of Samuel E. Cornish and John B. Russwurm here is further buttressed by the apparent influence they as abolitionists and *Freedom's Journal*'s credo had on one of its agents, a free black named DAVID WALKER [9], author of *Walker's Appeal* for the universal emancipation of blacks.

Samuel E. Cornish died on November 6, 1858, in Brooklyn, several months after John Brown held an antislavery convention in Chatham, Canada, to recruit whites and blacks for his attack on Harpers Ferry, West Virginia, a year later.

John B. Russwurm died in Liberia in 1851, the year the first extensive history of black Americans appeared: *Services of Colored Americans in the Wars of 1776 and 1812*, by William Nell.

9

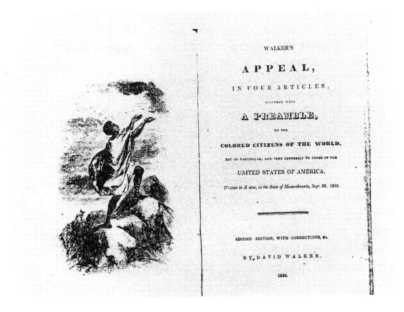

David Walker

1785–1830

Ethiopians! open your minds to reason; let therein weigh the
effects of truth, wisdom, and justice, (and a regard to your
individual as general good,) and the spirit of these our words,
we know full well, cannot but produce the effect for which they
are by us herefrom intended. Know, then, in your present state
or standing, in your sphere of government in any nation within
which you reside, we hold and contend you enjoy but few of
your rights of government within them....

Beware! know thyselves [slaveholders] to be but mortal
men doomed to the good or evil, as your works shall merit from
you....

But learn, slaveholders, thine will rests not in thine hand:
God decrees to thy slave his rights as a man. This we issue forth
as the spirit of the black man or Ethiopian's right, established
from the Ethiopian's Rock, the foundation of his civil and
religious rights, which hereafter will be exemplified in the
order of its course.... As came John the Baptist, of old, to
spread abroad the forthcoming of his master, so alike are
intended these our words, to denote to the black African or
Ethiopian people, that God has prepared for them a leader, who
awaits but his season to proclaim to them his birthright....

ROBERT ALEXANDER YOUNG

Almost twenty-nine years after an aborted slave rebellion by Gabriel
Prosser with about one thousand slaves; twenty-five years after Jean
Jacques Dessalines declared the independence of Haiti; nearly seven
years after Denmark Vesey's sabotaged slave conspiracy; and a full six
months before *Walker's Appeal*, the above words—self-published by
activist Robert Alexander Young in 1829, a free Negro from New York—
were issued as a summons to blacks (Ethiopians) to honor the will of
God and rise up against slaveholders and take back their birthrights of
freedom and other civil and religious rights.

Young's "mystical" words may or may not have influenced *Walker's
Appeal*, but his words reveal and underscore the pervasive climate of
rebellions, revolts, insurrections, and calls for slavery's abolition—led
by Blacks—that would make David Walker, writer/abolitionist, one of
the most feared (by whites) and most influential black leaders of his
time.

David Walker was born free in Wilmington, North Carolina on
September 28, 1785. In 1820, he migrated to Boston, Massachusetts,
where he became a dealer in used clothes. There he was an active
abolitionist and, in 1827, became an agent, or representative, of
Freedom's Journal and one of its contributing writers.

Like Young, David Walker saw blacks as instruments of God in
eradicating slavery and its evils and, generally, man's inhumanity to
man: "We must and shall be free I say, in spite of you [white America],"
Walker said. "You may do your best to keep us in wretchedness and
misery, to enrich you and your children, but God will deliver us from
under you." (The reader is referred to the author's *What Color Is Your
God?* for further discussion on a theology of black liberation.)

Walker's Appeal appears as a pamphlet of about eighty pages, with the full title begin *Walker's Appeal, in Four Articles: Together With a Preamble, to the Coloured Citizen of the World, But in Particular, and Very Expressly, to Those of the United States of America. Written in Boston, State of Massachusetts, September 28, 1829.* In most respects it is a religious document, viewing slavery as an evil, allied with forces of darkness and avarice and giving blacks the obligation—with the help of God—to eradicate it.

Although premised on religious tenets, *Walker's Appeal* advocated the use of violence by blacks if whites (slaveholders) continued to deny their freedom:

> If you commence, make sure work—do not trifle, for they will not trifle with you—they want us for their slaves, and think nothing of murdering us in order to subject us to that wretched condition—therefore, if there is an attempt made by us, kill or be killed. Now, I ask you, had you not rather be killed than to be a slave to a tyrant, who takes the life of your mother, wife, and dear little children? Look upon your mother, wife, and children, and answer God Almighty; and believe this, that it is no more harm for you to kill a man, who is trying to kill you, than it is for you to take a drink of water when thirsty; in fact, the man who will stand still and let another murder him, is worse than an infidel, and, if he has common sense, ought not to be pitied....

Although asserting that blacks would be free in spite of whites, Walker saw a different kind of America if whites would listen and repent:

> Treat us like men, and there is no danger but we will all live in peace and happiness together. For we are not like you, hard hearted, unmerciful, and unforgiving. What a happy country this will be, if the whites will listen. What nation under heaven, will be able do any thing with us, unless God gives us up into its hand? But Americans, I declare to you, while you keep our children in bondage, and treat us like brutes, to make us support you and your families, we cannot be your friends. And there is not a doubt in my mind, but that the whole of the past will be sunk into oblivion, and we

yet, under God, will become a united and happy people. The whites may say it is impossible, but remember that nothing is impossible with God.

Walker's ranking here acknowledges his having seen blacks—"coloured citizens"—as part of a world community needing to and being obligated to unite in order to throw off slavery and oppression and, also, for his reinforcing the climate for direct attacks—even violent instrumental ones—against slavery and its companion evil, white racism.

Walker's influence as author and main distributor of the *Appeal* is further evidenced by the fear he created and the tocsin he provided throughout the United States, especially in slaveholding states like Georgia and North Carolina, and slave cities like New Orleans, Richmond, and Savannah, where governors and city officials held special meetings to deal with its obvious implications.

Walker died under mysterious circumstances during 1830, within a year of the successful slave rebellion of NAT TURNER [10] in Southampton County, Virginia. "What a happy country this will be, if the whites will listen."

10

Nat Turner

1800–1831

The Patriotic Nathaniel Turner followed Denmark Veazie
[Vesey]. He was goaded to desperation by wrong and injustice.
By despotism, his name has been recorded on the list of infamy,
and future generations will remember him among the noble and
brave.

REV. HENRY HIGHLAND GARNET

At the national Convention of Colored Citizens held in Buffalo, New
York, in 1843—almost twelve years to the day after Nat Turner's
rebellion—Garnet's words revealed the esteem in which Nat Turner was
held by blacks. His ranking here is consistent with the influence his
vision and actions, as a revolutionary for black freedom, exerted during
one of the most critical moments in United States history.

Admittedly, it's difficult to quantify what Nathaniel "Nat" Turner knew about Denmark Vesey's slave plot, which was further described by HENRY HIGHLAND GARNET [14] as "a plan for the liberation of his fellow men. In the whole of human efforts to overthrow slavery, a more complicated and tremendous plan was never formed." Vesey's plan was betrayed by a house slave in May 1822; in July 1822 he was hanged with five of his associates at Blake's Landing, Charleston, South Carolina. It's equally problematic to conclude that Nat Turner was influenced by the betrayed and aborted slave plot of Gabriel Prosser—hanged two days after Nat's birth some thirty-one years earlier. It is a fact, however, that Nat Turner's slave rebellion in Southampton County, Virginia, in August 1831, was the culmination of some two hundred years of rebellions and plots against slavery by blacks in America, and the catalyst for blacks like Garnet and whites to push more urgently for the abolition of slavery in America. Turner would be the leader activist Robert Alexander Young "prophesied" that God would prepare "to proclaim to them his birthright."

Nat Turner's revolt.

Born a slave to Benjamin Turner on October 2, 1800, Nat Turner had the "indelible impression" as a child that he would be "a prophet as the Lord had shown me things that had happened before my birth. And my mother and grandmother strengthened me in this my first impression, saying, in my presence, I was intended for some great purpose. . . ." This view of blacks as prophets, agents, and leaders of God's opposition to the evils of slavery is consistent with views of Gabriel Prosser, Denmark Vesey, Robert Alexander Young, and David Walker, and, later, Henry Highland Garnet. Turner and they are the early black liberationist theologians. Turner also knew as a child: "I had too much sense to be raised, and, if I was, I would never be of any service to any one as a slave."

Turner as a young man was convinced of his "divine agency" and "superior judgment" and decided to alter his life accordingly: "Having soon discovered to be great, I must appear so, and therefore studiously avoided mixing in society, and wrapped myself in mystery, devoting my time to fasting and prayer."

Some years later he would run away, as his father had done many years earlier. However, he returned thirty days later at the bidding of the "spirit," at which time he had the vision that would justify his rebellion:

> And about this time I had a vision—and I saw white spirits and black spirits engaged in battle, and the sun was darkened—the thunder rolled in the heavens, and blood flowed in streams—and I heard a voice saying, "Such is your luck, such you are called to see; and let it come rough or smooth, you must surely bear it."

Awaiting further signs from heaven, Turner in February 1831 received one with the eclipse of the sun:

> On the appearance of the sign, I should arise and prepare myself, and slay my enemies with their own weapons. And immediately on the sign appearing in the heavens, the seal was removed from my lips, and I communicated the great work laid out for me to do, to four in whom I had the greatest confidence (Henry, Hark, Nelson, and Sam). It was intended by us to have begun the work of death on the 4th of July last. Many were the plans formed and rejected by us, and it

affected my mind to such a degree that I fell sick, and the time passed without our coming to any determination how to commence—still forming new schemes and rejecting them when the sign appeared again, which determined me not to wait longer.

After the delay due to his illness on July 4, Nat Turner and his associates ultimately decided to start their rebellion on Sunday night, August 21, at the house of Mr. Joseph Travis: "And until we had armed and equipped ourselves, and gathered sufficient force, neither age nor sex was to be spared—which was invariably adhered to...."

The rebellion lasted for almost three days, killing nearly sixty whites and resulting in the death of over one hundred black rebels. Three free blacks and thirteen slaves were tried and hanged immediately. Nat Turner, eluding his captors for nearly two months, was caught and hanged in Jerusalem, Virginia, on November 11, 1831, "willing to suffer the fate that awaits me."

11

James Forten

1766–1842

If the times of 1830 were eventful, there were among our
people...men equal to the occasion. We had giants in those
days! There were...James Forten, the merchant prince...

THE ANGLO-AFRICAN
OCTOBER 1859

Less than a month before the birth of FREDERICK DOUGLASS [2],
James Forten, "the merchant prince," stood up at a gathering of blacks at
the Bethel Church in Philadelphia to provide leadership in the protest
against the attempts of the American Colonization Society to send
blacks back to Africa. Historian Benjamin Quarles provides more details
on this historic meeting in 1817:

Never before had such a large number of Negro Americans assembled, not fewer than three thousand persons sitting and standing in the main floor and the U-shaped balcony. On the platform stood James Forten, a wealthy sail-maker who owned a country residence and kept a carriage. . . .

There was only one issue that could bring together a Negro gathering so numerous, of such diverse sponsorship, and of a mixture of the well-to-do and literate with the poor and unschooled. This binding issue was that of colonization, of sending Negroes to the west coast of Africa. Such a program had been proclaimed a month earlier by the newly formed American Colonization Society from its headquarters at the nation's capital. Any ambiguity in its official title, "American Society for Colonizing the Free People of Color in the United States," was removed by its avowed intent of sending the Negroes across the Atlantic.

As the chair of this meeting, Forten guided through the assemblage the following unanimously approved resolutions to protest the exiling of blacks "from the land of our nativity":

Whereas our ancestors (not of choice) were the first successful cultivators of the wilds of America, we their descendants feel ourselves entitled to participate in the blessing of her luxuriant soil, which their blood and sweat manured; and that any measure or system of measures, having a tendency to banish us from her bosom, would not only be cruel, but in direct violation of those principles, which have been the boast of this republic. . . .

Resolved, That we never will separate ourselves voluntarily from the slave population in this country; they are our brethren by the ties of consanguinity, of suffering, and of wrong; and we feel that there is more virtue in suffering privations with them, than fancied advantages for a season. . . .

Resolved, That having the strongest confidence in the Justice of God, and philanthropy of the free states, we cheerfully submit our destinies to the guidance of Him who suffers not a sparrow to fall, without his special providence.

James Forten was born in Philadelphia of free black parents. At fifteen, he served in the Continental Army as a powder boy on a ship that was captured by the British. He was imprisoned in England for seven months. Returning to the United States, he worked for Robert Bridges, a sailmaker. After Bridges retired, Forten bought the company, and as an inventor-entrepreneur of a device for handling sails, he built a highly successful business, accumulating a considerable fortune.

Forten was among "the several friends" whom Richard Allen and Absalom Jones led out of the predominantly white St. George Methodist Episcopal Church in November 1787. He was later among those who with Richard Allen formed the independent Bethel African Methodist Episcopal Church.

James Forten's influence as an abolitionist-entrepreneur against the colonization of blacks (a measure of his influence on this issue is his having convinced the white abolitionist, William Lloyd Garrison, that colonization was wrong); his equally forceful role in leading resistance to the state of Pennsylvania's attempts to restrict the immigration of blacks from the South; and his prominence and influence as a cofounder of the Pennsylvania Augustine Society "for the education of people of colour"—one of the earliest such societies—warrant his ranking here.

According to CARTER G. WOODSON [25], Forten used his considerable fortune to influence and shape the black abolitionist movement and was thus remembered by the *Anglo-African* in 1859 as a "giant" and "merchant prince" among blacks. Forten died in Philadelphia in 1842. His funeral was attended by a large group of blacks and whites, influential people as well as common folk of the time.

12

Harriet Tubman

1820(?)–1913

Her name deserves to be handed down to posterity, side by side
with the names of Jeanne D'Arc, Grace Darling, and Florence
Nightingale, for not one of these women, noble and brave as
they were, has shown more courage, and power of endurance,
in facing danger and death to relieve human suffering, than this
poor black woman.

SARAH BRADFORD

God hath chosen the weak things of the world to confound the
things which are mighty.

I CORINTHIANS 1:27

"This poor black woman," Harriet Tubman, like no other woman, has come to symbolize the indomitable spirit of blacks in their quest *to be* against the peculiar institution of slavery, with its intent and design to destroy their spiritual essence as human beings. Her ranking here recognizes the influence this "weak" (poor and illiterate) former slave had in helping to topple the institution of slavery in America. "No fear of the lash, the blood-hound, or the fiery stake," said Samuel M. Hopkins, "could divert her from her self-imposed task of leading as many as possible of her people from the land of Egypt, from the house of bondage."

Harriet, born Araminta Ross, was a child of the slave quarters on the Broadas Plantation in Dorchester County, Maryland, in 1820 or 1821, approximately twenty-eight years after the perfection of the cotton gin by Eli Whitney (which increased the wealth of cotton farming and the demand and market value of slaves) and the passage by Congress of the first Fugitive Slave Law (establishing the legal basis for returning runaway slaves to their masters wherever found in the United States).

Araminta was the granddaughter of slaves, and her parents, Benjamin Ross and Harriet Greene, were slaves. As a young girl, she took her mother's name, Harriet. At the age of six or seven, Harriet was taken from her mother and hired out to live with James Cook, a trapper whose wife was a weaver. Harriet refused to learn this trade and ran away. She was hired out again and again, running away each time. In her early teens, she started working as a field hand with her parents and brothers and sisters. While working in the fields, she heard stories of runaway and rebellious slaves, among them the story of NAT TURNER [10]. Like Turner, Harriet had dreams of freedom and often heard voices and had visionary powers that made her even more obsessed with being free. She said: "Sometime prior to the late war of the rebellion I married John Tubman [a free black—probably in 1844] who died in the state of Maryland on the 30th day of September, 1867."

Sometime during the summer of 1849, almost two years after Frederick Douglass published the first edition of the *North Star*, Harriet Tubman escaped from slavery in Maryland by using a "tool of rebellion": her feet. She followed the North Star in the sky and eventually came to Philadelphia, where she found shelter and friends. It was here she learned about the Underground Railroad, a secret network of abolitionists, freed blacks, sympathetic whites, and Quakers who helped runaway slaves. The Underground Railroad was a widespread

Harriet Tubman, Union spy.

system for aiding escaped slaves to freedom. Stations were set up along several routes from South to North and used such code words as *agent*, *conductor*, *station*, etc., to help runaway slaves find their way to the underground houses and people who sheltered them. The routes ran through the coastal states of the South to Philadelphia, New York, and Boston and from the middle South by way of Cincinnati to the Great Lakes and Canada. The Underground Railroad came to an end with the abolition of slavery (see *Black Abolitionists* by Benjamin Quarles for more discussion of the vital roles blacks played in the Underground Railroad).

　　Harriet Tubman became the most influential of the black "conductors"; repeatedly, she returned through the Underground Railroad to free her family, altogether, in nineteen trips, freeing three hundred slaves. The extraordinary courage of this black woman had the impact "to shake the nation that was deaf to her cries" for freedom for blacks. During the Civil War, Harriet Tubman distinguished herself as a nurse, spy, and scout in the Union Army. As historian Lerone Bennett has written:

The most remarkable of all Union spies was a woman—the celebrated abolitionist Harriet Tubman. Working in South Carolina and other states, she organized slave intelligence networks behind enemy lines and led scouting raids. She also became the first and possibly the last woman to lead U.S. Army troops in battle.

Corroborating the significance of Harriet Tubman in the struggle of blacks for freedom and equality in America are the words of Frederick Douglass in a letter to Harriet dated August 29, 1869:

> You ask for what you do not need when you call upon me for a word of commendation. I need such words from you far more than you can need them from me, especially where your superior labors and devotion to the cause of the lately enslaved of our land are known as I know them. The difference between us is very marked. Most that I have done and suffered in the service of our cause has been in public, and I have received much encouragement at every step of the way. You, on the other hand, have labored in a private way. I have wrought in the day—you in the night. I have had the applause of the crowd and the satisfaction that comes of being approved by the multitude, while the most that you have done has been witnessed by a few trembling, scarred, and foot-sore bondmen and women, whom you had led out of the house of bondage.... The midnight sky and the silent stars have been the witness of your devotion to freedom and of your heroism....
>
> Much that you have done would seem improbable to those who do not know you as I know you.

Harriet Tubman died penniless in Auburn, New York, on March 10, 1913, nearly fifty years after the Emancipation Proclamation.

13

Martin R. Delany

1812–1885

It is not our "little faith," that makes us anxious to leave this country or that we do not believe in the ultimate triumph of the principles of FREEDOM, but that the life-sustaining resources which slavery is capable of commanding may enable the institution to prolong its existence to an indefinite period of time. You must remember that slavery is not a foreign element in this government nor is it really antagonistic to the feelings of the American people. On the contrary, it is an element commencing with our medieval existence, receiving the sanction of the early Fathers of the Republic, sustained by their descendants through a period of nearly three centuries, deep

and firmly laid in our organization. Completely interwoven into
the passions and prejudices of the American people...

I can hate this Government without being disloyal,
because it has stricken down my manhood, and treated me as a
saleable commodity....

I am willing to forget the endearing name of home and
country, and as an unwilling exile seek on other shores the
freedom which has been denied me in the land of my birth.

H. FORD DOUGLASS

By 1854, the issue of black voluntary emigration and colonization had
so crystallized that during the antebellum period probably no single
issue more divided black and white abolitionists. The National Negro
Emigration Convention in Cleveland enthusiastically received the
above words of nationalist H. Ford Douglass, offering the plan of some
prominent blacks to voluntarily separate themselves, leaving a republic
in which slavery and its ideology and practices had led to the thingafica-
tion of blacks and had become "completely interwoven into the passions
and prejudice" of white America. Among those blacks was Martin R.
Delany, the "father of black nationalism" in America. Nearly two years
earlier, the same year Harriet Beecher Stowe's *Uncle Tom's Cabin* was
published, Delany self-published the manifesto of black nationalism,
*The Condition, Elevation, Emigration and Destiny of the Colored
People of the United States, Politically Considered.*

The counterpoint of black nationalism as espoused by Martin R.
Delany and others (that is, white America could not change to accept
blacks as human beings and therefore they should separate to form a
new nation) to the integrationist view of Frederick Douglass and others
(white America could be changed to accept the basic humanity of
blacks) and the influence Delany exerted during the antebellum period
over black and white leaders, forcing them to clarify their definitions of
freedom and equality and their strategies for achieving them, justify his
ranking here.

During the year of the War of 1812, Martin R. Delany was born
free in Charles Town, West Virginia. His father was a slave, and his
mother was free. His grandparents were slaves brought directly from
Africa, where one of his great-grandfathers had been a chief and the
other a prince.

In his early days as an abolitionist, Delany was more in agreement with the ideology and tactics of Frederick Douglass. As coeditors of the *North Star* newspaper, Delany and Douglass in an editorial in 1847 declared:

> It is neither a reflection on the fidelity, nor a disparagement of the ability of our friends and fellow-laborers, to assert what "common sense affirms and only folly denies," that the man who has *suffered the wrong* is the man to *demand redress*— that the man STRUCK is the man to CRY OUT—and that he who has *endured the cruel pangs of Slavery* is the man to *advocate Liberty*. It is evident we must be our own representatives and advocates, not exclusively, but peculiarly—not distinct from, but in connection with our white friends. In the grand struggle for liberty and equality now waging, it is meet, right and essential that there should arise in our ranks authors and editors, as well as orators.

Five years later, in his book, Delany had a different view and a nationalistic approach to the black struggle for liberty and equality:

> Except the character of an individual is known, there can be no just appreciation of his worth; and as with individuals, so it is with classes.
>
> The colored people are not yet known, even to their most professed friends among the white Americans; for the reason, that politicians, religionists, colonizationists, and Abolitionists, have each and all, at different times, presumed to *think* for, dictate to, and *know* better what suited colored people, than they knew for themselves; and consequently, there has been no other knowledge of them obtained, than that which has been obtained through these mediums. Their history, past, present and future, has been written by them, who, for reasons well known, which are named in this volume, are not their representatives, and, therefore, do not properly nor fairly present their wants and claims among their fellows. . . .
>
> Every people should be the originators of their own designs, the projectors of their own schemes, and creators of the events that lead to their destiny—the consummation of their desires.
>
> Situated as we are, in the United States, many, and

almost insurmountable obstacles present themselves. We are four-and-a-half million in numbers, free and bond; six hundred thousand free, and three-and-a-half-million bond....

But we have been, by our oppressors, despoiled of our purity, and corrupted in our native characteristics, so that we have inherited their vices, and but few of their virtues, leaving us in character, really a *broken people....*

The claims of no people, according to established policy and usage, are respected by any nation, until they are presented in a national capacity.

To achieve this independent black nation, Delany details a process for creating a council, representative of the colored people of the United States, who would survey the:

EASTERN COAST OF AFRICA, to make researches for a suitable location on that section of the coast, for the settlement of colored adventurers from the United States, and elsewhere....

The land is ours—there it lies with inexhaustible resources; let us go and possess it. In Eastern Africa must rise up a nation, to whom all the world must pay commercial tribute.

We must MAKE an ISSUE, CREATE an EVENT, and ESTABLISH a NATIONAL POSITION for OURSELVES: and never may expect to be respected as men and women, until we have undertaken, some fearless, bold, and adventurous deeds of daring—contending against every odds— regardless of every consequence.

Delany's vision and black nationalist rhetoric would later influence such nationalists as REV. HENRY M. TURNER [39], MARCUS GARVEY [21], and ELIJAH MUHAMMAD [51].

With the advent of the Civil War and the Emancipation Proclamation, Delany would later apparently retreat from his nationalistic visions by serving in the Union Army, rising to the rank of major and later, during Reconstruction, becoming involved in the tortured politics of South Carolina. Although Delany didn't play out his nationalistic agenda in his last days, "the message is greater than the messenger."

Martin Delany died in Wilberforce, Ohio, in January 1885, within days of the swearing-in of Grover Cleveland as President of the United States, the first Democratic president since the Civil War.

14

Henry H. Garnet

1815–1882

Resolved, That we still adhere to the doctrine of urging the slave to leave immediately with his hoe on his shoulder, for a land of liberty, and would accordingly recommend that five hundred copies of Walker's Appeal, and Henry H. Garnet's Address to the Slaves be obtained in the name of the Convention, and gratuitously circulated.

RESOLUTION 12
STATE CONVENTION OF OHIO NEGROES, 1849

The influence of DAVID WALKER [9] and his *Appeal* and Henry Highland Garnet and his "Address to the Slaves of the United States of America" on another generation of blacks and their thinking and strategizing are indicated by the above resolution. Walker's significance has already been discussed. Garnet's influence as an abolitionist, emigrationist, and black liberationist theologian—like Gabriel Prosser, Denmark Vesey, Robert Young, and David Walker before him—places him here among *The Black 100*.

Henry Highland Garnet was born a slave of William Spenser in Kent County, Maryland, on December 23, 1815, one year before the organization of the American Colonization Society by the U.S. Congress. He escaped from slavery with his parents in 1824, moving to New Hope, Pennsylvania. He graduated form Oneida Institute—an abolitionist school near Utica, New York—in 1840. Garnet studied theology and pastored churches in New York City and Washington, D.C. He later served as president of Avery College in Allegheny, Pennsylvania, a school founded by Rev. Charles Avery in 1849 "to train young Negroes for teaching and the ministry."

While attending the National Convention of Colored Citizens in Buffalo, New York, in August 1843, Garnet—the abolitionist-theologian—issued his celebrated "Address to the Slaves of the United States," urging slave revolts and calling for the total annihilation of slavery as a "sin against God":

> Brethren and Fellow Citizens: Your brethren of the North, East and West have been accustomed to meet together in National Conventions, to sympathize with each other, and to weep over your unhappy condition. In these meetings we have addressed all classes of the free, but we have never, until this time, sent a word of consolation and advice to you....
>
> Slavery! How much misery is comprehended in that single word. What mind is there that does not shrink from its direful effects? Unless the image of God be obliterated from the soul, all men cherish the love of Liberty....
>
> In every man's mind the good seeds of liberty are planted, and he who brings his fellow down so low, as to make him contented with a condition of slavery, commits the highest crime against God and man. Brethren, your oppressors aim to do this. They endeavor to make you as much like brutes as possible....
>
> TO SUCH DEGRADATION IT IS SINFUL IN THE EXTREME FOR YOU TO MAKE VOLUNTARY SUBMISSION. The divine commandments you are in duty bound to

reverence and obey. If you do not obey them, you will surely meet with the displeasure of the Almighty. . . .

Your condition does not absolve you from your moral obligation. The diabolical injustice by which your liberties are cloven down, NEITHER GOD, NOR ANGELS, OR JUST MEN, COMMAND YOU TO SUFFER FOR A SINGLE MOMENT. THEREFORE IT IS YOUR SOLEMN AND IMPERATIVE DUTY TO USE EVERY MEANS, BOTH MORAL, INTELLECTUAL, AND PHYSICAL THAT PROMISES SUCCESS. . . .

You had better all die—*die immediately*, than live slaves and entail your wretchedness upon your posterity. If you would be free in this generation, here is your only hope. However much you and all of us may desire it, there is not much hope of redemption without the shedding of blood. If you must bleed, let it all come at once—rather *die freemen, than live to be slaves. . . .*

Brethren, arise, arise! Strike for your lives and liberties. Now is the day and the hour. Let every slave throughout the land do this, and the days of slavery are numbered. You cannot be more oppressed than you have been—you cannot suffer greater cruelties than you have already. *Rather die freemen than live to be slaves.* Remember that you are FOUR MILLION! . . .

Let your motto be resistance! *Resistance!* RESISTANCE! No oppressed people have ever secured their liberty without resistance.

With this address, Garnet galvanized a whole nation—black and white abolitionists, slaveholders and slaves, pro and anti-colonizationists—to deal with America's great sin and lie: slavery.

Garnet also influenced, during the antebellum period, a corollary issued of slavery: colonization. Believing with other black leaders like Martin Delany and James Theodore Holly that blacks would never realize their rights and freedoms in the United States, Garnet became a prominent advocate of the voluntary colonization and emigration of blacks to any country that would guarantee their rights. Benjamin Quarles described him as "one of emigration's greatest proselytes." Garnet, in a letter to Frederick Douglass printed in the *North Star*, January 26, 1848, wrote, "I would rather see a man free in Liberia than a slave in the United States." With the passage of the 1850 Fugitive Slave Act, he and other emigrationists began to consider Africa, Haiti, South America, and Central America as possible countries for black expatriation. At the National Emigration Convention of 1854, such possibilities were explored.

Garnet's calling slavery the "highest crime against God and man" and his pronouncement of the "moral obligation" of blacks to destroy slavery, underscored the role of religion—Christian or non-Christian, in the "freedom-striving tradition" of the black church in America. These views would later be embraced and acted on by leaders like REV. HENRY M. TURNER [39], MARCUS GARVEY [21], ELIJAH MUHAMMAD [51], MALCOLM X [23], and DR. MARTIN LUTHER KING, JR. [1].

Henry Highland Garnet was named minister of Liberia in June 1881. He died in Monrovia, Liberia, on February 13, 1882.

15

Sojourner Truth

1797–1883

I don't get scared when fascism gets near.... The spirit of
Harriet Tubman, Sojourner Truth, Frederick Douglass fills me
with courage and determination that every Negro boy and girl,
yes and every white boy and girl, shall walk this land, free and
with dignity.

PAUL ROBESON

Born a slave in Hurley, New York, sometime during 1797, the year PRINCE HALL [7] and his associates created the first black interstate institution, the black Masonic lodges, Isabella, Belle, or Isabelle changed her name in 1843 to Sojourner Truth. She would become an influential abolitionist and women's suffrage figure as an itinerant lecturer, "walk[ing] this land, free and with dignity" during the antebellum and reconstruction periods and even reaching mystically into the twentieth century to give "courage and determination" to the influential PAUL ROBESON [24].

Granted her freedom by the abolition of slavery in New York State on Independence Day, 1827 (New York instituted slavery in 1664), Isabella, "of the slaves who were freed," said Benjamin Quarles, "was destined to be the most remarkable."

She took the name Sojourner Truth after her conversion to Christianity: *Sojourner* "because I was to travel up and down the land showing people their sins and being a sign to them," and *Truth* "because I was to declare the truth unto the people." Illiterate all her life, Sojourner Truth's courage and candid, homespun utterances against the evils of slavery and the denial of women's rights made her a major presence in her day and thus accords her ranking here. Adding to her importance was her early advocacy, with Martin R. Delany, for a black or "Negro State"; influencing the discussion among blacks and whites about black nationalism and emigrationism.

Sojourner Truth died in Battle Creek, Michigan on November 26, 1883, nearly one month after the United States Supreme Court declared unconstitutional the Civil Rights Act of 1875, which gave equal rights to the treatment of blacks in public places. She was remembered by the *New York Globe* on December 1 of that year:

> Sojourner Truth stands preeminently as the only colored woman who gained a national reputation on the lecture platform in the days before the [Civil] War.

16

Benjamin Banneker

1731–1806

This, Sir, was a time when you clearly saw into the injustice of a state of slavery, and in which you had just apprehensions of the horror of its condition. It was now that your abhorrence thereof was so excited, that you publicly held forth this true and invaluable doctrine, which is worthy to be recorded and remembered in all succeeding ages: "We hold these truths to be self-evident, that all men are created equal; that they are endowed by their Creator with certain unalienable rights, and that among these are, life, liberty, and the pursuit of happiness."

But, Sir, how pitiable is it to reflect, that although you were so fully convinced of the benevolence of the Father of Mankind, and of his equal and impartial distribution of these rights and privileges, which he hath conferred upon them, that you should at the same time counteract his mercies, in detaining by fraud and violence so numerous a part of my brethren, under groaning captivity, and cruel oppression, that you should at the same time be found guilty of that most criminal act which you professedly detested in others with respect to yourselves.

BENJAMIN BANNEKER

Benjamin Banneker was born free in Ellicott's Mills, Maryland, on November 9, 1731, some thirty-three years after Maryland had passed the first antimiscegenation law in the English colonies. (An indicator of the inefficacy of this law was that Molly Walsh, one of Banneker's grandmothers, was a white indentured servant from England.)

Although one of the most brilliant and influential inventors and scientists during the colonial and post-revolutionary periods, Benjamin Banneker earns his ranking through the impact of his activism against slavery and its contradictions in the lives of the white "founding fathers" of the Republic.

A contemporary of George Washington, Banneker used his renown as a mathematician, astronomer, surveyor, and writer to champion the cause of enslaved blacks against a government—through its leaders—that had declared that "All men are created equal; that they are endowed by their Creator with certain unalienable rights...life, liberty, and the pursuit of happiness." One such leader was the author of the Declaration of Independence, Thomas Jefferson.

In 1791, while Jefferson was secretary of state in George Washington's administration, Banneker sent Jefferson the above letter confronting his hypocrisy—if not indeed the hypocrisy of white America—in enslaving blacks while at the same time declaring the "true and invaluable doctrine" of the "natural rights" of humankind. Jefferson was affected by Banneker's letter and eleven days later wrote to him:

I thank you sincerely for your letter of the 19th instant. Nobody wishes more than I do to see such proofs as you exhibit, that nature has given to our black brethren talents

equal to those of the other colors of men; and that the
appearance of the want of them is owing merely to the
degraded condition of their existence both in Africa and
America. I can add with truth that nobody wishes more
ardently to see a good system commenced for raising the
condition, both of their body and mind, to what it ought to
be, as far as the imbecility of their present existence and
other circumstances, which cannot be neglected, will admit.

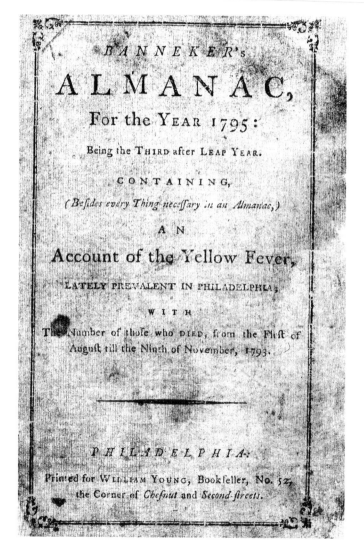

These letters became a part of a long correspondence between Jefferson and Banneker, which would influence the thoughts and behavior of this "founding father." Jefferson would go on to become the third president of the United States, and would also be the subject of accounts and stories (some more reliable than others) of being a slavemaster who fathered several slave daughters whom he sold or freed. The reader is guided to William Wells Brown's *Clotel, or The President's Daughter*, the first novel by a black American, as an example of such accounts.

Benjamin Banneker the astronomer and inventor would be internationally recognized by the scientific community for his precise calculations of celestial bodies and eclipses, and for what was the first clock in America, made of wood, which kept perfect time for over forty years. In the same year he wrote the above letter to Jefferson, also the year of the beginning of the Haitian Revolution, Banneker, as one of a team of three surveyors, planned and surveyed the location for the present city of Washington, D.C.

As a writer "through my own assiduous application of Astronomical Study," Banneker started producing in 1792 the first in a series of annual Almanacs, which also contained antislavery material.

In 1806, almost two years after Jean Jacques Dessalines declared independence for Haiti, Benjamin Banneker died in the town of his birth.

17

Crispus Attucks

1723–1770

The time has gone by for colored people to talk patriotism. ... The first blood shed in the American Revolution (that of Attucks, who fell in Boston) was that of a colored man. ...

The liberty purchased by the revolutionary men was used to enslave and degrade the colored man.

THE LIBERATOR
APRIL 10, 1857

There is no doubt that the first American to die on March 5, 1770 in the Boston Massacre at the hands of hated British soldiers, was Crispus Attucks, a black man. However, there is considerable dispute as to the impact of this event on the subsequent events of the Revolutionary War and the impact of the sacrifice of Attucks's death on the lot of black slaves in pre-revolutionary and post-revolutionary America.

The above quotes from *The Liberator*, an abolitionist journal, provide a black perspective on the irony of Crispus Attucks's death as a patriot, in view of the horrors unleashed on blacks through the continuation of slavery by white American "founding fathers" like George Washington, who said of Attucks and the Boston Massacre: "When the Colonists were staggering wearily under the cross of woe, a Negro came to the front and bore the cross to the victory of the glorious martyrdom." John Adams, the second U.S. president, said, "On that night [March 5, 1770], the foundation of American independence was laid."

Crispus Attucks's death came to symbolize for black America the American lie: a declaration of the rights of all men and the simultaneous denial of those rights to people of African ancestry. For over ninety-three years after Attucks's death, until the Emancipation Proclamation, "the liberty purchased by the revolutionary men was used to enslave and degrade the colored man."

Crispus Attucks's ranking here is not an acknowledgment of what his death meant or did not mean to the causes and effects of the American Revolution, but is a recognition of his impact as a symbol of the contribution of "colored people" to the fight for liberty in and for America. Attucks's ranking here also points to the difficulty of applying criteria of importance or influence among African-Americans from one period of history to another. One could argue that his death with that of four whites had marginal importance to the politics of the founding of America. Even if this is the case, Crispus Attucks has become an important symbol of the courage of blacks in their struggle for full rights and equality in America and proof of black contributions—in blood—to the shaping of this country.

Attucks was probably born a slave of Deacon William Brown in Framingham, Massachusetts, sometime during 1723. He escaped from slavery in November 1750 and reportedly became a seaman on whaling ships until the day of the Boston Massacre—an event that to many historians marks the beginning of the mass anti-British sentiments leading to the Revolutionary War of 1776.

Beyond symbolizing blacks' courage and sacrifice in the struggle to be free in America, Attucks's influence can be seen in the naming of several black military companies after him during the antebellum period; in the celebration by both whites and blacks in Boston of Crispus Attucks Day on March 5, from 1858 to 1870 (until the abolition of slavery was achieved and July 4, Independence Day, was substituted); and by blacks successfully getting the Massachusetts Legislature to pass a bill erecting a monument to Attucks, and the other four who died, on Boston Common, October 13, 1888.

18

Paul Laurence Dunbar

1872–1906

We should also develop a literature. Negroes should read some
things written by their own people that they may be inspired
thereby....

In this literature you will get the inspiration you need to
be like Frederick Douglass, Booker T. Washington, S.
Coleridge-Taylor, or Paul Laurence Dunbar. If you can
contribute to the world what those men have you will have no
reason to regret that you cannot be a George Washington or a
Thomas Jefferson, because you will still be identified with some
of the greatest men who have ever appeared in the history of
the world.

CARTER G. WOODSON

M any might take exception to listing Paul Laurence Dunbar in this volume, and his ranking here, because of his reputation politically as an accommodationist much like BOOKER T. WASHINGTON [3]. It is a fact that Dunbar's literary works were popular with and supported by white literary America, a fact illustrated by the words of praise and recommendation offered by William Dean Howells, the most respected white literary critic of the time, in an introduction to Dunbar's third collection of poetry, *Lyrics of Lowly Life*:

> What struck me in reading Mr. Dunbar's poetry was...here was the first instance of an American Negro who had evinced innate distinction in literature....So far as I could remember, Paul Dunbar was the only man of pure African blood and of American civilization to feel the Negro life aesthetically and express it lyrically....[He] studied the American Negro objectively, and to have represented him as he found him to be, with humor, with sympathy, and yet with what the reader must instinctively feel to be entire truthfulness.

Mr. Howells's patronizing and gratuitous pap aside, these words and others by white critics launched Paul Laurence Dunbar on his way to becoming the most popular and influential black writer of his time. The reader should understand that the author's recognition of the influence or importance of Dunbar among whites is not an endorsement of the right or wrong or good or bad of that influence, but is a more impartial view of the impact of Dunbar on the life of white and black America.

The above observations by CARTER G. WOODSON [25] about the need to create and develop black literature, and the inspiration and impact Dunbar and others have had in that process, show in part the esteem in which Dunbar was held and his influence in shaping a black literary experience in America.

Paul Laurence Dunbar was born to former slaves in Dayton, Ohio, on June 27, 1872, almost two years after the ratification of the Fifteenth Amendment, which gave blacks the right to vote. He attended elementary and high schools in Dayton and, while in high school, became a member of its literary society and wrote for the newspaper. He graduated high school in 1891, and because of a lack of money for college, started working as an elevator operator in Dayton.

During his off hours, Dunbar continued to develop his writing skills and in 1893 published *Oak and Ivy*, his first collection of poems. His second volume, *Majors and Minors*, which received favorable reviews, appeared in 1895. Dunbar gained national and international recognition and popularity with the publication of his third collection of verses, *Lyrics of Lowly Life*, in 1896, the year of *Plessy* v. *Ferguson*, the U.S. Supreme Court decision suporting the doctrine of "separate but equal" treatment of blacks in public accommodations. Between May 1898 and late 1905, Dunbar wrote four novels, four books of short stories, and three volumes of poetry.

Although much of his writing catered to white stereotypes of black attitudes and behaviors, such as being fun-loving, contented, happy-go-lucky, etc., Dunbar's greatest influence on blacks and black literature was his use of "dialect poetry," which revealed aspects of Negro life with "quaint charm and humor," according to LANGSTON HUGHES [34]. Examples of his dialect poetry are found in "The Co'n Pone's Hot," "A Confidence," "When Malindy Sings," and "Lovesome."

In August 1898, Dunbar influenced the public debate among blacks and whites about the merits of the industrial education espoused by Booker T. Washington and others by offering these observations:

> People are taking it for granted that he [the Negro] ought not to work with his head. And it is so easy for these people among whom we are living to believe this; it flatters and satisfies their self-complacency.
>
> At this late date the Negro has no need to prove his manual efficiency. That was settled fifty years ago, when he was the plantation blacksmith and carpenter and shoemaker....
>
> I would not counsel a return to the madness of that first enthusiasm for classic and professional learning; but I would urge that the Negro temper this newer one with a right idea of the just proportion in life of industry, commerce, art, science and letters, of materialism and idealism, of utilitarianism and beauty!

A closer look at Dunbar's words reveals a few protest pieces like "The Hunted Oak," which has an antilynching theme, and "We Wear the Mask," which dealt with masked pain, rage, and suffering in an unjust America.

We Wear the Mask

We wear the mask that grins and lies,
It hides our cheeks and shades our eyes,
This debt we pay to human guile;
With torn and bleeding hearts we smile,
And mouth with myriad subtleties.

Why should the world be over-wise,
In counting all our tears and sighs?
Nay, let them only see us, while
    We wear the mask.

We smile, but, O great Christ, our cries
To thee from tortured souls arise.
We sing, but oh the clay is vile
Beneath our feet, and long the mile;
But let the world dream otherwise,
    We wear the mask!

The collective impact of Paul Laurence Dunbar's life and writings is probably best expressed in author Benjamin Brawley's designation of him as "Poet of His People."

19

Phillis Wheatley

1753–1784

Negro poets [are] not new; their line goes back a long way in
Aframerican history. Between Phillis Wheatley, who as a girl of
eight or nine was landed in Boston from an African slave ship,
in 1761, and who published a volume of poems in 1773, and Paul
Laurence Dunbar, who died in 1906, there were more than
thirty Negroes who published volumes of verse.

JAMES WELDON JOHNSON

Phillis Wheatley was purchased directly off "an African slave ship, in
1761" by John and Susannah Wheatley, affluent white Bostonians.
Taught to read and write by the Wheatley family, Phillis would so

master the English language that in 1773 she published *Poems on Various Subjects, Religious and Moral*, the first book of poetry by an African-American woman. (The first published black poet was probably Jupiter Hammon, whose *An Evening Thought: Salvation by Christ, with Penetential Cries* was published in 1760.)

The impact of Wheatley's publication was a direct challenge to the prevailing racist and paternalistic attitudes held by whites in both North and South two years before the Revolutionary War. Blacks, whether slave or free, were supposed to lack the intellectual, spiritual, and moral powers and attributes necessary to be equal to whites, and thus were "deserving" of their dehumanizing treatment as chattels or things.

Although politically Phillis Weatley could be labeled an accommodationist to white views and behaviors toward blacks, her writings nonetheless influenced a significant element of white America to change its views about chattel slavery. Many so convinced became antislavery advocates or abolitionists. Examples of her effect can be seen in the reaction of a large number of influential whites to Wheatley's first published poem, "On the death of the Reverend George Whitefield" in 1770, and the use by abolitionists of her poems.

Phillis Wheatley's listing and ranking here is yet another example (see WASHINGTON [3] and DUNBAR [18]) of an influential black person affecting predominantly white America and its institutions but still having an influence on the black quest for equality and full participation in America. As the first major black poet in America, Phillis Wheatley influenced George Washington and his views about blacks through a poem and letter sent him honoring his appointment as commander in chief of the Continental army ("To His Excellency George Washington..."). In February 1776, Washington responded in part by saying:

> I thank you most sincerely for your polite notice of me, in the elegant lines you enclosed: and however undeserving I may be of such encomium and panegyric, the style and manner exhibited a striking proof of your poetical talents.... I would have published the poem, had I not been apprehensive that, while I only meant to give the world this new instance of your genius, I might have incurred the imputation of vanity.

Without making value judgments about her politics, JAMES WELDON JOHNSON [26] recognized Wheatley as a seminal poet in "Aframerican" history.

Phillis was manumitted by John and Susannah in 1773, months before the publication of *Poems on Various Subjects*. After the deaths of John and Susannah Wheatley, about 1778, Phillis met and married John Peters, a free black of some ill-repute. During an unhappy marriage with Peters, Wheatley lost all the inheritance she had received from the Wheatleys. In December 1784 she died, nearly destitute, in a poor section of Boston, within hours of the death of her one surviving child.

Phillis Wheatley's sensitivity to and awareness of her blackness is probably best seen in a poem she wrote to the Earl of Dartmouth late in her life:

> Should you, my lord, while you peruse my song,
> Wonder from whence my love of Freedom sprung,
> Whence flow these wishes for the common good,
> By feeling hearts alone best understood,
> I, young in life, by seeming cruel fate
> Was snatch'd from Afric's fancy'd happy seat:
> What pangs excruciating must molest,
> What sorrows labour in my parent's breast?
> Steel'd was that soul and by no misery mov'd
> That from a father seiz'd his babe belov'd:
> Such, such my case. And can I than but pray
> Others may never feel tyrannic sway?

20

P. B. S. Pinchback

1837–1921

Mr. Pinchback is the representative of a majority of the legal voters of Louisiana, and is entitled to a seat in the Senate. . . .

I desire, Mr. President, to make a personal reference to the Claimant [Pinchback]. I would not attempt one or deem one proper were it not that his personal character has been assailed.

As a father, I know him to be affectionate; as a husband, the idol of a pleasant home and cheerful fireside; as a citizen, loyal, brave, and true. And in his character and success we behold an admirable illustration of the excellence of our republican institution.

BLANCHE KELSO BRUCE

The above words were spoken on behalf of Pinckney Benton Stewart Pinchback by Blanche Kelso Bruce of Mississippi, the first black senator elected to a full six-year term in the U.S. Senate, in 1875. The challenge to P. B. S. Pinchback's election to the U.S. Senate in 1873, by white politicians, revealed but one aspect of white political resistance to black political power in the South following the Civil War, during a ten-year period known as Black Reconstruction (1867–1877). This period of Reconstruction has been the subject of much historical debate and controversy as to the impact of black political power over the lives of blacks and whites in the South, which enjoyed the support of radical white Reconstructionists in the North like Senator Charles Sumner of Massachusetts and Congressman Thaddeus Stevens of Pennsylvania.

Lerone Bennett graphically describes the extent of black power and control during Black Reconstruction by observing: "A man, in this age, went to mail a letter, and the postmaster was black. A man committed a crime, and, in some counties, was arrested by a black policeman, prosecuted by a black solicitor, weighed by a black and white jury and sentenced by a black judge."

No black politician had greater influence during this period than P. B. S. Pinchback of Louisiana and thus his ranking here. Pinchback came to symbolize what blacks could be when the shackles of slavery were removed. He held more principal political offices than any African-American in American history: in 1868, he was elected to the state senate, becoming president *pro tempore* in 1871. As *pro tempore*, he became lieutenant governor at the death of Oscar Dunn, a black incumbent, in 1871; from December 1872 to January 1873 he became governor upon the impeachment of the white incumbent; in 1872, he was elected to Congress but denied his seat when challenged by his white Democratic foe; and he was elected to the U.S. Senate in 1873 by the reconstructed Louisiana legislature. Challenged again, he was finally denied his senate seat by a vote of 32 to 29.

P. B. S. Pinchback was born on May 10, 1837, in Macon, Georgia, of a white Mississippi planter father and a black mother who had been a slave. He was educated as a free black in Ohio, attending high school in Cincinnati. His early adulthood was spent as a boatman, and, in 1870, he organized a business for operating steamboats on the Mississippi River. Also in 1870, he established the *Louisianan*, a newspaper, and would in 1875 enlarge his national reputation by becoming chairman of the Convention of Colored Newspaper Men held in Cincinnati in

August. At that convention, his vision of and call for black unity were expressed as follows:

> We are numerous enough, and all we need is to be intelligent enough to take care of ourselves. We are four millions, out of thirty millions who inhabit this country and we have rights as well as privileges to maintain and we must assert our manhood in their vindication.... With this force as a political element, as laborers, producers and consumers, we are an element of strength and wealth too powerful to be ignored by the American People. All we need is a just appreciation of our own power and our own manhood.

Pinchback's influence in this vital organization led to the formation of the Associated Negro Press.

In the early 1900s, Pinchback would broaden his political influence by aligning himself with Booker T. Washington's politics and tactics. He died in Washington, D.C., on December 21, 1921, nearly three months after the second Pan-African Congress, which met in London under the leadership of W. E. B. Du Bois [4].

21

Marcus Garvey

1887–1940

Marcus Garvey is without doubt the most dangerous enemy of
the Negro people.

W. E. B. Du Bois

But the followers of Marcus Garvey, who are legion and noisy as
a tambourine yard party, give him the crown of Negro
leadership.

Claude McKay

The point and counterpoint of Du Bois's characterization of Marcus
Mosiah Garvey as "the most dangerous enemy of the Negro people" to
that of Claude McKay's picture of Garvey—seen by his followers as

having "the crown of Negro leadership," reveal the extremes of the perceived influence of Marcus Garvey's views and tactics on African-Americans. Both views of Garvey contain misleading hyperbole and bombastic pap: it's more accurate to say that Garvey was "the most dangerous enemy" to the black intelligentsia and light-skinned Negroes whose prototype was Du Bois, than a menace to the lives of the so-called black masses. Garvey's rhetoric and economic and social programs forced the black intelligentsia to clarify its role in uplifting the black masses in America; Garvey with "the crown of Negro leadership" was more a latter-day Booker T. Washington type, with a nationalistic view of blacks living in Africa—as opposed to Tuskegee—and an expounder of a group divisive propaganda of the "darker" and "purer" black leading the economic, political, and cultural renaissance of blacks throughout the world.

Although Garvey was born in Jamaica (August 17, 1887), and never became a U.S. citizen, for the purposes of this book he will be treated as an African-American because his major successes and influences were realized in the context of the black struggle for freedom and equality in America, from 1916 to 1927.

Garvey was the youngest of eleven children of parents who were "pure"—as he would boast—"Black Negroes." A printer's apprentice at an early age, in 1907 Garvey participated in a failed printer's strike and out of this experience started to organize workers and publish a newspaper called *The Watchman*. He left Jamaica for a while to work in Costa Rica on a banana plantation and on newspapers in Port Limon and Colon, Panama. He returned to Jamaica in 1911 and, in 1912, went to London seeking finances for his vision of organizing the black masses in self-help programs. While in England, he was influenced by an Egyptian nationalist and by reading the views and philosophies of Booker T. Washington: "I read *Up From Slavery* . . . and then my doom—if I may so call it—of being a race leader dawned upon me in London after I had traveled through almost half of Europe. I asked, 'Where is the black man's Government?' 'Where is his King and Kingdom?' 'Where is his President, his country, and his ambassador, his army, his navy, his men of big affairs?' I could not find them, and then I decided, 'I will help to make them.'"

Returning to Jamaica in 1914, Garvey founded the Universal Negro Improvement Association and African Communities (Imperial) League (more popularly known as UNIA) to unite the black race through race pride, education, the redemption of Africa and economic development.

His first effort to realize these goals was a trade school copied after Tuskegee. The effort was a failure. However, Garvey was invited by Booker T. Washington to visit Tuskegee in 1915, but could not do so until March 1916, some four months after Washington's death.

Garvey described his views and efforts after arriving in the U.S. in 1916:

> Here I found a new and different problem. I immediately visited some of the then so-called Negro leaders, only to discover, after a close study of them, that they had no program, but were mere opportunists who were living off their so-called leadership while the poor people were groping in the dark. I traveled through thirty-eight States and everywhere found the same condition. I visited Tuskegee and paid my respects to the dead hero, Booker Washington, and then returned to New York, where I organized the New York division of the Universal Negro Improvement Association.

Garvey recruited thousands to UNIA and by 1918 started publishing *The Negro World*, a weekly with sections in English, French, and Spanish that reached a circulation of over 50,000 and was distributed throughout the United States, the West Indies, Latin America, and Africa. By 1919, UNIA had branches in thirty different cities and according to Garvey, a membership of over two million.

Marcus Garvey's rhetoric and vision of a black nation ("Back-to-Africa"), led by "pure," black-skinned not light-colored Negroes, with an independently viable economy, reached their zenith in June 1919 with the launching of the Black Star Line, three UNIA ships that demonstrated the economic prowess of blacks (all funds were raised by selling stock to blacks only). These ships were also to provide transportation to the "African Motherland."

Garvey's fame and popularity among blacks grew throughout America and the world. However, it was his influence as a black leader, by organizing the black masses into an economic, political, and cultural group called UNIA, and therefore obliging the Negro leadership of America to clarify its views and programs for the "uplifting" of blacks that warrants his ranking here. Although one can question Garvey's use of a racial purity credo to divide blacks of different hues against one another in his struggle for leadership and power among the masses, the impact of his ideological views and economic programs for the black masses in America was without rival among other black organizations, like the nascent NAACP and National Urban League.

Garvey's leadership in building UNIA, with its Black Star Line and *Negro World* publication, his Negro Factories Corporation for loans and technical assistance to small black business, and his "Back-to-Africa" movement, with projects in Liberia, document his influence in the struggle for black freedom and equality.

Garvey was not the first to advocate a return of blacks to the "African Motherland" (see HALL [7], DELANY [13], GARNET [14]); however, he was the first major black-skinned leader to insist that authentic black leadership could only come from "pure" blacks. Garvey's influence on this issue was shown by the millions of ordinary blacks who flocked to his UNIA and, at the same time, by his compelling leaders like Du Bois, A. Phillip Randolph, and others to devote their energies and organizations to countering the "Garvey movement." A dramatic example of this was a "symposium" on Garvey by Negro leaders in September 1922, conducted by Chandler Owen, executive secretary of the Friends of Negro Freedom, to ascertain what Negro leaders thought should be done with Garvey, who was having legal problems with the U.S. government.

In 1922, Garvey and several of his associates were arrested by U.S. officials and charged with using the mail to defraud in promoting the sale of Black Star Line stock. In 1923 serving as attorney *pro se*, Garvey alone was convicted of fraud and sentenced to five years in prison and fined $1,000. After an unsuccessful appeal of his conviction, he began serving time in Atlanta in 1925. In 1927 his sentence was commuted by President Coolidge. Garvey was deported to Jamaica and stayed there until he went to London in 1935, living there until his death from a stroke on June 10, 1940.

Dr. Martin Luther King, Jr., noted the importance of Marcus Garvey when, in 1965, placing a wreath on Garvey's grave, he said:

> He was the first man of color in the history of the United States to lead and develop a mass movement. He was the first man on a mass scale and level to give millions of Negroes a sense of dignity and destiny. And make the Negro feel that he was somebody.

22

Thurgood Marshall

1908–1993

I do not believe that the meaning of the Constitution was forever "fixed" at the Philadelphia Convention. Nor do I find the wisdom, foresight and sense of justice exhibited by the framers particularly profound. To the contrary, the government they devised was defective from the start, requiring several amendments, a civil war and momentous social transformation to attain the system of constitutional government, and its respect for the individual freedoms and human rights we hold as fundamental today.

THURGOOD MARSHALL

As an irreverent gadfly, in 1954 Thurgood Marshall led a team of legal social engineers spawned by CHARLES H. HOUSTON [5] to a momentous social transformation of our system of constitutional government through the U.S. Supreme Court decision *Brown* v. *Board of Education*, which eviscerated the "separate but equal" doctrine of *Plessy* v. *Ferguson* in public schools. Marshall, like the other African-Americans listed in this volume, confronted a "defective" and hypocritical system of government that denied blacks, women, and others equal rights and privileges. Marshall's life has come to symbolize American justice, and justice and equality for the downtrodden.

In June 1991, in *Payne* v. *Tennessee*, as an associate justice of the very court before which he won the epochal *Brown* decision, Marshall bluntly and defiantly dissented from a conservative majority opinion for the last time by saying: "The majority today sends a clear signal that scores of established constitutional liberties are now ripe for reconsideration.... Tomorrow's victims may be minorities, women or the indigent. Invariably this campaign to resurrect yesterday's 'spirited dissents' will squander the authority and the legitimacy of this court as a protector of the powerless." *Payne* v. *Tennessee* dealt with the admissibility of evidence concerning a victim and his or her death during the sentencing stage of a capital murder trial.

Thurgood Marshall's ranking here acknowledges the impact he had on the U.S. Supreme Court, that institution of American government most responsible for protecting the rights and liberties of all Americans. Marshall's influence on the law can be measured by his leadership of the NAACP Legal Defense Fund, Inc., his judgeship on the U.S. Court of Appeals, and his role as U.S. solicitor general. He held all these positions before he became the ninety-sixth man, and the first black, to sit on the U.S. Supreme Court, where for twenty-four years he wrote opinions affecting public policy on institutional racism, the death penalty, civil and human rights, and women's rights, including the right to abortion.

As the most prominent and influential of Charles H. Houston's social engineers, Thurgood Marshall's influence is arguably greater than that of his mentor and, thus ranks him higher than Houston. This argument points again to the difficulty and inexactitude of ranking influential black figures. Once again, the rankings in this volume are not intended to diminish the importance or contribution of any one person, but to show the different yet interrelated roles of *The Black 100* on the struggle for black equality in America. More specifically, I weighted Houston's influence as the architect of the legal strategies to eliminate legal segregation in America as had been in effect through *Plessy* v. *Ferguson*, to be of greater impact than Marshall and others' implementations of these strategies, while assaulting institutional racism during the fifties and sixties, climaxing with the *Brown* decision of 1954. On this point Genna Rae McNeil observed:

> The NAACP's victory of 1954 in *Brown* v. *Board of Education* was simultaneously the culmination of the legal campaign based on Charles Hamilton Houston's modified strategy carried forward by the NAACP's cadre of lawyers and a watershed decision in constitutional law with respect to equal protection of the laws.

Thurgood Marshall with other U.S. Supreme Court justices.

Thurgood Marshall was born in Baltimore, on July 2, 1908, six months before the founding of the NAACP. He was the great-grandson of slaves. His father, William, was a steward at an all-white country club on the Chesapeake Bay. His mother, Norma, was an elementary school teacher at an all-black school in Baltimore. Marshall said his father told him early on, "Son, if anyone ever calls you a nigger, you not only got my permission to fight him, you've got my order to fight him."

With this injunction to fight, Marshall attended all-black elementary and secondary schools and in 1930 graduated with a B.A. from Lincoln University, a black college in Oxford, Pennsylvania, as a pre-dental student. He decided instead to become a lawyer and was admitted to Howard University's Law School after being rejected at the University of Maryland's Law School. (Marshall would later, with Charles H. Houston, successfully challenge the University's admission policies in *University of Maryland* v. *Murray*.) In 1933 Marshall received his law degree from Howard, under Houston's tutelage.

In 1938, Marshall succeeded Houston as the head of the NAACP's Legal Defense Fund, Inc. For the next twenty-three years, he and his associates used the NAACP's "Inc. Fund," as it came to be called, as the cutting edge for challenges to institutionalized segregation as violations of the Fourteenth Amendment.

With the template developed while at Howard with Houston and others such as Edward Lovett, Oliver W. Hill, James G. Tyson, and Leslie S. Perry, Marshall, while head of the "Inc, Fund," won pivotal cases that directly attacked the separate but equal doctrine of *Plessy* v. *Ferguson: Sweatt* v. *Painter, Mclaurin* v. *Oklahoma State Regents*, and, the most monumental, *Brown* v. *Board of Education* in 1954. Altogether, Marshall would win twenty-nine of thirty-two cases before the U.S. Supreme Court.

Chief Justice Earl Warren, in *Brown* asked and answered a question blacks had asked and answered by struggle and protest (see HALL [7]) since the provenances of slavery, racism, and *Plessy*: "Does segregation of children in public schools solely on the basis of race, even though the physical facilities and other tangible factors may be equal, deprive the children of the minority group of equal educational opportunities? We believe it does."

The impact of this decision was to abolish legal American apartheid and shape the battleground for direct militant actions by blacks against political and economic barriers in American life.

Marshall joined these struggles as a judge on the U.S. Court of

Appeals (1961, nominated by John F. Kennedy), as U.S. solicitor general (1965, nominated by Lyndon B. Johnson), and as associate justice of the U.S. Supreme Court (1967, appointed by Johnson).

Thurgood Marshall, having always realized that American government is one of people and their views and values more than abstract laws, stepped down from the court on June 27, 1991, after offering some additional caustic and prophetic utterances in *Payne* v. *Tennessee*: "Power, not reason, is the new currency of this court's decision making... Neither the law nor the facts supporting [the law] underwent any change in the last four years. Only the personnel of this court did."

On July 1, 1991, President George Bush nominated CLARENCE THOMAS [98], a forty-three-year-old black man, an ideological opposite of Marshall, to succeed him and to become the one hundred and sixth person, but only the second black, to sit on the Supreme Court.

Thurgood Marshall died on January 24, 1993 in the Navy Medical Center, Bethesda, Maryland, of heart failure.

23

Malcolm X

1925–1965

I think it was eight years ago today that the Supreme Court
handed down the desegregation decision [*Brown* v. *Board of
Education*]. And despite the fact that eight years have gone
past, that decision hasn't been implemented yet. I don't have
that much faith. I don't have that much confidence. I don't have
that much patience. And I don't have that much ignorance. If
the Supreme Court, which is the highest law-making body in
the country, can pass a decision that can't get even eight
percent compliance within eight years, because it's for black
people, then my patience has run out.

MALCOLM X

This assessment by El-Hajj Malik El-Shabazz (Malcolm X's Muslim name) of the effect of the outlawing of segregation in public schools on the quality of black life in America reflected a widespread disenchantment with white institutions, with "integrationist" attitudes, and with the tactics and ideologies of nonviolent-action leaders, like DR. MARTIN LUTHER KING JR. [1], ROY WILKINS [33], A. PHILLIP RANDOLPH [31], and others. Indeed, Malcolm would force those he labeled "so-called Negro" leaders and Negro organizations to prove the effectiveness of both their religious and nonreligious ideologies and tactics in the face of the ineffective implementation of *Brown* and the overall lack of black progress toward full economic, social, and political equality in America. He described the situation graphically:

> I will never say that progress [for blacks] is being made. If you stick a knife in my back nine inches and pull it out six inches, there's no progress. You pull it all the way out, that's not progress. The progress is healing the wound that's below— that's below me. And they [white America] haven't even begun to pull the knife out, much less try to heal the wound.

Like Robert Alexander Young, DAVID WALKER [9], HENRY H. GARNET [14], and MARTIN R. DELANY [13] a hundred years before him, and MARCUS GARVEY [21] forty years before him, Malcolm would come to symbolize a black consciousness: the "knife" of white America was in the back of all blacks, regardless of their institutional labels and leadership cognomens:

> Let us remember that we're not brutalized because we're Baptists. We're not brutalized because we're Methodists. We're not brutalized because we're Muslims. We're not brutalized because we're Catholics. We're brutalized because we are black people in America. . .
>
> You and I learn a lesson from that. We are oppressed. We are exploited. We are downtrodden. We are denied not only civil rights, but even human rights. So the only way we're going to get some of this oppression and exploitation away from us, or aside from us, is to come together against a common enemy.

Malcolm's impact on the black struggle in America and throughout the world was demonstrated by his skill, like that of Dr. Martin Luther King, Jr., in fusing religion to the empowerment and liberation of blacks (in this regard, Malcolm is no less a black liberationist theologian than Nat Turner, Gabriel Prosser, David Walker, Henry H. Garnet, and others). Malcolm's belief that Islam and its God, Allah, could liberate blacks influenced the lives and actions of tens of thousands of blacks during the fifties and sixties. Malcolm's conversion to Islam while in prison in 1948, and the conversion of thousands of blacks through the teachings of ELIJAH MUHAMMAD [51] to his Nation of Islam, represented to many blacks the bankruptcy of white Christianity in the struggle for black freedom and power in America. (For more discussion on this issue, see the author's *What Color Is Your God?*) It should also be noted on this point that a perusal of *Walker's Appeal* and Garnet's *Address to Slaves* will rebut the notions that Christianity can't and will not aid in the liberation of blacks in America and throughout the world.

Malcolm's effective manipulation of the mass media—he was second only to Dr. King in this ability—to shape the thinking of "blacks in the diaspora" about issues relating to the legitimacy and use of violence, black institution building and its controls, black unity (in America and globally), black pride and identity, and the eradication of racism support Malcolm's ranking here. Although Malcolm saw the interrelatedness of all these issues, it was probably his demand that blacks use "any means necessary" in their struggle that made him the symbol of black resistance to white brutality and violence:

> If you think we are here to tell you to love the white man, you have come to the wrong place. And those of you who think that you, perhaps, came here to hear us tell you to turn the other cheek to the brutality of the white man, I say, again, you came to the wrong place. But no matter what happens, we don't teach you to turn the other cheek. We don't teach you to turn the other cheek in the South, and we don't teach you to turn the other cheek in the North. We teach you to obey the law. We teach you to carry yourselves in a respectable way. But, at the same time, we teach you that anyone who puts his hand on you, do your best to see that he doesn't put it on anybody else.

Malcolm was born Malcolm Little on May 19, 1925, in Omaha,

Nebraska, nearly three months after Marcus Garvey entered federal prison in Atlanta for mail fraud. Malcolm's father, Earl Little, was a Baptist Minister, who was also a local president of Marcus Garvey's Universal Negro Improvement Association. M. Louise Norton, his mother, was born in Grenada. The Little family was run out of Omaha by white terrorists and migrated to Lansing, Michigan. There, when Malcolm was six years old, his father was apparently murdered by white terrorists when thrown under a street car. Malcolm dropped out of school after finishing the eighth grade at Mason Junior High School in Lansing. He became a part of the mean streets of Detroit, Boston, and Harlem, as a hustler, pimp, thug, dealer and user of drugs, and burglar. In this last identity, he was arrested, convicted, and sent to prison for up to ten years at the age of twenty-one, in 1946—the year JACK JOHNSON [63] died. Malcolm described the period from the eighth grade to prison as follows: "I finished the eighth grade in Mason, Michigan. My high school was the black ghetto of Roxbury, Massachusetts. My college was in the streets of Harlem, and my Master's was taken in prison."

While in prison in 1948 Malcolm was converted to the teachings of Elijah Muhammad after being introduced to Islam by his younger brother Reginald. In August 1952, paroled from prison, Malcolm went to Detroit to live with an older brother, Wilfred, who was also a Muslim. Within a month, Malcolm met Elijah Muhammad in Chicago, while visiting with other Muslims the headquarters of the Nation of Islam. Shortly after this meeting, Muhammad gave Malcolm the "X" to replace his "slave surname" of Little. Elijah Muhammad would later invite Malcolm to Chicago to develop further his understanding of the Islamic religion. Malcolm would soon become second only to Muhammad as teacher and messenger to the "lost black sheep of the diaspora."

For nearly twelve years, Malcolm X was the most influential and effective spokesperson for the Nation of Islam and its messenger, Elijah Muhammad, organizing scores of Muslim temples from coast to coast and increasing the membership in the Nation of Islam to many thousands.

Malcolm's preaching the basic tenets of Islam not only affected those who called themselves Black Muslims but blacks in general, especially blacks who resonated with Malcolm's insistence on black pride and "black is beautiful." He would often say:

Who taught you to hate the texture of your hair? Who taught you to hate the color of your skin, to such extent that you

bleach it to get like the white man. Who taught you to hate
the shape of your nose and the shape of your lips? Who
taught you to hate yourself, from the top of your head to the
soles of your feet? Who taught you to hate your own kind?
Who taught you to hate the race that you belong to, so much
so that you don't want to be around each other? You know,
before you come asking Mr. Muhammad, does he teach hate,
you should ask yourselves who taught you to hate being what
God gave you. We teach you to love the hair that God gave
you.

After Elijah Muhammad suspended Malcolm for ninety days in
December 1963, for comments he made characterizing the assassination
of John F. Kennedy as "chickens coming home to roost," Malcolm quit
the Nation of Islam in March 1964 and formed his own Muslim Mosque,
Inc., in Harlem. Later that year he also began the Organization of Afro-
American Unity, with branches in Africa, Europe, and the United
States.

After a pilgrimage (hajj) to Mecca in spring 1964, Malcolm
converted to Orthodox Islam, changed his name to El-Hajj Malik El-
Shabazz, renounced Elijah Muhammad and his teachings, and embraced a more humanistic and global view of the "black problem" in
America and throughout the world.

After a series of threats and attempts on his life, following his break
from the Nation of Islam, Malcolm was shot and killed as he began to
speak to his followers at the Audubon Ballroom in Harlem on February
21, 1965.

At his funeral on Saturday morning, February 27, 1965, at the
Faith's Temple of God in Christ on Amsterdam Avenue and 150th street
in Harlem, renowned activist-artist OSSIE DAVIS [91] gave the eulogy:

Many will say, "Turn away, away from this man, for he is not a
man but a demon, a monster, a subverter and an enemy of
the black man." And we will smile. They will say that "He is
of hate, a fanatic, a racist who can only bring evil to the cause
for which you struggle." And we will answer and say unto
them, "Did you ever talk to Brother Malcolm? Did you ever
touch him or have him smile at you? Did you ever really
listen to him? Did he ever do a mean thing? Was he ever,
himself, associated with violence or any public disturbance?

For if you did, you would know him, and if you knew him, you would know why we must honor him. Malcolm was our manhood, our living black manhood. This was his meaning to his people. And in honoring him, we honor the best in ourselves." However much we differed with him or with each other about him and his values as a man, let his going from us serve only to bring us together now.

Consigning these mortal remains to Earth, the common mother of all, secure in the knowledge that what we place in the ground is no more, now, a man, but the seed, which after the winter of discontent, will come forth again to meet us. And we shall know him then for what he was and is—a prince, our own black, shining prince, who did not hesitate to die because he loved us so.

El-Hajj Malik El-Shabazz, as "prince" and "seed," is the fulfillment of the words of Christ:

Verily, verily, I say unto you, except a corn [seed] of wheat fall in the ground and die, it abideth alone: but if it die, it bringeth forth much fruit.

John 12:24

Dr. Martin Luther King, Jr., and Ralph Abernathy (background) with Malcolm X in 1964.

24

Paul Robeson

1898–1976

Robeson was a burning intellect and an exceptionally gifted
man who stood tallest among the tall because of the effective
way in which he used his gifts. Paul Robeson, a man of African
descent, and proud of it....

He was the first American artist who used his artistry as a
political weapon for his race. For this he suffered greatly in
America.

GIL NOBLE

Paul Robeson proclaimed, in 1934: "In my music, my plays, my films I want to carry always this central idea: to be African. Multitudes of men have died for less worthy ideals; it is even more eminently worth living for."

Robeson's ability and courage to politicize black aesthetics—and black culture—for the liberation of black people in America and throughout the world warrant his ranking here. Although he was as much a part of the cultural renaissance of the twenties and thirties as DU BOIS [4], LOCKE [36], JOHNSON [26], HUGHES [34], and others, he was without peer in his effectiveness in linking black culture to the struggle of the black and white working class in America and to the liberation of colonial peoples in Africa. In his performances in the United States and throughout the world, Robeson used elements of black culture such as Negro spirituals, black folk songs, and black dialect as his "weapons" to enlighten and sensitize whites and blacks to unjust conditions among African-Americans. The reader is encouraged to investigate the pioneering efforts of JAMES WELDON JOHNSON [26] in documenting the origins and meanings to the black struggle of Negro spirituals and black sermons. For example, see *The Book of American Negro Spirituals* (1925) and *God's Trombones, Seven Negro Sermons in Verse* (1927).

Philip S. Foner commented on the use of spirituals by Robeson:

> He never failed to point out that the Negro spirituals he brought into the concert halls of the United States and Europe were songs which had strengthened the slaves' determination to survive, and while they had given the slaves a certain measure of joy, they had also raised the collective spirit of an oppressed class. He always introduced "Go Down Moses" by explaining that it had helped the slaves in preparation to escape to freedom in the North, and that the heroic freedom fighter, Harriet Tubman, was identical with the figure of Moses in the spiritual, for, as an escaped slave herself, she had returned to the South again and again to rescue others who were still in bondage.

Paul Robeson's singleminded devotion "to be African" and his use of black culture for the liberation of black—and white—workers in America, Africa, and throughout the world caused him to "suffer greatly in America," as Gil Noble pointed out. This was exacerbated by his admiration for and embrace of the Soviet Union and its people, in the thirties, forties, and fifties. In 1935, after visiting the Soviet Union, Robeson said:

> In Soviet Russia I breathe freely for the first time in my life. It is clear, whether a Negro is politically a Communist or not, that of all the nations in the world, the modern Russians are our best friends.

In 1949 Robeson declared:

> The Soviet Union is the friend of the African and West Indian peoples. And no imperialist wolf disguised as a benevolent watchdog, and not Tito disguised as a revolutionary, can convince them that Moscow oppresses the small nations. Africa knows the Soviet Union is the defender and champion of the rights of all nations—large and small—to control their own destinies.
>
> To those who dare to question my patriotism, who have the unmitigated insolence to question my love for the true America and my right to be an American—to question me, whose father and forefathers fertilized the very soil of this country with their toil and with their bodies—to such people I answer that those and *only* those who work for a policy of friendship with the Soviet Union are genuine American patriots.

In April 1949, at the World Congress of the Defenders of Peace in Paris, Robeson would say: "It is unthinkable...that American Negroes would go to war on behalf of those who have oppressed us for generations [the United States] against a country [the Soviet Union] which in one generation has raised our people to full human dignity of mankind."

Robeson in 1937 cofounded the influential Council of African Affairs for the "struggle of the African masses"; the dissemination of "accurate information concerning Africa and its people; and the strengthening of the alliance of progressive Americans, black and white, with the people of Africa and other lands in the common struggle for world peace and freedom." For a while, he cochaired the council with W. E. B. Du Bois.

Like Du Bois, Robeson's political views and activities brought him into conflict with both the white and black establishment. His association with the Soviet government and its people placed on him the labels communist and socialist during the early fifties through the sixties. In 1950 the U.S. State Department denied Robeson a passport because of his refusal to sign an affidavit as to his membership in the Communist party. The passport division said: "The action was taken because the Department considers that Paul Robeson's travel abroad at this time would be contrary to the best interest of the United States."

Paul Bustill Robeson was born in Princeton, New Jersey, on April 9, 1898, twelve days before the beginning of the Spanish-American War. His father had been a runaway slave from a plantation in North Carolina, served with the Union Army during the Civil War, and later worked his way through Lincoln University to become minister of the Witherspoon Street Presbyterian Church in Princeton. Paul's mother, Maria Louisa Bustill Robeson, bore five children, of whom he was the youngest, and died in 1904 from burns suffered in a house fire.

In 1909 Robeson's family moved to Somerville, New Jersey, where his father became pastor of St. Thomas A.M.E. Zion Church. Robeson attended predominantly white Somerville High School. In 1915, he entered Rutgers College in New Brunswick, where he became a scholar-athlete: Phi Beta Kappa and twelve letters in football, track, baseball, basketball. His senior thesis was titled "The Fourteenth Amendment, the Sleeping Giant of the American Constitution."

After graduating in 1919 from Rutgers, Robeson moved to Harlem and in 1920 entered Columbia University Law School. While in law school he played professional football to earn money for school. He graduated from Columbia in 1923 and in 1924 began working in a white law firm, which he quit the same year because a white secretary refused to take dictation from him.

Robeson's career as an actor and singer began with appearances in *Taboo* (1922) and two plays (1925) by Eugene O'Neill, *All God's Chillun* and the revival of *The Emperor Jones*. Also in April 1925, Robeson performed a concert consisting of all Negro or black music—spirituals, folk and dialect songs—thus launching the use of black culture to assist the black struggle in America and throughout the world.

From 1927 to 1939 Paul Robeson spent most of his time in Europe, linking the black struggle for freedom and equality with nonblack working-class people, concluding that "the Negro must be conscious of himself and yet internationally linked with the nations which are culturally akin to him." He traveled extensively throughout the world, including the Soviet Union, Asia, and Europe.

OSSIE DAVIS [91] iconographically describes Robeson as a man who was greater than the sum of his parts:

> Paul was a man and a half, and we have no category, even now, to hold the size of him. Something about him escapes our widest, most comprehensive embrace, and we've never been able to put our finger on exactly what it is. Athletic champion, yes; Phi Beta Kappa scholar, singer, actor, spokesman, activist, leader—yes! Africanist, socialist, black Nationalist—all that, too, but something more, something new, something different.
>
> Paul spoke twenty-five languages not as an exercise but as a source through which he could absorb the many cultures into which he had not been born, but to which he was instinctively determined to belong. He consumed a language for the cultural essences it contained, and became in practice, in custom, and in habit, a loyal member of all the groups whose songs he sang. He studied many life styles till they became his by second nature, was himself transfigured by what he learned, and became by *accident* what socialist societies are meant to produce by design.

Paul Robeson's quest "to be African" in all his thoughts and deeds has come to symbolize the duty of all African-Americans to utilize their diverse, rich culture, to promote a black aesthetics and to liberate blacks and all people, everywhere.

Eric Bentley said: "Robeson the activist shows himself really significant...[By his] alignment with the future, Paul Robeson was a brother of Malcolm X, Stokely Carmichael, Rap Brown, Huey Newton, Eldridge Cleaver, before they were to take his hand."

Paul Robeson died January 23, 1976, in Philadelphia, one year to the day before *Roots* by ALEX HALEY [48] appeared on national television.

Paul Robeson and others picketing Ford's Theater in Baltimore, in 1947.

25

Carter G. Woodson

1875–1950

We have a wonderful history behind us....

It reads like the history of people in an heroic age....

If you read the history of Africa, the history of your ancestors—people of whom you should feel proud—you will realize that they have a history that is worthwhile. They have traditions that have value of which you can boast and upon which you can base a claim for the right to share in the blessings of democracy.

We are going back to that beautiful history and it is going to inspire us to greater achievements.

CARTER G. WOODSON

By going back scientifically to that "beautiful history" of blacks in America, Africa, and throughout the world, Carter Godwin Woodson earned the title "Father of Negro History." Woodson's "black historiography," an objective black perspective of history wedded to scientific methods and procedures, liberated black history from the racist biases and stereotypes of white historians and their "unscientific historiography." (The reader should note that W. E. B. DU BOIS [4] pioneered black historiography with *The Suppression of the African Slave Trade* and *Black Reconstruction.*)

Carter Woodson's influence in causing both blacks and whites to reexamine black history through a black historiography justifies his ranking here. Additional measures of Woodson's influence can be seen in his cofounding the Association for the Study of Negro Life and History (1915); his establishment of the seminal *Journal of Negro History* (1916); his incorporation of Associated Publishers to produce black history textbooks and learning materials (1921); his initiation and institutionalization of Negro History Week (1926); and his creation of the *Negro History Bulletin* (1937) to provide supplementary instructional tools for teaching history in the elementary and secondary grades.

Further supporting Woodson's ranking here are his scholarly writings, among which are *The Education of the Negro Prior to 1861* (1915); *The History of the Negro Church* (1921), *A Century of Negro Migration* (1918), and *The African Background Outlined* (1936). Woodson also wrote and edited other widely used, popular volumes such as *Negro Orators and Their Orations* (1925), *The Mind of the Negro as Reflected in Letters Written During the Crisis, 1800–1860* (1926), *The Miseducation of the Negro* (1933), and *African Heroes and Heroines* (1939). His cumulative accomplishments as a historian, writer, and educator would become vital elements of the historic cultural infrastructure upon which blacks could "boast" and "base" their "claim for the right to share in the blessings of democracy!"

Carter Woodson was born on December 19, 1875, in New Canton, Virginia, to James Woodson and Anne Eliza (Riddle) Woodson, former slaves, within a month of the apogee of black political representation during Black Reconstruction, with eight blacks in the Forty-Fourth United States Congress. Woodson was the eldest of nine children and was forced to work at an early age to help his parents make ends meet. This precluded his attending school until he was twenty years old. At twenty, self-educated, he entered Douglass High School in West

Virginia part-time, and finished there in 1896. Woodson later attended Berea College in Kentucky and received his bachelor's degree in 1903.

After teaching for several years in West Virginia, serving for three years as supervisor of schools in the Philippines (1903–1906), and traveling abroad to Europe, Africa, and Asia, Woodson returned to the United States to finish his studies for a B.A. begun during the summer of 1902 at the University of Chicago. He received his degree in the spring of 1908 and, in late summer of the same year, was also awarded an M.A. by the University of Chicago. He completed studies for his Ph.D. at Harvard University in 1912.

As an historiographer, Woodson greatly influenced the black experience—the American experience. However, his influences as an educator and activist shouldn't be overlooked. Woodson during the thirties and forties shaped the debate among black scholars and activists about the purpose and utility of formal education to the "uplift" of black people. Woodson said on these issues: "For me, education means to inspire people to live more abundantly, to learn to begin with life as they find it and make it better." He further specified, in *The Miseducation of the Negro*, that educated Negroes were not meeting these goals or providing a "better life" for the black masses:

> The large majority of the Negroes who have put on the finishing touches of our best colleges, however, are all but worthless in the uplift of their people. If, after leaving school, they have the opportunity to give out to Negroes what traducers of the race have taught them, such person may earn a living by teaching or preaching to Negroes what someone would like to have them know, but they never become a constructive force in the elevating of those far down. They become estranged from the masses and the gap between widens as the years go by.

Needless to say, Woodson's positions on these issues, on education in general and on the obligation of the black educated class to "uplift" the black masses in particular, continue to shape contemporary debate among blacks from all walks of life who are committed to the liberation of blacks in America and throughout the world.

A lasting monument to Woodson's influence as a historian-activist is his organizing for the second week of February in 1926, the first Negro History Week celebration. Negro History Week has now become Black

Carter G. Woodson,
with collection of
his publications.

History Month, because, in large part, Woodson became his own words
to black people and all Americans: a person "to inspire us to greater
achievements."

Like two of his contemporaries, Marcus Garvey and W. E. B. Du
Bois, Carter Woodson saw the need for black economic independence
as the best and *only* way for blacks to protect and further their political,
social, and cultural interests and to ensure the blessings of "real
democracy." He declared prophetically in 1922:

> In the first place, we need to attain economic independence.
> You may talk about rights and all that sort of thing. The
> people who own this country will rule this country. They
> always have done so and they always will. The people who
> control the coal and iron, the banks, the stock markets, and
> all that sort of thing, those are the people who will dictate
> exactly what shall be done for every group in this land. More
> than that, liberty is to come to the Negro, not as a bequest,
> but as a conquest. When I speak of it as a conquest, I mean
> that the Negro must contribute something to the good of his
> race, something to the good of his country, and something to
> the honor and glory of God. Economic independence is the
> first step in that direction.

Carter Woodson died on April 3, 1950, in Washington, D.C.,
nineteen days before the death of CHARLES H. HOUSTON [5].

26

James Weldon Johnson

1871–1938

And we ought to gather inspiration from the fact that we are in the right. We are contending for only what we are entitled to under the organic law of the land, and by any high standard of civilization, of morality, or of decency. Black America is called upon to stand as the protagonist of tolerance, of fair play, of justice, and of good will. Until white America heeds, we shall never let its conscience sleep. For the responsibility for the outcome is not ours alone. White America cannot save itself if it prevents us from being saved. But, in the nature of things, white America is not going to yield what rightfully belongs to us without a struggle kept up by us. In that struggle our watchword needs to be, "Work, work, work!" and our rallying cry, "Fight, fight, fight!"

JAMES WELDON JOHNSON

James Weldon Johnson significantly influenced black America's ability to stand "as the protagonist of tolerance, of fair play, of justice, and of good will" during the first thirty-five years of the twentieth century.

Like two of his contemporaries, W. E. B. DU BOIS [4] and CARTER G. WOODSON [25], James Weldon Johnson was a Renaissance man, a writer, poet, educator, lawyer, diplomat, civil rights activist, and lyricist. In this last identity, in 1900 Johnson wrote the lyrics (his brother, J. Rosamond Johnson wrote the music) for what would come to be known as the Negro National Anthem, "Lift Every Voice and Sing." In the first stanza he reaffirmed the black struggle for that which "rightfully belongs to us":

> Lift ev'ry voice and sing
> Till earth and heaven ring
> Ring with the harmonies of Liberty;
> Let our rejoicing rise
> High as the list'ning skies,
> Let it resound loud as the rolling sea.
> Sing a song full of the faith that the
> dark past has taught us.
> Sing a song full of the hope that the
> present has brought us.
> Facing the rising sun of our new day begun,
> Let us march on till victory is won.

Although Johnson exerted influence in many arenas, his ranking here recognizes his significant impact on the black struggle for freedom in America through his affiliation with the National Association for the Advancement of Colored People (NAACP) from 1916 to 1930, first as a field secretary and later as its executive secretary, from 1920 to 1930, and his leading role during the cultural movement known as the Negro or Harlem Renaissance of the 1920s and thirties.

While serving as field secretary for the NAACP in 1917, Johnson reported in the *Branch Bulletin* for March his effectiveness at organizing branches throughout principal cities in the South:

> Up to the present, branches have been organized in Richmond, Norfolk, Raleigh, Durham, Greensboro, N.C., Atlanta, Athens, Augusta, Columbia, Charleston, Savannah and Jacksonville.

The response of our people in the South to the call being made to them shows the wisdom of the Association in taking the step to organize south of Washington. In every city that I have visited I have found the thinking men and women of the race alive to the situation and ready to take part in the work that must be done. They also realize that the condition that has been brought about by the movement of colored people from the South to the North gives the greatest opportunity that has come in the last forty years for a demand to be made for those things to which the Negro is rightly entitled.

[For example]...The branch formed in Savannah has suggested a united effort of all the newly organized Georgia branches to right the present "Jim Crow" condition. There is no doubt that the new organizations in all of the southern cities will soon be actively engaged in work to change and better conditions in the communities which they represent.

In 1920, Johnson became the first black secretary of the NAACP. Under his leadership the Association continued to organize new branches throughout the country, to organize antilynching marches and promote antilynching legislation, and promulgate its integrationist policies and goals. Johnson also played an influential role in mediating clashes and disputes between followers of W. E. B. Du Bois and those of Booker T. Washington. In this role he gained the reputation of cautious conservative, to which he later responded in *Negro Americans, What Now*?:

To revolutionary elements it will no doubt appear that what I have outlined is too conservative. If it does, it is not because I am unconscious of the need of fundamental social change, but because I am considering the realities of the situation. Conservatism and radicalism are relative terms. It is as radical for a black American in Mississippi to claim his full rights under the Constitution and the law as it is for a white American in any state to advocate the overthrow of the existing national government. The black American in many instances puts life in jeopardy, and anything more radical than that cannot reasonably be required.

James Weldon Johnson's position in the Negro or Harlem Renaissance can be gathered from his publications during this period: *The Book of American Negro Spirituals* (1925); *The Second Book of American Negro Spirituals* (1926); *The Autobiography of an Ex-Colored Man* (1912, reprinted 1927); *God's Trombones, Seven Negro Sermons in Verse* (1927); *Black Manhattan* (1930); and *Negro American, What Now?* (1934). These works proved conclusively the rich and diverse contribution of blacks not only to black life and culture but also to the general American culture. In 1925, in an important essay in *Harpers Magazine* dealing with his writings and the significance of the work during the Renaissance of others such as his brother J. Rosamond Johnson, Claude McKay, Jean Toomer, Rudolph Fisher, Marion Anderson, Alain Locke, Langston Hughes, and Edmonia Lewis, James Weldon Johnson concluded that the Renaissance debunked:

> the common idea... that the Negro reached America intellectually, culturally, and morally empty, and that he is here to be filled—filled with education, filled with religion, filled with morality, filled with culture. In a word, the stereotype is that the Negro is nothing more than a beggar at the gate of the nation, waiting to be thrown crumbs of civilization. Through his artistic efforts the Negro is smashing this immemorial stereotype faster than he has ever done through any other method he has been able to use. He is making it realized that he is the possessor of a wealth of natural endowments and that he has long been a generous giver to America. He is impressing upon the national mind the conviction that he is an active and important force in American life; that he is a creator as well as a creature; that he has given as well as received; that he is the potential giver of larger and richer contributions.
>
> In this way the Negro is bringing about an entirely new national conception of himself; he has placed himself in an entirely new light before the American people. I do not think it too much to say that through artistic achievement the Negro has found a means of getting at the very core of the prejudice against him, by challenging the Nordic superiority complex. A great deal has been accomplished in this decade of "renaissance."

James William Johnson was born on June 17, 1871, in Jacksonville, Florida (he changed his middle name to Weldon in 1913). His father, James, was a freeman born in Richmond, Virginia, and his mother, Helen Louise, was born in Nassau, Bahamas. James was the second of three children; the oldest, a sister, died shortly after her birth and his brother, John [J.] Rosamond was born in 1873.

Johnson attended elementary schools in Jacksonville and, because there were no secondary schools for blacks in Jacksonville, attended secondary school at Atlanta University, where he also completed his undergraduate education in 1894. After getting his B.A., he returned to Jacksonville and became principal of the Stanton School from 1894 to 1901. In 1899 he became the first black person admitted to the Florida bar.

In 1901, he and his musically gifted brother moved to New York City to get involved in the music business. From 1900 to 1906 they collaborated on songs like "Since You Went Away," "Congo Love Song," and the famous "Lift Every Voice and Sing." They also teamed up with Robert Cole to write several successful songs for Broadway productions, such as "Under the Bamboo Tree" and "Didn't He Ramble." They also wrote and produced in 1903 the *Evolution of Ragtime: A Musical Suite of Six Songs Tracing and Illustrating Negro Music.*

In 1906, Johnson was appointed by President Theodore Roosevelt U.S. consul in Venezuela, and in 1909 he became consul in Nicaragua.

In 1912 Johnson published his benchmark novel *The Autobiography of an Ex-Colored Man*, in which he detailed the experience of a light-skinned Negro passing for white in America. In 1913, after leading a diplomatic life, he became editor of the *New York Age*. In 1916 he began his association with the NAACP.

On his birthday, in 1938, en route to his summer home in Maine, James Weldon Johnson was mortally injured when a train struck his car. He died on June 26.

He wrote his own epitaph:

I will not allow one prejudiced person or one million or one hundred million to blight my life, I will not let prejudice or any of its attendant humiliations and injustices bear me down to spiritual defeat. My inner life is mine, and I shall defend and maintain its integrity against all the powers of Hell.

27

George Washington Carver
1864(?)–1943

I can't offer you money, position or fame. The first two you have; the last, from the place you now occupy, you will no doubt achieve. These things I now ask you to give up, I offer you in their place work—hard, hard work—the task of bringing a people from degradation, poverty, and waste to full manhood.
BOOKER T. WASHINGTON

I am coming.
GEORGE WASHINGTON CARVER

"I am coming." With these simple words, in 1896, George Washington Carver accepted Booker T. Washington's offer to become the director of Agricultural Research and Experimental Station at Tuskegee Normal and Industrial Institute in Alabama, of which Washington was principal and founder. Accepting Washington's challenge, Carver over the next forty years or so used agriculture as a tool to open the "door of freedom to our people," through his scientific creativity in developing and producing crops and their by-products that would renew the viability of southern soils ravaged by the single-crop system—cotton or tobacco—associated with slavery. Carver's discoveries had their greatest impact in the improvement of the quality of life, economically, for the disproportionate number of blacks still residing in the South at this time, whose livelihood was tied to the soil as tenant farmers, farm workers, and sharecroppers. Carver's discoveries also benefited white farmers; the most prominent of them a peanut farmer from Plains, Georgia, who would become President of the United States: Jimmy Carter.

Not since BENJAMIN BANNEKER [16] had an African-American man of science had as much direct influence on the black struggle for full equality in America. Thus George Washington Carver's ranking here. This ranking is not intended to diminish the scientific contributions of black scientists like Norbert Rillieux (1806–1894, sugar refining), Jan Matzeliger (1852–1889, shoe manufacturing), Lewis H. Latimer (1848–1928, electric lighting), and others, but only illustrates, again, the author's application of his own criteria of the importance and influence of Carver's discoveries on black people and others. Surely, Carver's major role in the restoration of Southern agriculture meets these criteria.

George Washington Carver was born on the Moses and Susan Carver Plantation in Diamond Grove, Missouri, of slave parents in an unknown year—believed to be around 1864—after the Emancipation Proclamation and at the height of the Civil War. By one account he and his mother were kidnapped by a band of white slave-raiders and sold into slavery in Arkansas, where later his owner paid a ransom of a race horse for his return (his mother mysteriously disappeared).

After Emancipation, Carver continued to live with the Carvers. He learned to read and write and later attended an all-Negro school in Neosho, Missouri, and, after a period of meandering, completed high school in Minneapolis, Kansas.

Carver became interested in botany and applied for admission to Highland University in Kansas, where he was first accepted on his academic record but because he was black, was later rejected when he appeared to start his studies. He later attended Simpson College in Iowa (1890–91) and in 1891 Iowa State College at Ames (Iowa Agricultural

George Washington Carver in laboratory at Tuskegee.

College), with interests in agriculture and botany. He received a bachelor of science degree with honors from Iowa State in 1894. His thesis was "Plants as Modified by Man." Two years later he received his master's degree from Iowa State and joined the faculty with an ever-increasing reputation as an expert in mycology (fungi) and horticulture. He remained there until Booker T. Washington invited him to join the faculty at Tuskegee.

At Tuskegee, Carver took the twenty acres assigned to his unit and conducted research experiments on legumes like peanuts and cow peas, nitrogen producing plants that convert nitrogen into nitrates, which act as fertilizers for enriching soil. When coordinated with soil management and crop rotations, these provided Southern farmers—black and white—with hundreds of by-products that returned Southern agriculture to prominence as a supplier of new agricultural products to America and the world.

Carver is most famous for his work with the peanut, from which he derived some three hundred products. Of the potency of the peanut in enriching the ravaged soil of the South, he said:

> Plant peanuts. They are excellent legumes, they enrich the soil, they are easy to plant, easy to grow, and easy to harvest, they are rich in protein and good for feeding livestock, they yield a high percentage of oil of a superior quality. A pound of peanuts contains a little more of the bodybuilding nutrients than a pound of sirloin steak.

Carver also produced from the sweet potato over a hundred products.

George Washington Carver died on the grounds of Tuskegee—where he spent his life after 1896—on January 5, 1943, having significantly helped "a people from degradation, poverty, and waste to full manhood."

28

William M. Trotter

1872–1934

As soon as I began speaking, the leaders, stationed in various parts of the house, began asking questions.

In this and in a number of other ways they tried to make it impossible for me to speak. Naturally the rest of the audience resented this, and eventually it was necessary to call in the police and arrest the disturbers.

Of course, as soon as the disturbance was over, most of those who had participated in it were ashamed of what they had done. Many of those who had classed themselves with "The Intellectuals" before, hastened to disavow any sympathy with the methods of the men who had organized the disturbance. Many who had before been lukewarm in their friendship became my closest friends. Of course the two leaders, who were afterward convicted and compelled to serve a sentence in the Charles Street Jail, remained unrepentant.

BOOKER T. WASHINGTON

"Two years ago," said Mr. Trotter, "you were thought to be a
second Abraham Lincoln." [President Wilson] tried to
interrupt, asking that personalities be left out of the discussion.
Mr. Trotter continued to speak and the president finally told
him that if the organization he represented wished to approach
him again it must choose another spokesman. The president told
Mr. Trotter that he was an American citizen as fully as anybody
else, but that he [Trotter] was the only American citizen who
had ever come into the White House and addressed the
president in such a tone and with such a background of passion.

CHICAGO DEFENDER

The two incidents well depict the substance and style of William
Monroe Trotter: "unrepentant," as Booker T. Washington described
him, after Trotter and Greenville Martin, another demonstrator, had
served thirty days in jail for protesting at a church meeting at which
Washington had spoken in July 1903; and passionate—during his "man
to man" talk with Woodrow Wilson in 1914, when Trotter challenged the
increasing segregation of blacks in government departments during
Wilson's administration.

Trotter's direct actions against Booker T. Washington and his
"Tuskegee Movement," and Trotter's temerity in confronting nonblacks
and other black leaders of his day on issues affecting blacks earned him a
reputation as the first influential "militant" black leader of the twentieth
century. Trotter joined W. E. B. Du Bois and others in opposing
Washington's accommodationist policies and tactics. In 1905, with Du
Bois and others, Trotter put the "backbone in the platform" of the
Niagara Movement, the forerunner organization of the National Association for the Advancement of Colored People (NAACP), which was
founded 1909.

Trotter's influence in cofounding the Niagara Movement and his
founding of the Boston *Guardian* to provide a radical voice to the black
struggle support his ranking here. The significance of Trotter as a
militant activist and his "anti-Washington campaign"—using the Boston
Guardian—has been summarized by Lerone Bennett:

William Monroe Trotter, who was the advance man of a new
breed of black activists who fleshed out the renaissance of the
black soul. A throwback to the activists of the antislavery era
and an anticipation of the rebels of the 1960s...

Raised on the myths of the abolitionist period, he made himself over into an image of the old abolitionist, dedicating himself and all he had to the destruction of the Booker T. Washington image and the Booker T. Washington idea. In 1901, at the height of the reaction, he opened his anti-Washington campaign by founding the Boston *Guardian*. To make sure no one missed the point, he opened the newspaper office in the same building that had housed William Lloyd Garrison's *Liberator*.

Trotter's ranking here is further supported by his founding of the National Equal Rights League (1908) as an alternative for blacks to more white-dominated and supported organizations like the NAACP.

William Monroe Trotter was born on April 7, 1872, in Chillicothe, Ohio, nearly three months before the birth of PAUL LAURENCE DUNBAR [18] and nine months before P. B. S. PINCHBACK [20] became governor of Louisiana. Trotter was one of three children born to James Monroe Trotter and Virginia Isaac Trotter. When he was young, his family moved to Boston, where his father worked in the post office and later became involved in real estate. Monroe was the only black in his high school. After graduating, he worked for a year and, in 1891, entered Harvard College, where he became the first black to be honored with membership in Phi Beta Kappa. After finishing Harvard in 1894, he started a career in real estate with a white-owned company and, in 1899, went into business for himself.

In 1901, Trotter plighted his personal fortune to establish the Boston *Guardian* as a tool—in his arsenal of ideas and tactics—for attacking Booker T. Washington and all that Washington stood for. Although instrumental in establishing the Niagara Movement, he never joined or aligned himself with its progeny, the NAACP. He shared the fears and doubts of another fellow militant and cofounder, IDA B. WELLS-BARNETT [29] that the founding of the NAACP was yet another circumstance of liberal whites "betraying us again—these white friends of ours." (However, Wells-Barnett did later join the NAACP's Executive Committee.)

William Monroe Trotter died an apparent suicide on his birthday in 1934, nearly three months before W. E. B. Du Bois resigned from the NAACP because of his more militant views of the need for strategic, voluntary, racial segregation to promote the interests of blacks in America.

29

Ida B. Wells-Barnett

1862–1931

For nearly twenty years lynching crimes, . . . have been committed and permitted by this Christian nation. Nowhere in the civilized world save the United States of America do men, possessing all civil and political power, go out in bands of 50 to 5,000 to hunt down, shoot, hang or burn to death a single individual, unarmed and absolutely powerless. Statistics show that nearly 10,000 American citizens have been lynched in the past 20 years. To our appeals for justice the stereotyped reply has been that the government could not interfere in a state matter . . .

We refuse to believe this country, so powerful to defend its citizens abroad, is unable to protect its citizens at home.

IDA B. WELLS-BARNETT

Nearly seventy years after the first account of a lynching of a black man in America appeared in *Freedom's Journal*, the first black newspaper, Ida B. Wells-Barnett and a delegation from Chicago called on President William McKinley to protest the apathy of "this Christian nation" and the White House to the "nearly 10,000 American citizens... lynched in the past 20 years"—mostly black men. Wells-Barnett's role in leading antilynching crusades, for blacks and whites, at the end of the nineteenth and at the turn of the twentieth century, justify her ranking here.

Ida Bell Wells was born on July 6, 1862, in Holly Springs, Mississippi, to slave parents, James Wells and Lissie Bell. Wells attended high school at Rust University in Holly Springs, and Fisk University in Nashville for one year. She began teaching school in the rural South when she was fourteen years old and taught in the Memphis schools until her dismissal in 1891 for protesting about conditions in black schools.

In 1892, she became part owner of the *Memphis Free Speech*, a black newspaper, and began her antilynching campaign with editorials about the lynchings of three black males who allegedly raped three white women. In the spring of 1892, a white mob destroyed the offices of the *Memphis Free Speech* and ran her out of town.

Wells settled in Chicago and became associated with the *Chicago Conservator* and its editor, Ferdinand Lee Barnett. She married Barnett in 1895 and, for the next two years, lectured on lynching throughout the United States and Europe. In 1895, she published the first statistical record on lynching, *The Red Record*, which challenged the "universally declared cause for lynching," the rape of white women. *The Red Record* supported the conclusion that the real purpose of lynching—of blacks by whites—was to terrorize blacks into accepting an inferior, unequal, and subordinate condition in American life.

Wells-Barnett's ranking here is further buttressed by her leading role, with W. E. B. Du Bois [4], WILLIAM M. TROTTER [28], and others, in the founding of the Niagara Movement, the precursor of the National Association for the Advancement of Colored People, the NAACP. Wells-Barnett's influence can also be seen in her founding of the Alpha Suffrage Club of Chicago, the first black women's suffrage organization in America. In 1913, she marched with thousands in the suffrage parade the day before Woodrow Wilson took his oath of office.

Ida B. Wells-Barnett died in Chicago on March 25, 1931, a week before nine black youths who came to be known as the "Scottsboro Boys" went on trial for the alleged rape of two white women traveling as hobos on a freight train in Scottsboro, Alabama.

SOUTHERN HORRORS.

LYNCH LAW

IN ALL

ITS PHASES

Miss IDA B. WELLS,

Price, · · · Fifteen Cents.

THE NEW YORK AGE PRINT.

30

Madame C. J. Walker

1867–1919

Mrs. C. J. Walker, a woman who was an organizer of business
on a national scale.... She taught the masses of coloured women
a secret age-old, but lost to them—the secret every woman
ought to know. She taught them the secret of feminine beauty.

                                                JAMES WELDON JOHNSON

Madame C. J. Walker has been falsely associated by some with those
indicted by MALCOLM X [23] in his probing questioning of those
responsible for a "negative" concept of black beauty: "Who taught you to
hate the texture of your hair? Who taught you to hate the color of your

skin, to such extent that you bleach to get like the white man." The more accurate observations by JAMES WELDON JOHNSON [26] of the influence of Madame Walker on women of color by showing "them the secret of feminine beauty" also rebuts views held by some that Walker's "secret" was based on making black women (and men) into the image of whites at a time when one of her contemporaries, MARCUS GARVEY [21], was expressing "black pride," "black is beautiful," and the virtues of "black purity."

James Weldon Johnson's observations do not go far enough in emphasizing the influence of Madame Walker on black women and thus, the black experience in America, since Walker's beauty care products business was more an international than a national enterprise. Walker's network influenced the way millions of people of color, especially black women, saw and projected themselves positively as human beings, in the United States, Europe, Africa, and the West Indies.

Not only did Walker's beauty products provide expression for the unique "feminine beauty" of women of color, but her business also provided thousands of jobs for these women throughout the world. By providing for black women—in a black-owned business, with different roles and occupations as salespersons, managers, accountants, product makers, etc., at the turn of the twentieth century—Madame C. J. Walker helped to bring about a radical change in how blacks, especially black women, viewed themselves as providers in the workplace, and in the larger society as human beings. Surely, Walker and these black women were catalysts for the contemporary feminist movement. Walker's ranking here is in recognition of her above cited influences.

Born Sarah Breedlove in Delta, Georgia, Walker was the daughter of Owen and Minerva Breedlove, former slaves. She was orphaned at an early age and raised by an older sister. Breedlove was married when she was fourteen to a man named McWilliams, and was widowed and left with a small daughter at the age of twenty.

In 1887, she and her daughter moved to St. Louis, where she supported them by working in a laundry. In 1905, now Sarah Mc-Williams, she invented a metal "hot" comb and a hair conditioner erroneously referred to by many as a "hair straightener" for black women. Walker did not use and would not permit her associates to use the term "hair straightener" for her hair conditioning products. She saw all her products as enhancing the beauty of blacks, not making them white.

In 1906, she married Charles J. Walker in Denver, Colorado, and began door-to-door sales of her beauty care products and her invention for hair care. For the next four years, Walker recruited and trained others in her methods and ideas of enhancing black "feminine beauty" and, in 1910, built a factory in Indianapolis, Indiana, for Madame Walker beauty products. She amassed a fortune from her cosmetics business and "Walker Schools," and became the first known African-American female millionaire.

Madame C. J. Walker died on May 25, 1919, at her estate, Villa Lewaro, at Irvington-on-Hudson, New York, within days of Marcus Garvey's launching of his Black Star Line.

31

A. Philip Randolph

1889–1979

The task of realizing full citizenship for the Negro people is largely in the hands of the Negro people themselves.... Freedom is never given; it is won. And the Negro people must win their freedom. They must achieve justice. This involves struggle, continuous struggle.

True liberation can be acquired and maintained only when the Negro people possess power; and power is the product and flower of organization—organization of the masses, the masses in the mills and mines, on the farms, in the factories, in churches, in fraternal organizations, in homes, colleges, women's clubs, student groups, trade unions, tenants' leagues, in cooperative guilds, political organizations and civil rights associations.

A. PHILIP RANDOLPH

As an organizer of the diverse black masses for "true liberation," third only to Marcus Garvey and Dr. Martin Luther King, Jr., in this regard, A. Philip Randolph had a signal influence on the "continuous struggle" of African-Americans for economic, political, and social equality in America. Specifically, his impact as an organizer of the black masses— "in the mills and mines, on the farms, in the factories, in churches, in fraternal organizations, in homes, colleges, women's clubs, student groups, trade unions, tenants' leagues, in cooperative guilds, political organizations and civil rights associations"—warrant his ranking here.

Measures of Randolph's influence as an organizer are seen in his cofounding of *The Messenger*, a socialist weekly, in 1917; his organizing, in 1925, the Brotherhood of Sleeping Car Porters and Maids (BSCP), the first black trade union; his cofounding of the National Negro Congress, a loose coalition of 585 organizations, in 1936 (he served as its first president); and his helping to pressure President Franklin D. Roosevelt to form the Fair Employment Practice Commission (FEPC) in 1941, after threatening to march a hundred thousand demonstrators to Washington to protest "discrimination on account of race or color in the war industry."

In cofounding *The Messenger* with Chandler Owen, his friend and political ally, Randolph sought to provide blacks with a publication to rival the NAACP's *Crisis* and the National Urban League's *Opportunity*. Randolph and Owen ambitiously subtitled *The Messenger* the "Only Radical Negro Magazine in America." Although *The Messenger* didn't live up to either of these expectations, like *Crisis* and *Opportunity*—for which Randolph later wrote—it did publish the works of many of the black artists and intellectuals of the twenties like Countee Cullen, CLAUDE McKAY [37], and LANGSTON HUGHES [34].

The significance of A. Philip Randolph's role in organizing the first black trade union and gaining recognition of it by the Pullman Company some twelve years later was succinctly reported by economist T. Arnold Hill:

> The organization of the Brotherhood of Sleeping Car Porters and Maids is the one advanced step in unionism among Negroes. It came after continuous and persistent activity extending over a period of twelve years. Before union recognition was granted, the minimum wage paid porters was never higher than $77.50 per month. Hours averaged

A. Philip Randolph and others picketing against apartheid in South Africa.

from 400 to 600 a month, and overtime, if and when granted, began after a porter had traveled 11,000 miles during the month. Each porter was expected to report four hours before train time each trip without pay, to prepare his car for service.

Under the direction of A. Philip Randolph as president, the Brotherhood grew to that point where the Pullman Company was forced to recognize the right of the union to bargain collectively for porters and maids. The contract as recently signed grants a 240-hour month, time and one-half for overtime, a minimum wage of $89.50 a month for the first year with progressive increases to $110.50, and abolition of the company union known as the Pullman Porters and Maids Protective Association. Over 8,000 porters and maids benefited by a wage increase of $1,152,000 for 1937.

While organizing the BSCP, Randolph came into conflict with one of his chief enemies of the era, MARCUS GARVEY [21] and joined others in an anti-Garvey movement. It was in his many battles with Garvey over philosophy and tactics and his efforts to organize the masses away from Garvey's movement that Randolph admitted that his actions as a socialist and union organizer were having less influence than Garvey's:

What you needed to follow Garvey was a leap of the imagination, but socialism and trade unionism called for rigorous social struggle—hard work and programs—and few people wanted to think about that. Against the emotional power of Garveyism, what I was preaching didn't stand a chance.

It was while Randolph was President of the National Negro Congress, in 1936, that he called for a united front among the 585 organizations making up the Congress. He advocated the use of tactics like "mass demonstrations, such as parades, picketing, boycotting, mass protest, the mass distribution of propaganda literature, as well as legal action," to expose discrimination, racism, and segregation in American life. Randolph was so effective in organizing mass demonstrations and using them as political tools in the black struggle that in June 1941 he used a scheduled march on Washington of a hundred thousand people to "persuade" President Roosevelt to issue Executive Order No. 8802, forbidding racial discrimination in the defense industry. Twenty-two years later, with DR. MARTIN LUTHER KING, JR. [1], ROY WILKINS [33], BAYARD RUSTIN [59], and others, Randolph led the epochal March on Washington of 1963.

Asa Philip Randolph was born in Crescent City, Florida, on April 15, 1889, to James William Randolph and Elizabeth Robinson Randolph. At the age of two, he moved with his family to Jacksonville, Florida, where his father, a minister, took over a small black church. Randolph attended high school in Jacksonville at the Cookman Institute, which in 1923 merged with Daytona Normal and Industrial School, to become Bethune-Cookman College. He was graduated from Cookman in 1907 as class valedictorian.

For the next four years, Randolph worked as a collector of premiums for an insurance company, clerk in a grocery store, laborer in a lumber yard, and at other assorted jobs. In 1911, he moved to Harlem, New York, and lived there until his death on May 16, 1979.

A. Philip Randolph once said:

By fighting for their rights now, American Negroes are helping to make America a moral and spiritual arsenal of democracy. Their fight against the poll tax, against lynch law, segregation, and Jim Crow, their fight for economic, political, and social equality, thus becomes part of the global war for freedom.

32

Walter F. White

1 8 9 3 – 1 9 5 5

> In the final analysis, lynching and mob violence, disenfranchisement, unequal distribution of school funds, the Ku Klux Klan and all other forms of racial prejudice are for one great purpose —that of keeping the Negro in the position where he is economically exploitable.
>
> WALTER F. WHITE

In the crucible of the Atlanta Race Riot in August 1906, Walter F. White—then thirteen—had indelibly impressed on his consciousness the "one great purpose" of white violence and other forms of racial prejudice: "keeping the Negro in the position where he is economically exploitable." This experience, in which ten blacks were killed, and other moments in his native Atlanta and the deep South, at the turn of the twentieth century, influenced White to become involved with the struggle and resistance of blacks to all forms of racism and prejudice in American society.

Walter Francis White was born in Atlanta, Georgia, on July 1, 1893, to George and Madeline White. He attended segregated elementary and secondary schools in Atlanta and graduated from Atlanta University in 1916. After graduation, he joined a local branch of the National Association for the Advancement of Colored People (NAACP), which had been organized through the efforts of JAMES WELDON JOHNSON [26]. White became local secretary of the NAACP and through his outstanding management of the affairs of the local branch, built a relationship with Johnson, then the field secretary, and was recommended by Johnson to become an assistant secretary in the NAACP's New York office in 1918. During his tenure as assistant secretary, White built a reputation as a management expert and as a major voice against lynching, probably second only to IDA B. WELLS-BARNETT [29].

White's ability to capture in reports the abominations and atrocities of lynching—in order to galvanize "good people" to action in eradicating its roots, legally and politically—is seen in this excerpt from an account of the lynching of a pregnant black woman in Georgia, in the spring of 1918:

> At the time she was lynched, Mary Turner was in her eighth month of pregnancy. The delicate state of her health, one month or less previous to delivery, may be imagined, but this fact had no effect on the tender feelings of the mob. Her ankles were tied together and she was hung to the tree, head downward. Gasoline and oil from the automobiles were thrown on her clothing and while she writhed in agony and the mob howled in glee, a match was applied and her clothes burned from her person. When this had been done and while she was yet alive, a knife, evidently one such as is used in splitting hogs, was taken and the woman's abdomen was cut open, the unborn babe falling from her womb to the ground. The infant, prematurely born, gave two feeble cries and then its head was crushed by a member of the mob with his heel. Hundreds of bullets were then fired into the body of the woman, now mercifully dead, and the work was done.

A culmination of White's efforts in the antilynching crusade at the NAACP came with the U.S. Supreme Court decision in *Moore* v. *Dempsey*. "The Supreme Court decision," he wrote "thus becomes one of the milestones in the Negro's fight for justice—an achievement that is as important as any event since the signing of the Emancipation Proclamation." *Moore* v. *Dempsey* involved the denial of the constitutional rights of black sharecroppers and tenant farmers to organize as the Progressive Farmers Household Union of America against white landlords in Phillips County, Arkansas, who sought to keep them in perpetual peonage and servitude through the sharecropping "accounting" system. (GEORGE WASHINGTON CARVER [27] also played a role in the lives of black and white sharecroppers and tenant farmers.)

Not only does White's influential role in the antilynching campaigns in the twenties and thirties warrant his ranking here, but also his influence in transforming the NAACP into the major civil rights organization of the thirties, forties, and fifties. White's administrative skills must also be acknowledged, along with his legal plan for helping to attack the doctrines and practices of "separate but equal," which included hiring Charles Hamilton Houston for the NAACP's Legal Defense Fund, Inc. White is also significant because of his shifting power from whites, who had dominated the policies and affairs of the NAACP, to black professionals and himself, as secretary.

With his ascendancy as secretary, White demonstrated his power and influence within the NAACP in 1934 by causing W. E. B. Du Bois to resign as editor of *Crisis* and director of research and publicity. Du Bois's views on voluntary segregation of blacks in America were in opposition to the Association's integrationist policies. White reiterated his and the Association's views on this issue by stating that:

> the Negro must, without yielding, continue the grim struggle *for* integration and *against* segregation for his own physical, moral and spiritual well-being and for that of white America and of the world at large.

Walter White also contributed to the Negro Renaissance of the twenties through his writings: *Rope and Faggot* (1920) and *The Fire in the Flint* (1924), which dealt with antilynching, and *Flight* (1926), on the subject of passing for white.

Walter White died on March 12, 1955, in New York City, nearly nine months before ROSA PARKS [100] refused to give up her seat to a white man on a bus in Montgomery, Alabama.

33

Roy Wilkins

1901–1981

Here was a Negro who would not "act right." Furthermore he had killed a sheriff—a white man. The lid was off. It was a free-for-all. Anybody could do anything. The white race must be vindicated. White supremacy must be maintained. The ordained of God must not be challenged. The Negro must be kept in the place the Lord made for him. So the five thousand against two. So the machine guns against shotguns. So the carving of bloody, roasted flesh.

Roy Wilkins

With bitter eloquence, Roy Wilkins described the "cruel and bestial" acts of a white mob of five thousand in Gordonville, Virginia, in the spring of 1934. Those killed were an elderly black man and his sixty-two-year-old sister, after the man had resisted the mob's attempts to remove them from land seized by "eminent domain" for the building of a cemetery by the local municipality. Wilkins went on to observe that in the tradition of white American lynchers, the mob was not satisfied with just shooting the two, but "like a pack of maniacs, the killers rushed in and chopped up the bodies for souvenirs to carry home. Even pieces of bone were carried away."

Roy Wilkins, like predecessors JAMES WELDON JOHNSON [26] and WALTER F. WHITE [32], was exposed to and reported on acts of violence directed against black Americans because of their skin color and African descent. He, too, committed his adult life to the eradication of the legal and political conditions that sought to maintain white supremacy in America, also mainly through the institution of the National Association for the Advancement of Colored People (NAACP), from the thirties through the sixties, the last two decades as its executive secretary.

As executive secretary of the NAACP, Wilkins effected a change in the Association's role in the civil rights struggle after World War II and the decision in *Brown* v. *Board of Education*. New organizations and new leaders having different ideologies, tactics, and agendas for the liberation of blacks in America and throughout the world were emerging: the Southern Christian Leadership Conference (SCLC) under Dr. Martin Luther King, Jr.; the Student Nonviolent Coordinating Committee (SNCC) under Stokely Carmichael and H. Rap Brown; the Black Panther Party led by Bobby Seale, Huey Newton, and Eldridge Cleaver; Malcolm X and others. As Malcolm said:

> You and I are living at a time when there's a revolution going on, a worldwide revolution. It goes beyond Mississippi, it goes beyond Alabama, it goes beyond Harlem. There's a worldwide revolution going...[and]...what is it revolting against? The power structure. The American power structure? No. The French power structure? No. The English power structure? No. Then what power structure? An international Western power structure.

Wilkins led the NAACP to accept that it was no longer *the* leading civil rights organization but still an influential one and that the challenge was to collaborate with other black rights' organizations and labor leaders. The challenges that Wilkins and the NAACP had to meet in the maelstrom of the civil rights struggle of the fifties and sixties were also seen by A. PHILIP RANDOLPH [31] in 1936:

> The Negro peoples should not place their problems for solution down at the feet of their white sympathetic allies which has been and is the common fashion of the old school Negro leadership, for, in the final analysis, the salvation of the Negro, like the workers, must come from within.

Wilkins's ranking here serves to recognize his influence in the transformation of the NAACP, during this new era of the black struggle—a protracted and persistent struggle! Measures of this transformation can be seen in NAACP support for the momentous March on Washington in 1963; its work toward the passage of the Civil Rights Act of 1964; and Wilkins's chairmanship of the Leadership Conference on Civil Rights, a coalition of a hundred labor, religious, and civil rights groups.

Roy Wilkins was born on August 30, 1901, in St. Paul, Minnesota. He was raised by an aunt and uncle and attended integrated public elementary and secondary schools in St. Paul. In 1923, he graduated from the University of Minnesota with a B.A. After graduation, he joined the staff of the Kansas City *Call*, a black weekly, in Missouri.

In 1931, he left the *Call* to join the NAACP as assistant secretary under Walter F. White. In 1934, after W. E. B. Du Bois resigned from the NAACP, Wilkins took on the additional role of editor of *Crisis*, a position he held until 1949. In 1949, during Walter White's leave of absence, Wilkins became acting secretary. When White returned in 1950, he was given the title executive secretary, and most of the authority for day-to-day operations remained with Wilkins. After White's death in 1955, Wilkins was appointed executive secretary and served in that capacity until 1977—a most turbulent two decades in the continuum of the black struggle in America.

Roy Wilkins died on September 8, 1981, in New York City.

34

Langston Hughes

1902–1967

We younger Negro artists who create now intend to express our individual dark-skinned selves without fear or shame. If white people are pleased we are glad. If they are not, it doesn't matter. We know we are beautiful. And ugly too. The tom-tom cries and the tom-tom laughs. If colored people are pleased we are glad. If they are not, their displeasure doesn't matter either. We build our temples for tomorrow, strong as we know how, and we stand on top of the mountain, free within ourselves.

LANGSTON HUGHES

As one of the most prominent black artists of the Negro Renaissance of the twenties and thirties, Langston Hughes, like his contemporary, PAUL ROBESON [24], used black culture as weapons in the struggle of African-Americans against racism and discrimination. Hughes believed that authentic and legitimate Negro artists were obliged to associate their art with the "eternal tom-tom beating in the Negro soul—the tom-tom of revolt against weariness in a white world, a world of subway trains, and work, work, work; the tom-tom of joy and laughter, and pain swallowed in a smile."

James Langston Hughes's ranking here is warranted by his use of the experiences of ordinary black people as material for his diverse writings in order to influence and bring about a positive change in the black condition in America. "There are certain practical things American Negro writers can do, and must do," Hughes said, "There's a song that says, 'the time ain't long,' that song is right; something has got to change in America—and change soon. We must help that change to come."

For over forty years, Langston Hughes helped to bring about change in America—for blacks and whites—as a writer of both fiction and nonfiction, as playwright, columnist, and poet. In his columns for the *Chicago Defender* in the early forties and in fiction in the fifties, Hughes used his character Jesse B. Semple to symbolize the values and daily reality of ordinary black people, in such works as *Simple Speaks His Mind* (1950), *Simple Takes a Wife* (1953), *Simple Stakes a Claim* (1957), and *Simple's Uncle Sam* (1965).

Although Hughes was a multifaceted artist, his greatest impact in bringing black experience to American literature was as a poet, and he would become known as "the Poet Laureate of the Negro Race." In the tradition of PAUL LAURENCE DUNBAR [18], Hughes used black folk material to protest the treatment and conditions of blacks in America. Examples can be seen in his *The Weary Blues* (1926), *Fine Clothes to the Jew* (1927), *One Way Ticket* (1949), *Montage of a Dream Deferred* (1951), and *The Panther and the Lash* (his last volume, 1967).

Hughes was born in Joplin, Missouri, on February 1, 1902, to James and Carrie Hughes. By the time he was twelve, he had lived in seven different cities scattered across the Midwest and in Mexico City, Mexico.

He moved to Lincoln, Illinois in 1914, after his parents had separated, where he lived with his mother and stepfather. He graduated from elementary school in Lincoln and finished high school in Cleveland, Ohio in 1920, after moving there in 1916.

In 1921, he published one of his first poems, "The Negro Speaks of Rivers," in *Crisis*, then edited by W. E. B. DU BOIS [4]. In 1926, Hughes matriculated at Lincoln University. After graduating from Lincoln, he went on a lecture tour of some fifty black schools and colleges throughout the East, South, and West. At the end of his tour, he concluded that these schools were mid-Victorian in their values and as strict as in the "witch-burning" days of the Puritans, because the black faculties discouraged black students from getting involved with the culture and politics of black life. As Hughes specifically charged:

> Many of our institutions apparently are not trying to make men and women of their students at all—they are doing their best to produce spineless Uncle Toms, uninformed, and full of mental and moral evasions.

Langston Hughes with fellow Harlem Renaissance figures Charles S. Johnson, E. Franklin Frazier, Rudolph Fisher, and Herbert Delany.

Hughes's agitation on this issue—during and after his tour of black colleges in 1931–32—planted seeds of student and faculty unrest, forcing a reexamination of the proper role of black colleges in the black struggle, leading to the fusion of the black student protest movement with the civil rights movement during the fifties and sixties.

Hughes died on May 22, 1967, in New York City—days before Thurgood Marshall was sworn in as the first black Supreme Court justice.

Langston Hughes, the poet-prophet, saw his life and art as inextricably linked to that of black people (like the works of AUGUST WILSON [96]) and could thus say with poignancy and insight:

> I am both a Negro and poor. And that combination of color and of poverty gives me the right then to speak for the most oppressed group in America, that group that has known so little of American democracy, the fifteen million Negroes who dwell within our borders...
>
> We Negroes of America are tired of a world divided superficially on the basis of blood and color, but in reality on the basis of poverty and power—the rich over the poor, no matter what their color.

35

Mary McLeod Bethune

1875–1955

It should not be necessary to struggle forever against popular prejudice, and with us as colored women, this struggle becomes two-fold, first, because we are women and second, because we are colored women....

By her peculiar position the colored woman has gained clear powers of observation and judgment—exactly the sort of powers which are today peculiarly necessary to the building of an ideal country.

MARY B. TALBERT

Like HARRIET TUBMAN [12], SOJOURNER TRUTH [15], PHILLIS WHEATLEY [19], IDA B. WELLS-BARNETT [29], MADAME C. J. WALKER [30], and the other black women in this volume, Mary McLeod Bethune symbolizes the significant role of black women in the African-American quest to participate fully and equally in "the building of an ideal country."

Mary McLeod Bethune's impact on issues and matters related to the struggle of African-American women are evinced by her serving two terms (1924–28) as president of the National Association of Colored Women (founded in 1896 as a "social, economic and moral force" among women of color), and her founding and serving as president of the powerful National Council of Negro Women (1935–49, a coalition of black women's organizations throughout the United States). Bethune had a significant impact on general women's issues in her role as special assistant to the secretary of war, in the establishment and implementation of the Women's Army Corps (WAC) in 1945.

Mary McLeod Bethune's greatest impact on the black struggle came with her applying her "powers of observation and judgment" about the needs of blacks for a well-rounded education in the founding of the Daytona Normal and Industrial School for Negro Girls in 1904. With $1.50 and a vision of and a commitment to community-centered education for blacks in the Daytona Beach, Florida, area, Bethune and a few dedicated and resourceful others built, on what was mostly a garbage dump, a citadel to black learning and education in the twentieth century. In 1923 the Industrial School merged with the Cookman Institute for Men (alma Mater of A. Philip Randolph) and became Bethune-Cookman College.

Bethune was born Mary Jane McLeod on July 10, 1875, in Mayesville, South Carolina, during the waning days of Black Reconstruction. Her parents, Samuel and Patsy McLeod, were former slaves. Mary Jane was born free, the fifteenth of their children. She attended a local Presbyterian school and later attended Scotia Seminary in Concord, North Carolina, graduating in 1893. In 1895, she graduated from the Moody Bible Institute of Chicago, where she was the only black student.

After teaching at various schools in the South from 1895 to 1897, she married Albertus Bethune in 1897. In 1899, Bethune accepted a teaching job in the Palatka Mission School for blacks and in 1904 moved to Daytona Beach, Florida, where she founded the above-mentioned

Normal and Industrial School for Negro Girls, later Bethune-Cookman College. She served two terms as its president, 1904-42 and 1946-47.

From her founding of the National Council of Negro Women (1935) to her serving in the Roosevelt Administration as director of the Division of Negro Affairs and as special assistant to the president on minority affairs, to her death in 1955, Bethune was one of the most visible and influential African-Americans.

Mary McLeod Bethune died on May 18, 1955, in Daytona Beach, Florida, almost a year after the *Brown* v. *Board of Education* decision.

36

Alain Locke

1885–1954

The Negro question is too often put forward merely as the
Negro question. It is just as much, and even more seriously, the
question of democracy. The position of the Negro in American
society is its one great outstanding anomaly.

ALAIN LOCKE

Alain Leroy Locke's quest, and his accomplishments in removing the
Negro as America's "one great outstanding anomaly," support his
ranking here. The pith of Locke's thoughts and actions on the black
struggle in America has been brilliantly summarized by Leonard
Harris: "Locke helped build a cultural movement, the Harlem Renais-

sance, that was enlivened by his value theory. The adult education movement, and the central role that critical thinking skills have in educational curricula, are both indebted to Locke's stalwart efforts. The Black Aesthetic movement, African Philosophy, and debates on Black Philosophy have frequently relied on some feature of Locke's philosophy to frame their discussion."

Locke's landmark *The New Negro* (1925) guaranteed his prominent role with that of W. E. B. DU BOIS [4] and JAMES WELDON JOHNSON [26] in the Harlem Renaissance during the twenties and thirties. His ranking here revisits the difficulty of ranking the *Black 100*. Although Locke in many ways was as much a leader during the Renaissance as Du Bois and Johnson, it is the author's view, by the application of my criteria of influence, that Du Bois and Johnson used a powerful institution, the NAACP, to affect to a greater extent the thoughts and lives of blacks in their ongoing struggle for equality in America.

However, Locke's cumulative effect on the black experience, as author-activist and educator, were considerable. *The New Negro* signaled "the New Negro Movement" in America, which would eradicate immemorial stereotypes by whites and blacks of black culture as empty and void. In place of these stereotypes Locke asserted the uniqueness of the "Negro Soul." His ideas and understanding of the "Negro Soul" directly influenced the sociological perspectives on race relations held by E. FRANKLIN FRAZIER [38].

Locke's greatest impact on "the Black Aesthetic Movement, African Philosophy and Black Philosophy" came as a professor at Howard University. From 1912 to 1925, Locke advocated that Howard become the intellectual center for black thought and culture. This was to be achieved through an emphasis on higher order thinking and reasoning in the arts and the social and natural sciences. In this regard, Locke directly influenced Howard's first black president and educational innovator, MORDECAI JOHNSON [40].

During this period at Howard, Locke also proposed the development of courses dealing specifically with race and race relations. In 1915, he began a series of lectures on "Race Contacts and Inter-Racial Relations: A Study in the Theory and Practice of Race." In large part because of Locke's efforts to direct Howard University toward black culture, he was dismissed in 1925 by Stanley Durkee, the last white president of Howard. Locke was rehired by Mordecai Johnson in 1928 to help him redirect Howard to the equipping of blacks for educational and political equality in America.

Upon his return to Howard in 1928, Locke set in motion the organizational and pedagogical systems for an African Studies program (not fully implemented until after his death), and the Social Science and Philosophy Divisions, which would later be headed by E. Franklin Frazier. He was also influential in the American Association for Adult Education, dealing with adult education, Negro folk education, and intergroup relations. He retired from Howard in June 1953.

Locke was born on September 13, 1885, in Philadelphia, Pennsylvania, to free Negro parents, Pliny Ishmael and Mary Locke, who named him Arthur (no one knows when Locke changed his name to Alain). His father graduated from Howard University Law School in 1874.

Locke attended a private elementary school and Central High in Philadelphia, from which he received a B.A. in 1902. He received another B.A. from Harvard—magna cum laude as a Phi Beta Kappa—in 1907. Also in 1907, Locke was selected as the first black Rhodes Scholar, attending Hertford College in England from 1907 to 1910. In 1910–11, he attended the University of Berlin. In 1918, he received a Ph.D. from Harvard University.

Locke died on June 9, 1954, in New York City, nearly a month after *Brown* v. *Board of Education* was decided. His quest to destroy the idea of blacks as an "anomaly" in American life had one major goal: cultural recognition. Locke would say on this point:

> Cultural recognition...means the removal of wholesale social proscription and, therefore, the conscious scrapping of the mood and creed of "White Supremacy." It means an open society instead of a closed ethnic shop. For what? For making possible free and unbiased contacts between the races on the selective basis of common interests and mutual consent, in contrast with what prevails at present—dictated relations of inequality based on caste psychology and class exploitation.

37

Claude McKay

1889–1948

The Summer of 1919 was a terrifying period for the American Negro. There were race riots in Chicago and in Washington and in Omaha and in Phillips County, Arkansas; and in Longview, Texas; and in Knoxville, Tennessee; and in Norfolk, Virginia; and in other communities. Colored men and women, by dozens and by scores, were chased and beaten and killed in the streets.

JAMES WELDON JOHNSON

During the "Red Summer" of 1919—called that because of the extensive bloody acts of violence against blacks as described by Johnson and others—Claude McKay declared the defiant intentions of yet another generation of blacks to resist and struggle against white racism and violence:

> If we must die—let it not be like hogs
> Hunted and penned in an inglorious spot,...
> Oh, Kinsmen! We must meet the common foe;
> Though far outnumbered, let us show us brave,
> And for their thousands blows deal one death-blow!
> What though before us lies the open grave?
> Like men we'll face the murderous, cowardly pack,
> Pressed to the wall, dying, but fighting back!

McKay's poem "If We Must Die," and his poetry volumes *Spring in New Hampshire* (1920) and *Harlem Shadows* (1922), are considered by many to have signaled the Harlem Renaissance, a flowering of black culture in protest literature and the arts (see JAMES WELDON JOHNSON, [26]) and leading to a new generation of civil rights protest—culminating with Dr. Martin Luther King, Jr., and others in the fifties and sixties.

McKay, as poet, critic, writer, and activist, had a significant impact in changing the way blacks saw themselves as a people and their unique culture, in the struggle against injustice in America. Through his novels *Home to Harlem* (1928), *Banjo: A Story Without a Plot* (1929), and *Banana Bottom* (1933), McKay depicted black life with nuances that often permitted his critics to accuse him of catering to white negative stereotypes of black attitudes and behaviors, like those often associated with the writings of PAUL LAURENCE DUNBAR [18].

As an activist-critic, McKay, like DU BOIS [4], TROTTER [28], RANDOLPH [31], and others, countered the propaganda and tactics of MARCUS GARVEY [21], organizer of the black masses in the twenties. Among Garvey's many ideas and tactics to which McKay took exception was the "Back-to-Africa" proposal: "The most puzzling thing about the 'Back-to-Africa' propaganda is the leader's repudiation of all the fundamentals of the black worker's economic struggle... All those who think broadly on social conditions are amazed at Garvey's ignorance and his intolerance of modern social ideas... He talks of Africa as if it were a little island in the Caribbean Sea. Ignoring all geographical and political divisions, he gives his followers the idea that a vast continent of diverse tribes consists of a large homogeneous nation of natives struggling for freedom and waiting for the Western Negroes to come and help them drive out the European exploiters. He has never urged Negroes to organize in industrial unions."

Claude McKay was born on September 15, 1889, in Clarendon

Hills, Jamaica. His parents were farmers. At the age of six, he moved to Montego Bay to live with an older brother, a teacher and minister in the Anglican Church. His initial education was taken in Jamaica, where he demonstrated early a gift for poetry and writing. In 1912 he published two volumes of poetry: *Songs of Jamaica* and *Constab Ballads*.

Also in 1912, he came to the United States to study agriculture under GEORGE WASHINGTON CARVER [27] at Tuskegee Institute. After a year there, he began similar studies at Kansas State College but left after two years to pursue a career as a poet and writer in New York City. He worked at various marginal jobs, while writing. In 1919, *The Liberator* published his influential poem "If We Must Die."

From 1922 to 1934, McKay lived abroad in Russia, France, Spain, and Morocco. He returned from Europe in 1934 and, in 1937, wrote an autobiography *A Long Way From Home*. In 1940, McKay became a U.S. citizen. He converted to Roman Catholicism in 1944 and spent the rest of his life working for Roman Catholic causes among the poor in Chicago.

Claude McKay died in Chicago on May 28, 1948.

38

E. Franklin Frazier

1894–1962

The question of love is irrelevant.... The Negro does not want love. He wants justice. Modern political communities are not based upon the principles of love but upon certain principles of justice....

I am primarily interested in saving the Negro's self-respect. If the masses of Negroes can save their self-respect and remain free from hate, so much the better for their moral development. One's refusal to strike back is not always motivated by a belief in the superiority of moral force any more than retaliation is always inspired by courage. In the first case it is often pure cowardice while in the latter, the fear of the censure of the herd. I believe it would be better for the Negro's soul to be seared with hate than dwarfed by self-abasement.

E. FRANKLIN FRAZIER

Edward Franklin Frazier's commitment to "saving the Negro's self-respect" would make him to black sociology what Carter Woodson became to black history: the father and leading pioneer. In Frazier's black sociological perspectives, outlined in his seminal volume *The Negro Family in the United States* (1939), the African-American experience is positive and not maladaptive or defective. This had a singular impact on the way blacks saw themselves as human beings in their struggle against white racism. Equally significant, this volume affected race relations in America, then and now. Two other pioneers in this area were DU BOIS [4] in the field of black sociology (*The Philadelphia Negro*, 1899) and ALAIN LOCKE [36] (*The New Negro*, 1925).

Frazier's psychosociological insights into the proper or healthy response of the "Negro Soul" when confronted with white hate, violence, and hypocrisy were spoken in 1924: "Deploring of hatred and praise of love is as superficial as despicable. Hatred may have a positive moral value. A few choice souls may rise to a moral elevation where they can love those who oppress them. But the mass of mankind either become accommodated to an enforced inferior status with sentiments consonant with their situation, or save themselves by hating the oppression and the oppressors. In the latter case, hatred is a positive moral force. So if hatred is necessary to prevent the Negro from becoming accommodated to his present state, how can anyone preach love?"

These insights into the healthy response of blacks—or any group—to discrimination and hate permitted Frazier to pioneer sociological theories and explanations of how best to understand black group behaviors vis-à-vis nonblacks and thus foster better race relations among all groups in a multiethnic and multicolored America. Examples of Frazier's systematic treatment of race relation issues are in his *Traditions and Patterns of Negro Family Life* (1934), *The Negro in the United States* (1949), and *Race and Culture Contacts in the Modern World* (1957).

Frazier's *Negro Church in America* (1962) also had an influence on the understanding of blacks and whites of the history and role of the black church in black assertion and survival in America.

The Black Bourgeoisie (1957), Frazier's most controversial work, and in some ways his most influential, provided a black sociological perspective on the new Negro middle class estrangement from normative black culture and reality to "a world of make-believe." See CARTER G. WOODSON's [25] concern for this estrangement.

Edward Franklin Frazier was born in Baltimore, Maryland, on September 24, 1894, nearly five months before the death of Frederick Douglass. He attended elementary and secondary schools in Baltimore. In 1912, he entered Howard University and graduated with honors in 1916. From 1916 to 1919 he taught at several different schools. In 1919, he entered Clark University in Massachusetts and received an M.A. in sociology in 1920. He received his Ph.D. in sociology from the University of Chicago in 1931.

Frazier taught at Morehouse College (1922–1924), and served as director of Atlanta University's School of Social Work from 1922 to 1927. He taught at Fisk University from 1931 to 1934. In 1934, he was appointed head of Howard University's Department of Sociology, serving there until 1959.

An additional measure of E. Franklin Frazier's influence on American life is seen in his becoming president of the predominantly white American Sociological Society, in 1948.

E. Franklin Frazier died on May 17, 1962, in Washington, D.C.

39

Henry McNeal Turner

1834–1915

Thousands of white people in this country are ever and anon
advising the colored people to keep out of politics, but they do
not advise themselves. If the Negro is a man in keeping with
other men, why should he be less concerned about politics than
any one else? Strange, too, that a number of would-be colored
leaders are ignorant and debased enough to proclaim the same
foolish jargon. For the Negro to stay out of politics is to level
himself with a horse or a cow, which is no politician, and the
Negro who does it proclaims his inability to take part in
political affairs. If the Negro is to be man, full and complete,
he must take part in everything that belongs to manhood. If he
omits a single duty, responsibility or privilege, to that extent he
is limited and incomplete.

HENRY MCNEAL TURNER

146

Henry McNeal Turner was born free on February 1, 1834, near Newberry, Abbeville, South Carolina, within months of two significant happenings: the founding of the American Anti-Slavery Society and the abolition of slavery in the British Empire. Turner's parents, Hardy and Sarah, were free Negroes. Reportedly, Turner's maternal grandfather was an African prince, freed from slavery because of British law that forbade the enslavement of African royalty.

As a young man, Turner worked in cotton fields, as an apprentice blacksmith, and as an aide in a law office. With the assistance of white and black friends, he learned how to read and write, using spelling books, history and law books, and the Bible. Turner's interest in religion and God came from his Bible readings, and, in 1851, he was converted to Christianity through the Methodist Episcopal Church, South. After being licensed by the white Methodist Episcopals to preach, he toured the South, preaching to blacks, slave and free, and in 1857 formally linked his life and message to the gospel of liberation of the African Methodist Episcopal Church, in the tradition of RICHARD ALLEN and ABSALOM JONES [6].

Like Allen and Jones, Henry H. Garnet, Gabriel Prosser, Denmark Vesey, Nat Turner, and others, Henry McNeal Turner became prominent in the development and practice of a black liberation theology that would influence latter-day black theologian-activists like Dr. Martin Luther King, Jr., Malcolm X, Elijah Muhammad, Adam Clayton Powell, and Jesse Jackson.

Henry McNeal Turner was a significant bridge from the early nineteenth-century black church—a political and social force for change—to the early twentieth-century needs and demands of blacks for a black God and a theology unequivocally supportive of the black struggle for freedom, as seen by William Pickens in 1919:

> Why, I ask you, is God always shown as white? It is because He is the white man's God. It is the God of our masters. (Yes, brother, that's it.) It's the God of those who persecute and despise the coloured people. Brothers, we've got to knock that white God down and put up a black God—we've got to rewrite the Old Testament and the New from a black man's point of view. Our theologians must get busy on a black God.

Turner was as "busy on a black God" as anyone during his

generation. However, his listing and ranking here are in further recognition of his unique influence in politicizing black theology, and thus the black church, by demanding direct involvement in the politics of American life, which would make the Negro a full and complete citizen. Turner not only did this through his rhetoric, but also by his actions. During Black Reconstruction, Turner organized emancipated slaves for the Republican Party in Georgia and, in 1867, was elected a state legislator by the Georgia Constitutional Convention.

In 1868, Turner and other elected blacks were declared ineligible to serve in the legislature by a new white Democratic majority that was seeking to undo black political representation. In a speech before the Georgia House of Representatives, Turner led the appeal for the reinstatement of his "fellow colored members" and himself by saying in part: "I hold that I am a member of this body. Therefore, sir, I shall neither fawn nor cringe before any party, nor stoop to beg them for my rights ... I am here to demand my rights, and to hurl thunderbolts at the men who would dare cross the threshold of my manhood." Turner and his black colleagues were returned to their seats, but he served only one term as a legislator, from 1868 to 1870.

After 1870, Turner became deeply involved with the African Methodist Episcopal Church and Morris Brown College in Atlanta, where he served as president for twelve years. He sought to use these institutions and their resources to better the Negro's condition in America. Shortly after Booker T. Washington's Atlanta Compromise address in 1895, Turner declared more stridently and urgently that blacks must return to Mother Africa to be fully free and great as a people. In this view he was like HENRY H. GARNET [14] and MARTIN R. DELANY [13] before him and MARCUS GARVEY [21] at the turn of the twentieth century. Turner said in 1896:

> I believe that the Negroid race has been free long enough now to begin to think for himself and plan for better conditions that he can lay claim to in this country or ever will. *There is no manhood future in the United States for the Negro.* He may eke out an existence for generations to come, but he can never be a *man*—full, symmetrical and und-warfed. . . . And as such, I believe that two or three millions of us should return to the land of our ancestors, and establish our own nation, civilization, laws, customs, style of manufac-ture, and not only give the world, like other race varieties,

the benefit of our individuality, but build up social conditions peculiarly our own, and cease to be grumblers, chronic complainers and a menace to the white man's country, or the country he claims and is bound to dominate.

Henry McNeal Turner would spend the rest of his life fusing his black theology of liberation with a "Back-to-Africa" propaganda, visiting and studying Africa, mainly Liberia. He made four trips to Africa between 1891 and 1898.

Turner died on May 8, 1915, in Windsor, Ontario, nearly six months before the death of Booker T. Washington, an arch rival for the leadership of and power over the minds and hearts of black people, in their struggle for full rights and freedoms in America and throughout the world.

40

Mordecai W. Johnson

1890–1976

The Negro people of America have been with us here for three hundred years. They have cut our forests, tilled our fields, built our railroads, fought our battles, and in all of their trials until now they have manifested a simple faith, a grateful heart, a cheerful spirit, and an undivided loyalty to the nation that has been a thing of beauty to behold. Now they have come to the place where their faith can no longer feed on the bread of repression and violence. They ask for the bread of liberty, of public equality, and public responsibility. It must not be denied them.

MORDECAI W. JOHNSON

In his commencement address at Harvard University, in June 1922, Mordecai Wyatt Johnson reasserted the "simple faith" of black people in their right to feed on "the bread of liberty, of public equality, and public responsibility." With his ascendancy as the first black president of Howard University in 1926, Mordecai Johnson would redirect this major institution of higher education to the equipping of blacks for educational and political equality so as to assist in the "uplift" of blacks in America and everywhere.

Like CARTER WOODSON [25], W. E. B. DU BOIS [4], MARY MCLEOD BETHUNE [35], CHARLES H. HOUSTON [5], PAUL LAURENCE DUNBAR [18], and others, Johnson believed that quality higher education was vital to black freedom in America. Howard University, influenced by his leadership and philosophies of education and learning strategies for developing the black intellect to the fullest, became the most notable educational institutional counterpoint to Booker T. Washington and his industrial educational citadel, Tuskegee Institute (see DU BOIS [4] for more discussion on these issues). (Howard wasn't the only black college or university that was teaching higher-order thinking and critical analysis skills, of course.)

Johnson's belief in the efficacy of higher learning for blacks was best expressed by him:

> If the Negro studies the human will, human motive, human organization, the philosophy of social life, in order to discover how he may become free...he is sure to discover something about the human will, something about human motives and human organization that may be to the advantage of mankind.

During a tenure of over thirty years as president of Howard, Johnson attracted some of the most distinguished black academics and scholars, such as CHARLES H. HOUSTON [5], E. FRANKLIN FRAZIER [38], CARTER WOODSON [25], ALAIN LOCKE [36] and BENJAMIN MAYS [53]. He also was responsible for twenty new buildings at Howard and doubled the volumes in the university libraries.

Mordecai Wyatt Johnson was born on January 12, 1890, in Paris, Tennessee. His father was minister of the Mt. Zion Baptist Church there. Through his father's influence, Mordecai became interested in religion. He received his B.A. from Morehouse College at the age of sixteen. He also received a B.A. from the University of Chicago in 1913.

Johnson's theological and biblical training consisted of a B.D. (Bachelor of Divinity) from Rochester Theological Seminary in 1916, a M.Th. (Master in Theology) from Harvard and D.D. (Doctor of Divinity) degrees from both Howard (1923) and Gammon Theological Seminary (1928).

Although Mordecai Johnson can be classified a black theologian, as much so as HENRY HIGHLAND GARNETT [14] and HENRY MCNEAL TURNER [39], he didn't embrace their belief in the bankruptcy of Christianity to blacks or their goal of blacks returning to Mother Africa for full freedom and dignity. Johnson said on these issues: "Another and larger group among us believes in religion and believes in the principles of democracy, but not in the white man's religion and in the white man's democracy... Whatever one may think of these radical movements and their destiny, one thing is certain: they are home-grown fruits, with roots deep sprung in a world of black American suffering. Their power lies in the appeal which they make to the Negro to find a way out of his trouble by new and self-reliant paths. The larger masses of the colored people do not belong to these more radical movements. They retain their belief in the Christian God, they love their country, and hope to work out their salvation within its bounds."

Mordecai Wyatt Johnson died on September 10, 1976, in Washington, D.C., nearly a month before the last of the Scottsboro Boys was granted a pardon by George Wallace, governor of Alabama (see IDA B. WELLS-BARNETT [29]).

41

Robert Abbott

1870–1940

Since 1914, it is variously estimated that between 500,000 and 1,500,000 Negroes have gone North. Without Negro labor the South will be bankrupt. With it and its great natural resources, it can become one of the richest sections of the country. It remains to be seen whether the better element among the whites can (and will) gain the ascendancy over the larger element of those who practice the policy laid down by the Dred Scott decision of regarding the Negro as "having no rights which a white man is bound to respect."

WALTER F. WHITE

The mass migration of blacks from the South to the North and West at the turn of the twentieth century was one of the most significant phenomena in American history. It was a "push-pull" phenomenon: the push of blacks to these areas from the South was due to several major factors: an agricultural depression in the South (see GEORGE WASHINGTON CARVER [27]), increased mechanization in the production of cotton; a series of summer floods in middle Alabama and Mississippi; the ravages of the boll weevil (injurious cotton-eating beetles); and terrorism against blacks, because whites continued to regard blacks as "having no rights which a white man is bound to respect"—as it was phrased in the *Dred Scott* opinion of the U.S. Supreme Court.

Several major factors pulling blacks from the South to the North and West were job opportunities in the industrializing North; a desire by blacks for a greater degree of personal liberty; and the representations of Robert Sengstacke Abbott, in the *Chicago Defender,* that the North was a "Promised Land" of opportunity, relatively free of the external forms and practices of discrimination, racism, and violence.

In the tradition of *Freedom's Journal,* founded seventy-eight years earlier by SAMUEL E. CORNISH and JOHN B. RUSSWURM [8], Robert Abbott built the *Chicago Defender* into the prototypical black weekly for the masses at the turn of the twentieth century. In this way he influenced, like none other in the newspaper industry, the mass exodus of blacks to the North. This resulted in the nationalization of the race problem, because of what would soon become evident: pervasive white racism in the North.

Robert Abbott was born in 1870 to former slave parents Thomas and Flora Abbott, the year of ratification of the Fifteenth Amendment, which gave black males, and all male citizens, the right to vote.

Abbott was raised by his mother and stepfather, John Hermann Henry Sengstacke. Later, in admiration of his stepfather, Abbott took his surname as his middle name. Abbott attended Hampton Institute and Kent College of Law in Chicago, receiving an LL.B. degree in 1898. After leaving Chicago to practice law in the Midwest for five years, he returned to Chicago in 1903. In 1905 he founded the *Chicago Defender,* reportedly with a capital investment of twenty-five cents. From the early days of the *Defender,* with only a door-to-door circulation, Abbott catered to issues and topics of interest to the black masses. He thereby built the circulation of the *Defender,* during the mass black exodus from the South, to nearly a quarter of a million.

As editor and publisher of the *Defender*, Abbott exposed the atrocities committed against blacks during the Chicago riots of 1919. He also editorialized in the *Defender* against Marcus Garvey and the Garvey movement. In an anti-Garvey symposium of Negro leaders in September of 1922, he stated that "Mr. Garvey's policy is not correct for the American Negro." Abbott was also a prominent leader in the anti-lynching crusades during the early twentieth century.

Robert Sengstacke Abbott died in Chicago, on February 29, 1940, the month Richard Wright's provocative *Native Son* was published.

42

Jackie Robinson
1919–1972

It was high time...that the Jim Crow pattern of baseball was changed. Black baseball fans were no longer willing to support a national game from whose ranks one-tenth of the nation was excluded. ...If Black players were brought into the Big Leagues an untapped reservoir of Black baseball patrons would be opened up.

Here was a new angle—white racism could be a barrier to greater profits. And yet, business was afraid of the juggernaut it might create.

WILLIAM L. PATTERSON

In 1947 Jack Roosevelt Robinson became the first black player in major league baseball. His pushing aside the juggernaut of racism warrants his ranking here. Robinson remains a compelling symbol of black persistence in their struggle to participate fully and equally in all aspects of American life, including a most lucrative and economically rewarding area: organized sports.

That other black ballplayers, like Satchel Paige and Josh Gibson, could have been the first to integrate baseball and so would have had the same impact as Robinson on opening the doors for other blacks cannot diminish Robinson's achievement in the black struggle. The fact is that Jackie Robinson was the first to integrate baseball and like so many other "black firsts" he benefited from the ongoing struggle of blacks to be free and to be treated justly and equally in America. Like many others, Robinson stood on the shoulders of those who felt every lash of the master's whip, led every revolt, every protest, every demonstration, every legal action for more than three centuries. Thus, the integration of baseball by Jackie Robinson should be viewed as a significant event in the evolution or maturation of the black struggle, a "continuous struggle," according to A. PHILIP RANDOLPH [31].

Author Jules Tygiel described the symbolic, social, and political significance of Jackie Robinson's integration of major league baseball: "The integration of baseball represented both a symbol of imminent racial challenge and a direct agent of social change. Jackie Robinson's campaign against the color line in 1946–47 captured the imagination of millions of Americans who had previously ignored the nation's racial dilemma. For civil rights advocates the baseball experience offered a model of peaceful transition through militant confrontation, economic pressure, and moral suasion."

The "whys" of Robinson's entry into major league baseball, and thus organized sports, were not all altruistic. Lawyer-activist William Patterson's observation of the pecuniary interests of an all-white ownership group to tap "the reservoir of black baseball patrons" should not be slighted or ignored. By removing the barrier to black participation in baseball and subsequently in other organized sports, white owners not only benefited from a higher caliber game (better players, a better game), but also from a broader economic base and additional profits, with black fans following their favorite black players.

Jackie Robinson's outstanding performance as a baseball player (1947–1956) had another impact on the economics of baseball and all organized sports: greater salaries and benefits for both black and white players which escalated in the nineties to multimillion-dollar yearly contracts.

Jack Roosevelt Robinson was born in Cairo, Georgia, on January 31, 1919, the year of the "Red Summer," a time of unprecedented bloody violence against blacks. Jackie (by which name he would later be called) was the youngest of five children of Jerry and Mallie Robinson. One of his grandfathers had been a slave. His father worked on a large plantation farm as "a half-cropper," Jackie said, "that means that, instead of working for a flat sum, he would get half the profits from whatever he produced from the earth." His father left the family before Jackie was two years old. Jackie's mother took him and the rest of the family to Pasadena, California, where he was raised and attended elementary and secondary schools.

Jackie attended Pasadena Junior College (1937–39) and UCLA (1939–41), where he played football, baseball, and basketball, and ran track. After his junior year, he left to play football for the Los Angeles Bulldogs. In May 1942 he was drafted into the army and applied for Officer's Candidate School, becoming a second lieutenant in January 1943. While in the army, as a black officer, Robinson had a heavy exposure to white racism. He later said, "I was naïve about the elaborate lengths to which racists in the armed forces would go to put a vocal black man in his place."

After leaving the army in 1944, Robinson started playing baseball for the Kansas City Monarchs of the Negro American League. In 1945, he was signed by Branch Rickey, president of the Brooklyn Dodgers, to a minor league contract. In 1947, he joined the Brooklyn Dodgers, thus becoming the first black in major league baseball. Robinson played for the Dodgers for ten years and had a career batting average of .311. In 1962, he was the first black man inducted into the Baseball Hall of Fame.

Jackie Robinson died on October 24, 1972, in Stanford, Connecticut, the same year SHIRLEY CHISHOLM [69] became the first black woman to have her name placed in nomination for the presidency of the United States.

43

Adam Clayton Powell, Jr.

1908–1972

The fifth anniversary of your chairmanship of the House
Education and Labor Committee reflects a brilliant record of
accomplishment. It represents the successful reporting to the
Congress of forty-nine pieces of bedrock legislation, and the
passage of every one of these bills attests to your ability to get
things done. Only with progressive leadership could so much
have been accomplished by one committee in so short a time. I
speak for the millions of Americans who benefit from these laws
when I say that I am truly grateful.

LYNDON B. JOHNSON

Adam Clayton Powell, Jr., used his influential position as chairman of the powerful House Education and Labor Committee to champion the cause of blacks and whites for full economic and political power in America. At the time of Powell's chairmanship, the Education and Labor Committee was responsible for over forty percent of all domestic legislation in the United States.

Powell—the fourth black congressman since Reconstruction (Oscar Depriest [1928], Arthur L. Mitchell [1934], and William L. Dawson [1942] were the first, second, and third)—became chairman of the House Education and Labor Committee in January 1961. While chairman, and thus the most powerful black in Congress, he influenced other legislation outside his committee that would further the rights and freedoms of blacks and all Americans: the Civil Rights Act (1964), the Economic Opportunity Act (1964), and the Voting Rights Act (1965). Among the "forty-nine pieces of bedrock legislation" affecting millions of Americans cited by President Johnson in his letter to Powell in 1966 were the Anti-Poverty Act; the Minimum Wage Act; the Manpower Development and Training Act; the Vocational Educational Act; and the National Defense Education Act. Each had the intent and economic features to alter positively the lives of millions of poor blacks and whites.

Within months of President Johnson's glowing words about Powell's progressive leadership, Powell was stripped of his chairmanship. He was expelled from the House of Representatives in March 1967, during the ninetieth Congress. The alleged reasons were misuse of congressional funds and other improprieties. Powell's censure and removal by a white male power block came to symbolize for black America the double standard white America held not just for the politically powerful like Adam Powell but for all blacks. Powell argued that his accusers were racist and hypocritical because they were guilty of the very behaviors of which he was accused. Protests by blacks against Powell's expulsion ensued across America, culminating with demonstrations in Washington, D.C.

In April 1967, Powell was reelected to his congressional seat by an overwhelming majority of voters in his Harlem district. He also decided to go to court to challenge the House's denial of his seat. While fighting in the courts, in November 1968, Powell was reelected to congress by an 85 percent majority. In January 1969, Congress reversed its earlier position on Powell's right to be seated: it seated him, fined him $25,000, and stripped him of all seniority and power. (In June 1969, the U.S.

Supreme Court ruled that Congress didn't have the right to expel him.) In 1970, Powell was defeated for reelection by Charles Rangel, so ending twenty-six years of congressional representation of the black masses of Harlem and throughout America.

Adam Clayton Powell, Jr., was born on December 23, 1908, in New Haven, Connecticut. His father, Adam Clayton Powell, Sr., was called to the ministry of the influential Abyssinian Baptist Church in Harlem, New York, during its centennial year. The family moved to Harlem when Adam Jr. was six months old. He attended Townsend Harris, then a prep school, and the City College of New York (CCNY), quitting after two years. He finished his undergraduate studies at Colgate University, with honors, after three and a half years. He also completed graduate studies at Teacher's College of Columbia University, with a master's degree in religious education.

While at Colgate in 1931, Powell had a mystical experience with the "voice of God." He believed that voice was calling him to the "Lord's work," as opposed to his desire to go to Harvard Medical School. "I'm a mystic. I believe in hearing the inaudible and touching the intangible and seeing the invisible," Powell said in describing this experience. "I was sitting there one night about two o'clock in the morning, marking up the papers of the freshman class in humanities, when this small voice in back of me said, 'What are you going to do, go to Harvard Medical School? Your father has the biggest church in Harlem. Who's going to succeed him?'"

Powell succeeded his father as pastor of Abyssinian Baptist Church in 1938 when he was thirty years old. Like other black theologian-activist ministers such as HENRY H. GARNET [14], HENRY M. TURNER [39], and RICHARD ALLEN [6], Powell linked his Christian theology and tenets to the liberation of the black masses socially, politically, and otherwise. His church would be a socioeconomic political tool, as many black churches had been from the beginning of the black experience in America. An example of Adam Powell's use of his church for the economic empowerment of blacks was his organization in 1938 of the Coordinating Committee for Employment to fight for jobs. The Committee, he said, "is now inaugurating a mass boycott and picketing of every enterprise in greater New York that refuses to employ Negroes." Adam Powell coined the phrase in the late thirties: "Don't buy where you can't work."

Powell's gospel of economic and political power for blacks in Harlem and throughout America got him elected to the City Council of

New York in 1941. In 1944, with the help of A. PHILIP RANDOLPH [31] and others, he had the political boundaries of Harlem changed, and that year he was elected Harlem's first black congressman.

Adam Clayton Powell, Jr., died on April 4, 1972. As man and leader, he has been described, sagely, by Gil Noble:

> Adam Clayton Powell represents still another chapter in a long story of black militant fighters against oppression and injustice here in America. He wasn't perfect, he had his faults. But don't we all. The point is, he was a fighter. If he did play, he worked harder than he played. Most of all, he was a fighter.

44

Whitney M. Young, Jr.

1921–1971

The Urban League must of necessity be involved in this feat of social engineering. To divorce ourselves from this would be an expression of irresponsibility; to isolate our organization from this activity would be to deny corporations, foundations and community funds a unique opportunity for representation and participation in a new era of social planning. The Urban League will be valueless to responsible institutions in our society if it does not maintain communication with and the respect of other responsible Negro organizations and the respect of the masses of Negro citizens.

WHITNEY M. YOUNG, JR.

163

Since its inception in 1911 as a merger of three organizations—the Committee for Improving the Industrial Conditions of Negroes in New York, the National League for the Protection of Colored Women, and the Committee on Urban Conditions—the National Urban League (NUL) has committed itself to the improvement of the economic and social conditions of blacks in urban areas.

Unlike the National Association for the Advancement of Colored People (NAACP, founded in 1909), the NUL didn't view itself as a civil rights, mass protest, and litigious organization. That's why the words of Whitney Moore Young, Jr., Executive Director of the NUL in 1963, committing the League to "this feat of social engineering," are so significant and revealing of his influence on the struggle for blacks for a more egalitarian America.

"This feat" was the 1963 March on Washington, "the crossing of the Rubicon in the African-American quest for equality in America" (see REV. DR. MARTIN LUTHER KING, JR. [1]). Whitney Young's role was to persuade the NUL leadership to adopt a tactic it had not previously used for improving the economic and social condition of blacks: a mass protest or mass demonstration. By involving the National Urban League in the March on Washington, Whitney Young not only linked the NUL with other Negro organizations but metamorphosed the NUL into a civil rights and economic and social organization, gaining—as never before—"the respect of the masses of Negro citizens."

Whitney Young's role in this metamorphosis of the NUL into a civil rights partnership with other black civil rights groups during the sixties and seventies justifies his ranking here. Nancy J. Weiss assessed the impact of Young in redirecting the NUL to the needs of the black masses during his ten-year tenure as its leader: "Through jobs and training programs, Young enlarged the economic opportunities available to black Americans. He gave powerful whites in the private sector a means of comprehending the problems of the ghetto and, in the most successful instances, making some contribution toward their amelioration. He threw his weight behind public policies to combat discrimination and poverty. He encouraged communication and understanding across racial lines at a time when turmoil and misunderstanding were driving whites and blacks apart."

Whitney Moore Young, Jr., was born on July 31, 1921, to Whitney Sr. and Laura Young in Lincoln Ridge, Kentucky, at the beginning of the black cultural renaissance of the twenties and thirties. Young attended the Lincoln Model School in Simpsonville, Kentucky, an all-black elementary school, and the all-black Lincoln Institute, a boarding high school in Lincoln Ridge headed by his father. He received a B.S. from Kentucky State College (1941) and a M.A. (1947) from the University of Minnesota. Young joined the St. Paul, Minnesota, Urban League in 1947 and became executive director of the Urban League in Omaha, Nebraska, in 1950. From 1954 to 1960, he was dean of the Atlanta University School of Social Work. After a year as a visiting scholar at Harvard University, Young was appointed executive director of the National Urban League, a position he held from 1961 to 1971, transforming the NUL into a socioeconomic organization with a civil rights focus.

Whitney died on March 11, 1971, in Lagos, Nigeria, while attending the African-American Dialogue, sponsored by the African-American Institute of New York.

45

Mary C. Terrell
1863–1954

Even if I believed that women should be denied the right of suffrage, wild horses could not drag such an admission from my pen or my lips...

What could be more absurd and ridiculous than that one group of individuals who are trying to throw off the yoke of oppression themselves, so as to get relief from conditions which handicap and injure them, should favor laws and customs which impede the progress of another unfortunate group and hinder them in every conceivable way. For the sake of consistency, therefore, if my sense of justice were not developed at all, and I could not reason intelligently, as a colored woman I should not tell my dearest friend that I opposed woman suffrage.

MARY CHURCH TERRELL

Mary Church Terrell's ranking here acknowledges the influential role she played in helping black and white women "throw off the yoke of oppression" of white racism and sexism in America. Terrell's "sense of justice" for black women led her to play a pivotal role in organizing the pioneering National Association of Colored Women (NACW) in 1896, a merger of the National Federation of Afro-American Women and the Colored Women's League. NACW was organized "as a social, economic and moral force" within two months of *Plessy* v. *Ferguson*, the United States Supreme Court decision upholding the doctrine of "separate but equal" treatment of blacks. (Also see MARY MCLEOD BETHUNE [35].)

Terrell's commitment to eradicating the Jim Crow effects of *Plessy* v. *Ferguson* led her, as one of two black women (the other was IDA B. WELLS-BARNETT [29]) to help found the Niagara Movement (1909), which was the forerunner of the National Association for the Advancement of Colored People (NAACP).

Other measures of Terrell's influence over women's rights issues were her active membership in the National American Woman Suffrage Association, whose activities led to the ratification of the Nineteenth Amendment to the U.S. Constitution, giving women the right to vote (1920); and her successful challenge to the racist policies of the Washington, D.C., branch of the American Association of University Women, which excluded blacks.

Mary Church Terrell was born in 1863, the year of the Emancipation Proclamation, in Memphis, Tennessee, to Robert and Louisa Church, former slaves. She was sent by her parents to Yellow Springs, Ohio, to be educated in the elementary and secondary schools there. Terrell received a B.A. (1884) and an M.A. from Oberlin College. While working on her master's, she taught at Wilberforce University (1885–87). In 1887, she began teaching in the segregated Washington, D.C., public schools and later became principal of Washington Colored High School (also known as M Street High School, later changed to Paul Laurence Dunbar High School). In 1891 she married Robert Herberton Terrell, who later became a Washington, D.C., municipal court judge. In 1895, Mary Terrell became the first black woman to be appointed to the Board of Education in Washington, D.C.

In the early nineteen-fifties Terrell utilized some of the tactics and strategies developed by A. PHILIP RANDOLPH [31] and ADAM CLAYTON POWELL, JR. [43], to help form the Coordinating Committee for the Enforcement of the District of Columbia Anti-Discrimination Laws.

She became chairman of this committee and successfully used it to attack segregation of restaurants in Washington through picketing, demonstrations, and litigation (*District of Columbia* v. *John R. Thompson Co.*). At the age of ninety, Terrell brought about the desegregation of restaurants and other businesses in Washington, D.C.

Mary Church Terrell died on July 24, 1954, in Annapolis, Maryland, nearly two months after *Brown* v. *Board of Education* delivered the legal death blow to the "separate but equal" doctrine of *Plessy* v. *Ferguson*.

46

John H. Johnson
1918–

To make *Ebony* and the Negro consumer market integral parts
of the marketing and advertising agendas of corporate America.
　　To accomplish this, we had to make four points: (1) that
Black consumers existed; (2) that they had disposable income;
(3) that they bought brand-name products; (4) that they could
and would buy additional products if they were appealed to
directly and personally.

JOHN H. JOHNSON

In the tradition of *Freedom's Journal, Crisis, Opportunity, Guardian,*
and *Messenger, Ebony* magazine (first issue November 1945) would
become a most important organ in giving visibility and expression to

black experiences, values, aspirations, and accomplishments and to the black quest for full equality in American life. However, *Ebony* and its publisher, John Harold Johnson, would have the seminal effect of making the *Ebony* reader an integral part of "the marketing and advertising agenda of corporate America" in a post-World War II, mass media, high tech advertising age.

Like MADAME C. J. WALKER [30], at the turn of the twentieth century, Johnson, through *Ebony*, would make blacks feel good about themselves and at the same time create economic opportunities for blacks and whites by catering to the needs, desires, and interests of a multibillion-dollar black consumer market. Johnson's business acumen in utilizing black consumerism to attract white corporate America's advertising dollars to his publications had another impact on black America. It led to the creation of a new generation of black entrepreneurs, committed to the economics of black consumerism, by spawning black-owned business; thus economically empowering black communities across America in their quest for an economic base to undergird full political and social participation.

Negro Digest (1942), Johnson's first publication targeted at the black consumer, was more traditional than *Ebony*. *Negro Digest* was "dedicated to the development of interracial understanding and the promotion of national unity." It was a technical and financial success, which led Johnson to publish *Ebony* in 1945. In 1950, he published *Tan*, and in 1951 *Jet*. By 1973, Johnson had diversified into a black cosmetics line, Fashion Fair Cosmetics, named after his nationally and internationally successful Ebony Fashion Show (begun in 1958).

By building on the black consumer base, John H. Johnson in the late eighties developed a business conglomerate—Supreme Life Insurance Co., Johnson Publishing Co., including Fashion Fair Cosmetics, Ebony/Jet Showcase (a nationally syndicated TV show), radio stations, and more—grossing nearly $175 million and employing nearly two thousand people. Johnson has been listed by *Forbes* magazine as one of the four hundred richest people in America.

John Harold Johnson's beginnings in Arkansas City, Arkansas, on January 19, 1918, didn't qualify him for the *Forbes* 400. He was the only child born to Gertrude and Leroy Johnson, "a handsome laborer who worked in the saw mills and helped out on the levee." His father died when Johnson was six years old. He was raised by his mother and stepfather, James Williams. John Harold attended a segregated elementary school in Arkansas City. In July 1933, he and his family moved to

Chicago, where he initially attended Wendell Phillips High School (which later burned) and transferred to Jean Baptiste Pointe Du Sable High School, from which he graduated in 1936. After graduating from Du Sable, Johnson started working full time at Supreme Life Insurance Company, attending the University of Chicago part time for two years, and after that attended Northwestern University School of Commerce.

It was while working as editor for Supreme's house publication, the *Guardian*, that Johnson got the idea to publish the *Negro Digest* in 1942, starting him on the path to becoming the most influential publisher to the Negro consumer market in American history. Like many of *The Black 100*, Johnson stood on the shoulders of the black activists who came before him: he was inspired by the entrepreneurial traditions of blacks like JAMES FORTEN [11].

47

Jesse Jackson

1941–

Future leaders, those who would lead the nation, must know that the flag is red, white and blue but the nation is not red, white and blue. It is red and yellow and brown and black and white.

JESSE JACKSON

The emergence of Jesse Louis Jackson in the 1980s as a political leader of the United States' diverse and multicolored people—"red and yellow and brown and black and white"—warrants his ranking here. By running for the Democratic nomination for the presidency in 1984 and 1988, Jackson demonstrated the maturation of African-American political leadership and its quest for the highest political offices in America.

Importantly, Jackson was backed by his "Rainbow Coalition" of multiethnic groups. In the legacy of P. B. S. PINCHBACK [20], HENRY M. TURNER [39], and ADAM CLAYTON POWELL, JR., [43], Jackson made of his campaign for the presidency more than the mere symbolic victory of running, in 1984; he proved in 1988 the true potential of a candidate of African descent for the White House.

Reflecting on his two campaigns for the Democratic nomination—against Vice President Walter Mondale (1984) and Governor Michael Dukakis (1988)—Jackson said: "I look at the impact of my campaign in Vermont and Maine, Puerto Rico. We won Alaska, Michigan, Mississippi, and we came in number one or number two in 46 or 54 states [and territories]. That changes the impact of our political aspirations, in some sense, forever. And so, there were victories all over the place, and there are still victories to be had, after all. Mondale got 6.7 million votes and won; I got seven million votes and lost; Dukakis got nine million."

Ordained a Baptist minister in 1968, Jesse Jackson was of the mold of black theologian-activists like Revs. HENRY H. GARNET [14], RICHARD ALLEN [6], ADAM CLAYTON POWELL, JR. [43], and MARTIN LUTHER KING, JR. [1], Jackson's mentor in the civil rights movement of

Jessie Jackson (center) with Dr. Martin Luther King, Jr., on the balcony of the Lorraine Motel, in Memphis, Tennessee, the day before Dr. King was killed.

the fifties and sixties. It was his association with King that catapulted Jackson into the national eye; in 1967, King appointed him to head the economic section of the Southern Christian Leadership Conference (SCLC, founded in 1957), known as Operation Breadbasket. This was a coalition of black businessmen and clergy seeking business and job opportunities for blacks with nonblack businesses conducting business in black communities.

Through Jesse's leadership in Chicago, Operation Breadbasket spread to major cities across America, gaining for blacks thousands of jobs and business opportunities with white and black businesses as suppliers, producers, and vendors. While national director of Breadbasket (1967–71), Jesse, like JOHN H. JOHNSON [46] and others, marshaled the economics of black consumerism, with the threat of boycotts of uncooperative businesses, to build a new generation of black entrepreneurs and black workers, both professional and nonprofessional.

After leaving Breadbasket in 1971, Jackson founded the influential People United to Save Humanity (PUSH), becoming its executive director. Over the next fifteen years, he utilized his superb organizing skills to expand PUSH into fourteen major cities across the United States. Among PUSH's strategic goals are:

> The development and expansion of black-owned and controlled financial/commercial businesses as institutions necessary to a healing, stable Afro-American survival; and the right of every child to a relevant, quality education, supported by taxation and free of charge, regardless of place of residence.

Measures of Jackson's ability to mobilize PUSH to deliver on these goals affecting the quality of life of blacks in America have been PUSH's national agreements with major corporations like Kentucky Fried Chicken, Burger King, and General Foods to provide more jobs for blacks; and the establishment of PUSH-EXCEL, a program designed to help motivate black student achievement in school.

Jesse Louis Jackson was born October 8, 1941, in Greenville, South Carolina, almost five months after A. PHILIP RANDOLPH [31] called off his threatened March to Washington of one hundred thousand demonstrators to protest discrimination against blacks in the war industry. Jesse Jackson was raised by his mother and stepfather, Charles H. Jackson, whose last name he assumed as a child. He attended all-black

Sterling High School and starred in football, baseball, and basketball. After graduating high school in 1959, he went to the University of Illinois on a football scholarship. Experiencing racism at Illinois on and off the field, Jackson decided to attend predominantly black North Carolina A&T College, in Greensboro, North Carolina.

At A&T he led student sit-ins at restaurants and other businesses in downtown Greensboro that refused to serve blacks and graduated with a B.S. in sociology in 1964. In 1965 he attended the Chicago Theological Seminary at the University of Chicago. After leaving the seminary in 1965, he joined Dr. Martin Luther King, Jr.'s Selma, Alabama, campaign and in 1966, SCLC's Chicago campaign.

Since his last run for the presidency, Jesse Jackson has continued to influence American thought—white and black—through a highly successful nationally syndicated TV show and as a shadow senator from Washington, D.C. "My agenda, really" he says, "is empowerment, and empowerment really means D.C. statehood."

48

Alex Haley

1921–1992

They [middle-class black America] have forgotten the struggle
and the hardships and the blood, sweat, and tears.... and they
have forgotten the road over which we have come and they are
not teaching it to their children. They are failing to teach their
children. To tell their children and to tell their children's
children....

RALPH DAVID ABERNATHY

Having been taught through stories told by his maternal grand-mother about his African ancestors, Alex Haley was inspired to search more deeply for his African origins. His landmark *Roots: The Saga of an American Family* (1976) inspired millions of African-Americans, along with other Americans of diverse backgrounds and cultures, to search for and rediscover their own family histories. In 1977 Haley's *Roots* won a Pulitzer Prize and was made into a TV miniseries of the same name, attracting over 130 million viewers, at that time the largest program audience ever.

The impact of *Roots* is best viewed as prodding middle class black Americans to remember and rediscover "the struggle and the hardships and the blood, sweat, and tears" that RALPH D. ABERNATHY [66] sorrowfully observed they had forgotten "to tell their children and to tell their children's children." *Roots*, the book, which took Haley twelve years to research, and the miniseries were powerful tools for reminding black and nonblack America of a continuum of African resistance, "a struggle waged in slave ships, a struggle waged as they crossed the Middle Passage," as Leonard Jeffries described it; and of a struggle waged in America, told through the story of Haley's progenitor Kunta Kinte and his progeny, who had been kidnapped from West Africa and brought to America as slaves.

The impact of Haley's *Roots* on black and nonblack America reveals a painful irony about the role of the media on the ability of a post–World War II, mass media, high-tech dominated black America to pass on the basic facts and truths about the African experience in America and Africa to "our children's children." Prior to the appearance of Haley's *Roots*, from approximately the late forties to the early seventies, blacks had been portrayed in the media as having little or no culture, history, or tradition that nonblacks were bound to respect. Usual representation of Africans on TV, in print, and in films, was as savages, with Tarzan and Jane characters devoid of culture and civility, potent images bombarding black and nonblack America with false stereotypes, and denying the truth of the black experience, past and present.

In order to gain a sense of how negative these media images were during this period, consider how much *less* influential Haley's *Roots* might have been on blacks prior to the emergence of the mass-media, high-tech era on a generation of blacks exposed to MARCUS GARVEY [21] and his movement at the turn of the century; or on a generation of African-Americans exposed to HENRY M. TURNER [39], whose maternal

Alex Haley with Maya Angelou and Levar Burton on location for *Roots*.

grandfather was an African prince; or on a generation of blacks influenced by the writers and artists of the black cultural renaissance of the twenties and thirties; or on the generation of PAUL ROBESON [24] (whose father was a runaway slave); or on CARTER WOODSON's [25] generation, which he urged to celebrate "the history of Africa, the history of your ancestors, people of whom you should feel proud." The reader is also reminded that MARTIN R. DELANY [13] was the great-grandson of an African prince and that PHILLIS WHEATLEY [19] was brought directly off a slave ship in Boston, after being "snatch' from Afric's fancy'd happy seat" in 1761, six years before the kidnapping of Kunta Kinte!

The point of these observations about black awareness of the African-American legacy is to show the extraordinary influence of Alex Haley's work in directing black America to rediscover the roots of the immemorial black struggle, which had been obscured and distorted by white-dominated media for over thirty years prior to the emergence of *Roots: The Saga of an American Family* and *Roots*, the TV miniseries.

Alex Haley was born the eldest of three boys in Ithaca, New York, on August 11, 1921, at the beginning of the Negro Renaissance. He spent his childhood with his grandparents in Henning, Tennessee (1921–29), where his maternal grandmother, Cynthia Murray Palmer, often sat on an open porch and told him stories about Africa and his African ancestors.

His father, Simon Haley, was a former sharecropper who became a college professor after getting a bachelor's degree at A&T College in Greensboro, North Carolina, and a master's degree in agriculture from Cornell University School of Agriculture. His mother was a schoolteacher. Alex finished high school in Ithaca when he was fifteen and attended college for two years before joining the U.S. Coast Guard in 1939, at the prodding of his father. In the Coast Guard he developed his writing skills and in 1959 returned to pursue a full-time career as a writer.

From 1954 to 1956 he free-lanced for publications such as *Reader's Digest*, *Atlantic Monthly* and *Playboy*, beginning for the last the monthly "Playboy interviews." His interview with MALCOLM X [23] led to a collaboration titled *The Autobiography of Malcolm X* (1965), completed just two weeks before its subject was killed. The *Autobiography* sold over six million copies.

Alex Haley's ranking here above both JAMES BALDWIN [49] and RICHARD WRIGHT [50] is not an assertion that he is a better or greater writer than the others. His ranking recognizes the fortuity of his being able to use the mass media—print and electronic—to influence both black and white America.

After *Roots*, Haley wrote only one other book, a novella titled *A Different Kind of Christmas* (1988). He was working on a book about MADAME C. J. WALKER [30] at his death on February 10, 1992, during the annual celebration of Black History Month.

49

James Baldwin

1924–1987

Where are the black writers who will dare to confront this racist nation? Who will illuminate the dream of the disenfranchised and sing the song of the voiceless? Who will remember that black men and black women left the African continent together, lay spoon fashion in the filthy hatches of slave ships together, stood on the auction block together, were sold again together, took the lash together? Baldwin's gigantic contribution to us answers those questions.

MAYA ANGELOU

James Arthur Baldwin was born in Harlem, New York, on August 2, 1924, during the black cultural renaissance. As a writer-activist who dared "to confront the racist nation" and who sought to "illuminate the dream of the disenfranchised and sing the song of the voiceless," Baldwin became one of the most prominent black intellectuals of the fifties and sixties, "who embarked," according to Lerone Bennett, "on a perilous journey of self-naming and self-legitimization. The grand outcome was a literary efflorescence which reached higher peaks than the Negro Renaissance of the twenties."

As a self-described "maverick outside writer," Baldwin shaped the thoughts and actions of thousands upon thousands of blacks, and nonblacks, during the vortex of change that took place in America during the fifties, sixties, and seventies. Although not taking sides with the general characterizations of the nonviolent tactics of DR. MARTIN LUTHER KING, JR. [1], vs. the more confrontational tactics of MALCOLM X [23], he always saw his role as a writer to give blacks a superior moral and spiritual sense, which would keep them from becoming as debased as racist whites in America. On this issue he said, "Whoever debases others is debasing himself. That is not a mystical statement but a most realistic one, which is proved by the eyes of an Alabama Sheriff—and I would not like to see Negroes ever arrive at so wretched a condition."

During the civil rights struggles of the fifties and sixties, Baldwin involved himself as a writer, reporter, and activist. Reflecting on this involvement, he said, "I had to go through the civil rights movement and I don't regret it at all. All those people trusted me. There was something very beautiful about that period, something life-giving for me to be there, to march, to be a part of a sit-in, to see it through my own eyes."

In addition to Baldwin's activism in the civil rights movement was his literary "gigantic contribution" to the black struggle for a more egalitarian America. Some of his titles: *Go Tell It on the Mountain* (1953, his first novel); *Notes of a Native Son* (1955, essays); *Giovanni's Room (1956, novel)*; *Nobody Knows My Name* (1960, essays); *Another Country* (1962, novel); *The Fire Next Time* (1963, essays); and *No Name in the Street* (1972, essays). Altogether, Baldwin published sixteen books. Two of his plays, *Blues for Mister Charlie* and *The Amen Corner*, received favorable reviews. His *One Day When I Was Lost*, a screenplay based on *The Autobiography of Malcolm X*, was a source of producer-director Spike Lee's 1992 film on Malcolm X. James Baldwin's last books were

The Evidence of Things Not Seen (1985) and *The Price of the Ticket: Collected Non-Fiction 1978–1985.*

Mel Watkins has cogently summarized the impact of James Baldwin as an artist-activist: "Along with Martin Luther King, Jr., he helped shape the idealism upon which the sixties' civil rights protest was based... Since he was a political leader, King's influence on the events of the sixties is readily understandable. The source of Baldwin's influence as a writer is less apparent, particularly since the ideological content of his essays was rarely new—among others, Frederick Douglass, W. E. B. Du Bois, and Richard Wright had previously dealt with many of the ideas that he presented. Aside from the accident of timing, it was the uniquely personal perspective and style in which Baldwin couched his ideas that set him apart. His essay style, in fact, set a literary precedent that would later develop into the 'new journalism.'"

James Baldwin died in the south of France, in Saint-Paul-de-Vence, on November 30, 1987. On December 8, 1987, approximately four thousand people gathered in New York at the Cathedral of St. John the Divine for his funeral. Among the speakers were MAYA ANGELOU [85] and TONI MORRISON [73] who eulogized Baldwin in part: "So, I have pored again through the 6,895 pages of your published work... No one possessed or inhabited language for me the way you did.... But for the thousands and thousands of those who embraced your text, who gave themselves permission to hear your language by that very gesture, they ennobled themselves, became civilized."

50

Richard Wright

1908–1960

Four centuries of oppression, of frustrated hopes, of black
bitterness, felt even in the bones of the bewildered young, were
rising to the surface....

Here's that *something*, that pent-up folk consciousness.
Here's a fleeting glimpse of the heart of the Negro, the heart
that beats and suffers and hopes—for freedom. Here's the fluid
something that's like iron. Here's the real dynamite that Joe
Louis uncovered!

RICHARD WRIGHT

Richard Wright was a twenty-seven-year-old writer for *New Masses*, a leftist publication, when he described the impact on and the reaction of Chicago blacks to Joe Louis's victory over Max Baer, the ex-heavyweight champion of the world, in October 1935. No one better described, and influenced more as a writer, the "pent-up folk consciousness" and "heart of the Negro" than Richard Wright.

His ranking here acknowledges his powerful influence on the African-American quest for freedom. His ranking behind JAMES BALD-WIN [49] is no determination as to who was the better writer, but my judgment that Wright had relatively less impact on a critical phase of the black struggle than Baldwin, who, though living in France, like Wright, came to the United States at strategic points to get involved directly with Dr. King and others, as a writer, reporter, and activist.

Examples of Richard Wright's ability to capture the "pent-up folk consciousness" of blacks are best seen in his *Uncle Tom's Children* (1938) and *Native Son* (1939). As PAUL ROBESON [24] described Wright's portrayal of the Negro in *Uncle Tom's Children*, "He was and is— courageous, and forever struggling to better his condition." Robeson further stated that "Richard Wright, flesh of the flesh of these virile, hard-working, suffering, but joyous Americans of African descent [created] people who everyone will feel really exist; characters straight out of the rich life of the folk who have contributed so much to the physical and cultural making of present-day America." In *Native Son*, his most famous book, Wright, through the character Bigger Thomas, showed the destructive impact of the forces of northern urban racism on blacks, who were isolated in ghetto after ghetto after their mass exodus from the South.

Richard Wright was born in Roxie, Mississippi, on September 4, 1908, to poor parents, Nathan and Ella Wright. After his father deserted the family in 1913, his mother moved the family first to Memphis and then to West Helena, Arkansas. When Richard's mother became ill and couldn't support him, he spent a little time in an orphanage, until his maternal grandparents took him into their care in Jackson, Mississippi. In Jackson, he was exposed to the virulent racism of the deep South.

After finishing the ninth grade, in 1925, he decided to move to Memphis. In 1927, he moved to Chicago. There, after a series of nonwriting jobs, he started writing for publications such as *Left Front* and *New Masses*. While in Chicago during the Depression, Wright got involved with federal government writing projects and further developed his writing skills. In 1937, he moved to New York, where in 1938 he wrote *Uncle Tom's Children*.

Among Wright's other significant volumes dealing with the black experience are the autobiographical *Black Boy* (1943) and *I Tried to Be a Communist* (1944).

In 1947, Richard Wright moved to France, where he lived until his death in Paris of a heart attack on November 28, 1960.

51

Elijah Muhammad

1897–1975

[Elijah] Muhammad has deeply shaken the Negro Christian community. Muhammad's recital of how the Christian faith has failed the Negro, "By their fruits ye shall know them," has sunk deeper into the hearts of the Negro masses than Negro clergymen will admit publicly.

Louis Lomax

Unlike RICHARD ALLEN and ABSALOM JONES [6], DAVID WALKER [9], NAT TURNER [10], HENRY M. TURNER [39], DR. MARTIN LUTHER KING, JR. [1], ADAM CLAYTON POWELL, JR. [43], and JESSE JACKSON [47], Elijah Muhammad shook the foundations of the "Negro Christian community" by completely repudiating Christianity as a tool of racist oppression and as the ideology of white devils who sought to perpetuate the exclusion of blacks from the benefits of American life. The other black theologians and activists cited above all in some way sought to restructure and redirect Christianity to meet the needs and aspirations of blacks in America and throughout the world.

The impact of Muhammad's efforts to get the "Negro masses" to embrace the teachings of the Nation of Islam in a post–Marcus Garvey era warrants his ranking here. "He went down in the mud and got the brother that nobody else wanted," said Louis Farrakhan. "He got the brother from prison, the brother from the alley, the brother from the poolroom, the sister from the corner and he polished us up." Among Muhammad's most notable rescuees were MALCOLM X [23], and LOUIS FARRAKHAN [80].

The Nation of Islam was formed in 1930 in Detroit by Wallace D. Fard, who adopted the Muslim name W. Farad Muhammad. W. Farad Muhammad was allegedly born in Mecca, Saudi Arabia, in 1877. He believed that he was summoned by Allah, the God of Islam, to redeem the original race of humankind: the black race. Farad Muhammad believed that only through a black nation, the Nation of Islam, could African-Americans realize full economic, political, and social rights by embracing a black God and the doctrines of the messenger, Farad. He emphasized self-help, self-love, and separation from whites. This Muslim faith asserted that blacks were Muslims by birth and must unite in their own nation, away from white devils and evil. (See DELANY [13], GARNET [14], GARVEY [21], and TURNER [39], for earlier black nationalist and separatist movements.)

In 1930, Elijah Muhammad met W. Farad Muhammad who had just established the first University of Islam and Temple No. 1 in Detroit. At this time he renounced Christianity and became one of Farad's several hundred disciples. In 1934, Farad mysteriously disappeared, but before leaving, he anointed Elijah Muhammad leader of the Nation of Islam, officially changing his name from Elijah Poole to Elijah Muhammad. Shortly thereafter he moved to Chicago and founded Temple No. 2, emerging as the leader of the Nation of Islam.

Elijah Poole was born on October 10, 1897, to tenant farmers Wally and Mary Poole in Sandersville, Georgia. Elijah was the seventh of thirteen children. Because he was forced to leave school at an early age, he was taught to read by one of his older sisters. In order to alleviate his family's poverty, he worked as a laborer and bricklayer in Sandersville and Macon, Georgia.

Elijah Poole converted to Christianity as a young man and became a Baptist minister. After experiencing various acts of racism directed toward him and his family, he moved to Detroit in 1923, where he worked in an automobile plant until 1929.

From 1934 until his death in 1975, Elijah Muhammad built a Black Muslim Nation of several hundred thousand by appealing to the black masses. He established over 150 temples in the United States and the Caribbean and nearly fifty universities of Islam. He acquired thousands of acres of land for farming in the deep South and sparked the entrepreneurial spirit among African-Americans in the sixties and seventies by starting and operating supermarkets, banks, newspapers, restaurants, and dry cleaners in every major American city. (Also see the role of J. H. JOHNSON [46] and JESSE L. JACKSON [47], regarding the development of black enterprises.)

Elijah Muhammad died on February 25, 1975, in Chicago. On February 26, 1975, he was succeeded by his son Wallace D. Muhammad, who in practicing orthodox Islam changed the Nation of Islam to the World Community of Islam and among other changes has permitted whites to join the community.

Wallace D. Muhammad has abandoned the goals of a "separate nation within a nation" as espoused by his father: "We can't think that way [separation], not and live in America and claim a share in the benefits of this country you know. If we are going to live in this country and claim a share in the fruits of this country, then we have to identify in the national aspirations of the people."

52

Zora Neale Hurston

1901–1960

There are certain practical things American Negro writers can do through their work.

We can reveal to the Negro masses, from whence we come, our potential power to transform the now ugly face of the Southland into a region of peace and plenty.

We can reveal to the white masses those Negro qualities which go beyond the mere ability to laugh and sing and dance and make music, and which are a part of the useful heritage that we place at the disposal of a future free America.

LANGSTON HUGHES

189

Zora Neale Hurston's pioneering folkloric works *Jonah's Gourd Vine* (1934), *Mules and Men* (1935), and *Tell My Horse* (1938) demonstrate her ability as a writer in revealing to "the Negro masses from whence we come" and her influential contribution in placing that "useful heritage, at the disposal of a future free America." Like fellow Black Renaissance writers HUGHES [34], MCKAY [37], and WRIGHT [50], Zora Neale Hurston captured the nuances of the average black person's struggle for freedom in America and throughout the world.

Although *Vine* and *Mules and Men* have been criticized for perpetuating white stereotypes of blacks (similar criticisms were leveled at MCKAY and DUNBAR [18]), Hurston's role as a participant, observer, and creative writer who revealed unique aspects of black folk life through American and Caribbean folktales has been a positive one in the African-American struggle for equality.

Zora Neale Hurston was born January, 1901 in Eatonville, Florida, an all-black town rich in black folklore and traditions. She was one of eight children born to Lucy and John Hurston. Her father was a minister who later became mayor of Eatonville. Lucy Hurston died when Zora was nine years old.

As a teenager, Hurston left Eatonville to work as a maid for a Gilbert and Sullivan traveling musical show. She settled in Baltimore where she graduated from Morgan Academy (the high school of Morgan State University) in 1918. From 1919 to 1924 she attended Howard University, where she met ALAIN LOCKE [36], who was also interested in Negro folk education, and developed her writing skills.

Drawing upon the folk traditions of Eatonville, she published her first short story, "John Redding Goes to Sea," in *Stylus* (1921). In 1924, she published another folk piece, "Drenched in Light," in *Opportunity*.

From 1925 to 1927, with a scholarship to Barnard College in New York, Zora studied anthropology under the renowned anthropologist Franz Boas. In 1926 she began her first collaboration with Black Renaissance writer Langston Hughes on a magazine, *Fire!!* She also collaborated with Hughes on the play *Mule Bone* in 1930.

Other important works by Zora Neale Hurston are: "Spunk" (1925, a short story in Locke's seminal *The New Negro*); *Their Eyes Were Watching God* (1937, a novel); *Moses, Man of the Mountain* (1939, folkloric); and *Dust Tracks on the Road* (1942, autobiographical).

Zora Neale Hurston died penniless on January 28, 1960, in Saint

Lucie County, Florida, within days of the historical sit-ins in Greensboro, North Carolina.

Biographer Robert E. Hemenway described the triumph and tragedy of Zora Neale Hurston's life as it mirrored the black experience in America: "Zora Neale Hurston was a nontragic person, a woman who rejoiced in print about the beauty of being black. When her blues came, when bigots and rednecks and crackers and liberals and racial missionaries got her down, she retreated into a privacy that protected her sense of self; publicly, she avoided confrontation by announcing that she didn't look at a person's color, only one's worth. She personally believed in an integrated society, but she spent her career trying to preserve and celebrate black cultural practices."

Zora Neale Hurston with Langston Hughes and Jessie Fauset at Tuskegee, 1927.

53

Benjamin E. Mays

1895–1984

We strive to desegregate and integrate America to the end that this great nation of ours, born in revolution and blood, "conceived in liberty, and dedicated to the proposition that all men are created equal" will truly become the lighthouse of freedom where none will be denied because his skin is black and none favored because his eyes are blue.

BENJAMIN E. MAYS

Benjamin Elijah Mays was born in post–Reconstruction America on August 1, 1895, in Epworth, South Carolina, nearly nine months before *Plessy* v. *Ferguson* established the "separate but equal" doctrine. His parents, Hezekiah Mays and Louvenia Carter Mays, were born slaves.

When he was nearly four years old, Mays was exposed to white mob violence against his father—"because his skin [was] black"—and other blacks, which led to the Phoenix riot in Greenwood County, South Carolina, in November of 1898, in which at least eight blacks were killed by whites.

In the practice of *Plessy* v. *Ferguson*, Mays attended a segregated elementary school. He graduated as class valedictorian from an all-black high school in Orangeburg, South Carolina, (the high school of South Carolina State College) in 1916. He was Phi Beta Kappa at Bates College in Maine, where he received a B.A. in 1920. Following graduation, he decided to enter the ministry. He was ordained a Baptist minister and later served as pastor of the Shiloh Baptist Church in Atlanta. Mays received an M.A. (1925) and a Ph.D. (1935) from the University of Chicago.

Benjamin E. Mays's ranking here recognizes the impact of his lifelong struggle "to desegregate and integrate America" and make it "the lighthouse of freedom where none will be denied because his skin is black and none favored because his eyes are blue."

One measure of Mays's influence on this struggle was his role as a black theologian-activist in fusing Christianity and the black church to the liberation struggle of blacks (in this he was like one of his outstanding students, DR. MARTIN LUTHER KING, JR. [1]). As president of Morehouse College he also played a crucial role in transforming the institution into a citadel of higher education for black men who, as he would say, were "honest men, men who can be trusted in public and private life—men who are sensitive to wrongs, the sufferings and injustices of society, and who are willing to accept responsibility for correcting the ills."

Beginning in the summer of 1930, Mays and fellow minister, Joseph W. Nicholson, documented the importance of the black church in the lives and aspirations of the black masses. Their work, *The Negro's Church*, is seminal in this regard. In 1968, Mays authored *The Negro's God* to further substantiate the centrality of God to the experiences and aspirations of black Americans. In 1934, Mays joined MORDECAI W. JOHNSON's [40] faculty at Howard University as dean of the School of

Religion and became one of the most influential Black Liberation theologian-activists of his day. He remained at Howard University until 1940. From 1940 to 1967, Mays helped shape the lives of thousands of "Morehouse Men," who directly influenced the struggle for equality in America by correcting its ills in their work as doctors, lawyers, engineers, ministers, writers, professors, and other professions.

In 1969, Mays was elected to the Atlanta School Board and later became its president. Until his retirement in 1981, he actively sought the collaboration of black churches and other organizations in helping to solve larger societal problems afflicting public schools such as drugs, vandalism, violence, truancy, and dropouts. Benjamin Elijah Mays died on March 28, 1984, in Atlanta, Georgia.

54

Muhammad Ali

1942–

He was arguably the greatest fighter of all time. But more importantly, he reflected and shaped the social and political currents of the age in which he reigned. Ali in the 1960s stood for the proposition that principles mattered, that equality among people was just and proper, that the war in Vietnam was wrong. . . . He is today a deeply religious man who evokes feelings of respect and love wherever he travels throughout the world.

THOMAS HAUSER

Muhammad Ali's transcendence from being arguably the greatest fighter that ever lived to the human rights persona who in the "1960s stood for the proposition that principles mattered...that the war in Vietnam was wrong" justifies his ranking here. Ali's beliefs in Islam—like his mentors MALCOLM X [23] and ELIJAH MUHAMMAD [51]—shook the foundations of racism in America by confronting a pervasive American lie: the declaration of equal rights for all Americans and the simultaneous denial of those rights to people of African descent.

Ali's most dramatic and forceful confrontation with this American lie occurred in 1967 when he refused to be inducted into the U.S. armed forces to fight in the Vietnam War. Ali explained his refusal by saying, "I'm not going to help nobody against something Negroes don't have. If I'm going to die, I'll die right here fighting you. If I'm going to die, you're my enemy. My enemy is the white people, not Viet Congs or Chinese or Japanese. You're my foes when I want freedom. You're my foes when I want justice. You're my foes when I want equality. You won't even stand up for me in America for my religious beliefs and you want me to go somewhere and fight, while you won't even stand up for me here at home."

Like JACKIE ROBINSON [42], JESSE OWENS [56], JACK JOHNSON [63], HENRY AARON [87], ARTHUR ASHE [98], and other athlete activists, Ali not only represents the athletic achievements of African-Americans but has become the prototypical symbol of the black athlete as an advocate in the struggle for freedom and equality during the last four decades of the twentieth century. Just as Elijah Muhammad, Malcolm X, and Louis Farrakhan rocked the black Christian community by embracing the teachings of the Nation of Islam, Muhammad Ali, by becoming a Black Muslim in the early 1960s represents the role of a non-Christian religion as an alternative means of eradicating the effects of racism against blacks in America. Ali's contribution to the black struggle is best summarized as his being the first African-American to merge the symbol of athletic accomplishment—the heavyweight boxing title—with a non-Christian religious ideology—Islam—in order to further the freedom and equality of blacks in America and throughout the world.

Ali paid dearly for his beliefs in Islam and his objection to the Vietnam War. DR. MARTIN LUTHER KING, JR. [1] was moved to comment on Ali's sacrifices due to his convictions: "No matter what you think of Mr. Muhammad Ali's religion, you certainly have to admire his courage. For here is a young man willing to give up fame if necessary, willing to give up millions of dollars in order to stand up for what conscience tells him is right."

Ali was born Cassius Marcellus Clay, Jr., in Louisville, Kentucky, on July 17, 1942, the same year William L. Dawson was elected to the U.S. Congress, only the third black since Reconstruction. His father, Cassius Marcellus Clay, Sr., was a sign painter and his mother, Odessa Grady Clay, was a domestic worker. Ali attended segregated elementary and secondary schools in Louisville and graduated in June 1960.

Ali started boxing when he was twelve years old after his bicycle was stolen. He sought to develop his pugilistic skills in order to "whup" whoever had stolen it. By the time he finished high school, Ali had fought 108 times as an amateur boxer, won six Kentucky Golden Gloves championships, two National Golden Glove tournaments, and two National Amateur Athletic Union titles. After winning the Olympic trials in 1960, he participated in the Olympics in Rome as a light-heavyweight where he won the gold medal and catapulted himself onto the global stage of history.

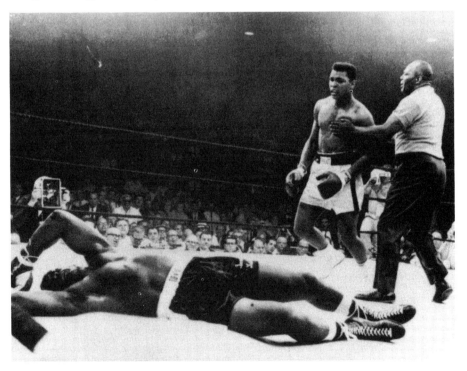

Muhammad Ali knocks out Sonny Liston in Lewiston, Maine, 1965.

Ali became a professional boxer after the Olympics and began his quest to become heavyweight champion of the world, using some of the antics and rhetoric of a famous white wrestler of the 1950s, Gorgeous George: "I saw Gorgeous George on TV. . . . He was a blond-haired wrestler, a white fellow. He said [things like] 'I'm the King, I'm going to destroy this bum. . . .' I said: 'That's a good idea.' So I started talking: 'I am the greatest. I'm pretty . . .'"

Ali's antics and rhetoric attracted the attention of the entire world. In February 1964, he fought the then unbeatable heavyweight champion, Sonny Liston, for the title. By beating Liston, Ali not only shook up the world of boxing but America as well. The day after the fight he announced that he had joined the Black Muslims and had taken the name Muhammad Ali, which was given to him by ELIJAH MUHAMMAD [51]. Ali had joined Elijah Muhammad, Malcolm X, and tens of thousands of other blacks in repudiating Christianity as a tool of racist oppression.

In 1967, at the Army Induction Center in Houston, Ali refused to be inducted into the armed forces, citing his religious beliefs as the reason for his refusal. As a result, he was convicted of draft evasion, his boxing license was revoked, and his title was stripped from him. All of these actions revealed the noxiousness of racism in American life. On June 28, 1971, Ali's conviction was reversed by the Supreme Court, which granted him conscientious objector status because of his religious beliefs.

Although Ali had already returned to boxing in 1970, before the Supreme Court decision, he continued his quest to be recognized as champion with greater furor and fame after the court's decision. He fought and beat George Foreman for the title in 1974. After losing the title to Leon Spinks in February 1978, Ali gained it a second time by beating Spinks in September 1978.*

With his retirement from boxing in 1981, Ali had already transcended the sport. He had become the most recognized and visible

---

*The author qualifies the popular view that Ali held the heavyweight title three times—the first fighter ever to do so. Those who hold this view count as his first loss the unjust and racially motivated stripping of his title in 1967, due to his refusal to fight in Vietnam. The facts are that racism in America stripped Ali of his title. Ali was vindicated by the Supreme Court's decision when given conscientious objector status and, thus, was justly and morally heavyweight champion of the world when he returned to boxing in 1970.

person in the world because of his manipulation of the media, his willingness and courage to stand up for the Islamic faith, and his commitment to the struggle for justice and equality for blacks and for all people.

Suffering the effects of Parkinson's Syndrome at the age of fifty, Ali best summarized the significance of his fame and renown in furthering the causes of Islam and human rights: "People say I had a full life, but I ain't dead yet. I'm just getting started. All of my boxing, all of my running around, all of my publicity was just the start of my life. Now my life is really starting. Fighting injustice, fighting racism, fighting crime, fighting illiteracy, fighting poverty, using this face the world knows so well, and going out and fighting for truth and different causes."

55

Arthur Schomburg

1874–1938

History must restore what slavery took away, for it is the social damage of slavery that the present generations must repair and offset.

But today, even if for the ultimate purpose of group justification, history has become less a matter of argument and more a matter of record. There is the definite desire and determination to have a history, well documented, widely known, at least within race circles, and administered as a stimulating and inspiring tradition for the coming generations.

ARTHUR A. SCHOMBURG

Arthur Alfonso Schomburg's obsession with making black history "less a matter of argument and more a matter of record" was his signal impact on the black struggle "to repair and offset" the damages of slavery and racism in America and throughout the world. Schomburg's ranking here acknowledges his influence as a prominent bibliophile and collector of African-American print materials and artifacts. For this reason, Schomburg has been called the Sherlock Holmes of Negro History.

As a contemporary of the Father of Negro History, CARTER WOODSON [25], Schomburg's vast collection of black history materials and artifacts documented the rich history of blacks in America and Africa and throughout the world. Schomburg's collection systematically and scientifically proved the three major conclusions he asserted in an essay, "The Negro Digs Up His Past," in 1925: "The Negro has been throughout the centuries of controversy an active collaborator, and often a pioneer, in the struggle for his own freedom and advancement... Negroes of attainment and genius have been unfairly disassociated from the group, and group credit lost.... [And] the remote racial origins of the Negro... offer a record of credible group achievement when scientifically viewed...."

Schomburg was born in San Juan, Puerto Rico, on January 24, 1874, to Carlos and Mary Schomburg—almost two weeks before Blanche Kelso Bruce, a black man, was elected to the U.S. Senate. Schomburg was educated in public schools in Puerto Rico and attended St. Thomas College in the Virgin Islands. As a young Puerto-Rican of African descent, Schomburg became interested in his African past and started collecting books and other materials on African history.

Schomburg came to the United States in 1891, started working at a law office, and continued to add to his black history collection. In 1906, he started working for Bankers Trust Co. and remained there until his retirement in 1929. In 1911, Schomburg and John E. Bruce founded the influential Negro Society for Historical Research. And in 1922, he was elected president of the American Negro Academy, the first major organization of the black intelligentsia, founded in 1897.

By 1925 Schomburg had collected several thousand documents, books, and artifacts and in May of the same year the New York Public Library dedicated its 135th Street Branch as the Department of Negro Literature and History to recognize this valuable collection. In 1926 the Carnegie Corporation purchased over five thousand items from Schomburg's collection for $10,000, donating them to the Department of Negro Literature and History in Harlem.

After retiring from Bankers Trust, Schomburg became curator of the Negro Collection at Fisk University. He remained there until 1932, when the Carnegie Corporation gave a grant to the New York Public Library to hire Schomburg as curator of the Division of Negro Literature, History, and Prints.

Schomburg died on June 10, 1938. The monument to his influence on the black experience in America and throughout the world is the Schomburg Center for Research in Black Culture—the former Division of Negro Literature, History, and Prints. With over one hundred thousand volumes of black history, and nearly 5 million artifacts, photographs, magazines, and manuscripts from throughout the world, the Schomburg Center in Harlem has become the mecca for those who wish to document black history in order "to restore what slavery took away...."

Arthur Schomburg (at right) with Marcus Garvey at the funeral of John E. Bruce.

56

Jesse Owens

1913–1980

How pitiable is it to reflect, that although you were so fully convinced of the benevolence of the Father of Mankind, and of his equal and impartial distribution of these rights and privileges, which he hath conferred upon them, that you should at the same time counteract his mercies.... That you should at the same time be found guilty of that most criminal act which you professedly detested in others with respect to yourselves.

BENJAMIN BANNEKER

Just as BENJAMIN BANNEKER [16] confronted Thomas Jefferson's hypocrisy and the hypocrisy of white America some 145 years earlier, James Cleveland [Jesse] Owens would, in 1936 at the Berlin Olympics, confront Aryan Supremacy as espoused and symbolized by Adolf Hitler. At the same time Owens revealed the inveterate lie of American society: a declaration of the equal rights of all men and the simultaneous denial of those rights to people of African descent.

Much like CRISPUS ATTUCKS [17] who was wrapped in the flag of American patriotism by the Founding Fathers, George Washington and John Adams, Jesse Owens's winning of four gold medals at the Berlin Games was used by white America to trumpet the superiority of American democracy over fascism. This occurred at a time when blacks continued to migrate from the South to the North in large numbers due to racism and violence, when blacks were disproportionately unemployed during the Great Depression because of discrimination, and when black organizations like the NAACP were designing legal campaigns to eviscerate the "separate but equal" practices of *Plessy* v. *Ferguson*.

Beyond the significance of his winning four gold medals in the face of the expectations of the Aryan supremacists, Owens came to symbolize the black struggle for equality. Owens also represented the ongoing contradiction of being "all-American" when it served the purpose of white America, but less than equal when constitutional rights and protections were sought by African-Americans. Owens himself experienced the American lie when he returned to the United States. "After I came home from the 1936 Olympics with my four medals," he said, "it became increasingly apparent that everyone was going to slap me on the back, want to shake my hand, or have me up to their suite. But no one was going to offer me a job."

Owens was born on September 12, 1913, in Oakville, Alabama, to Henry and Emma Owens, sharecroppers and the children of former slaves. Owens, nicknamed J.C. at an early age, was the youngest of ten children.

In 1922, the Owens family moved to Cleveland, Ohio, where he attended Fairmont Junior High School and started his career in track and field. He enrolled in East Technical High School at the age of seventeen, and while there was given the name "Jesse" because a teacher mispronounced his initials, J.C.

After breaking world records in the one hundred-yard and two hundred-yard dashes in 1933, Owens entered Ohio State University in Columbus, Ohio. In 1936, after qualifying for the Olympic Games by setting a world record in the one hundred-yard dash, Owens won four Olympic gold medals in the one hundred meters, two hundred meters, long jump, and four-hundred-meter relay.

Owens unequivocally rejected the much-publicized account of his having been snubbed by Adolf Hitler during the presentation of his medals. "I would be the first to criticize him [Hitler] for doing such a thing," Owens said, "but it never happened." Owens later explained that although not officially snubbed by Hitler—the Fuehrer watched him with unmasked disdain from the stands—it was he, Jesse Owens— a black athlete—who triumphed at the games. More important, Owens and his athletic records long outlived Adolf Hitler and the Third Reich. Jesse Owens died of lung cancer on March 31, 1980, in Tucson, Arizona.

Jesse Owens at medal ceremony at the Olympic Games, 1936.

57

Charles R. Drew

1904–1950

It was at Amherst, however, that an incident involving racism and prejudice took place. The track team went to Brown University for a track meet. After the meet, the Amherst team was scheduled to eat together at a nearby hotel. To the amazement of Drew and three other Afro-Americans on the team, the manager of the team informed them that the Narragansett Hotel would not serve the Afro-American members of the team. The four had to eat in the Brown University Commons while the rest of the team ate in luxury and comfort at the hotel. Needless to say, they left Brown, embittered and resentful, and Drew never forgot that incident.

LOUIS HABER

While an undergraduate at Amherst College in 1922, Charles Richard Drew experienced the incident of racism and prejudice described above. As a preeminent surgeon and blood plasma expert in 1941, Dr. Charles Richard Drew was exposed to the racist and white supremacist views of the U.S. armed forces when they ordered the American Red Cross Blood Bank in New York City, of which Drew was director, not to send "colored" blood for transfusions to white troops. If "colored" blood was to be used, it was to be segregated, as black soldiers and troops were.

During World War II, Drew addressed these irrational fears of whites about "Negro or colored" blood: "There are many who have a real fear born of ignorance that the blood of a Negro carries with it the possibility of their offspring having dark skin and other characteristics of the Negro race. Only extensive education, continued wise government, and an increasing fight on our part to disseminate the scientific facts and raise our levels of achievement can overcome this prejudice which to a large extent is founded on ignorance."

As a pioneer in blood plasma research, including its development and storage in what is known as blood banks, Drew deserves his listing and ranking in this volume. Drew's findings that blood plasma (liquid blood with the cells removed) produced more positive results than whole blood when used in transfusions revolutionized this branch of modern medicine. Additionally, Drew discovered that blood plasma could be stored longer and did not require blood typing and cross matching. The use of Drew's blood plasma by the British in World War II saved tens of thousands of lives. Since then, millions of civilians (white and black) have had blood plasma transfusions.

Drew's ranking is further supported by his direct impact on the training of hundreds of black doctors and students at Howard University Medical School from 1935 until his untimely death in April 1950. Drew was at Howard during the tenure of MORDECAI W. JOHNSON [40].

Drew was born on June 3, 1904, in Washington, D.C., four months before MARY MCLEOD BETHUNE [35] founded the Normal and Industrial School for Negro Girls. Drew was the oldest of five children of Richard Thomas Drew and Nora Burrell Drew. He attended segregated elementary and secondary schools in Washington. After graduating from M Street High School (later renamed Paul Laurence Dunbar High School) in 1922 with honors, Drew enrolled at Amherst College in Massachusetts, where he was an outstanding all-around athlete.

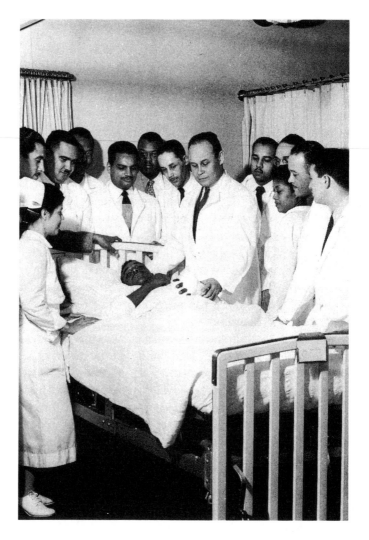

Charles Drew with medical students at Howard University.

After graduation from Amherst in 1926, Drew became a football coach at Morgan College until his acceptance at McGill University Medical School, in Canada, in 1928. It was at McGill that he started his research on blood. After graduating second in his class and interning for a year at the Montreal General Hospital, he joined the Howard University Medical School faculty, in 1935, as an instructor in pathology. He later became a professor of surgery, teaching and training scores of black doctors.

In 1938, Drew took a leave of absence from Howard, receiving a Rockefeller Foundation grant to continue his blood research at Columbia University. While at Columbia University and as a resident in surgery at Columbia Presbyterian Hospital Drew began his pioneering work with blood plasma storage and the creation of blood banks. Drew's doctoral thesis was titled "Banked Blood: A Study in Blood Preservation." In 1940, Drew received the doctor of medical science degree (Sc.D.) from Columbia University—the first black ever to receive this degree in the United States.

In 1940, Drew returned to Howard University to teach, but took another leave of absence in August to supervise the Blood Transfusion Association's plasma processing program for British soldiers with the British Red Cross. The following year Drew became the director of the Red Cross Blood Bank in New York City where he was responsible for providing blood plasma to American armed forces.

After the "colored blood" incident in 1941, Drew returned to teaching medical students, training surgeons, and writing articles for medical journals at Howard. On March 31, 1950, while driving to Tuskegee, Alabama, to deliver a lecture, Drew was fatally injured when he fell asleep at the wheel of his car. He died near Burlingston, North Carolina, on April 1, 1950, two days before the death of CARTER G. WOODSON [25].

58

John Hope

1868–1936

John Hope was a man of conviction and principle. . . . Hope was the only person from a Southern Black college to ally himself with this display of racial solidarity [Niagara Movement] and his participation was both daring and dangerous considering his position and the times.

ADDIE LOUISE JOYNER BUTLER

John Hope's conviction and principle in joining W. E. B. DU BOIS [4], WILLIAM M. TROTTER [28], IDA B. WELLS-BARNETT [29], MARY CHURCH TERRELL [45], and forty-eight others in February of 1905 to organize the Niagara Movement (which later became the National Association for the Advancement of Colored People, NAACP) to counteract BOOKER T. WASHINGTON [3] and his Tuskegee Movement showed his daring in speaking out for those causes which he felt advanced the struggle of blacks for full equality in America.

In June 1906, John Hope became the first black president of Atlanta Baptist College (which became Morehouse College). Like all Southern black college presidents, he was at the mercy of Northern white benefactors and one of the most powerful black Americans of the times, Booker T. Washington. Obviously, Washington didn't look favorably upon the "anti-Bookerite Niagara Movement" or upon John Hope, who was a friend and ally of Washington's archenemy, W. E. B. Du Bois.

In 1906 Hope furthered exposed himself to the wrath of Washington through a speech in Nashville attacking the basic tenets and tactics of Washington's landmark Atlanta Compromise address: "If we are not striving for equality, in heaven's name for what are we living? I regard it as cowardly and dishonest for any of our colored men to tell white people or colored people that we are not struggling for equality. . . . Yes, my friend, I want equality. Nothing less. . . . If equality, political, economic, and social, is the boon of other men in this great country of ours, then equality, political, economic, and social, is what we demand. . . . Rise, Brothers! Come let us possess this land. Never say: 'Let well enough alone.' Cease to console yourselves with adages that numb the moral sense. Be discontented. Be dissatisfied. . . . "

Hope's discontent and dissatisfaction went beyond his disagreement with Washington's "accommodationist" views and tactics. Hope would make a major contribution to black demands for equality by asserting "the need of a liberal education for us. The Negro must enter the higher fields of learning."

His impact went beyond shaping the Niagara Movement and other civil rights causes. In 1929, as the first president of the Atlanta University complex—an affiliation of Morehouse College (male, undergraduate), Spelman College (female, undergraduate), and Atlanta University (coed graduate and professional studies)—Hope established Atlanta University as a paragon for "higher fields of learning."

Other measures of Hope's influence include his position on the advisory board of the NAACP, his work as president of the National Association of Teachers of Colored Schools, and his tenure as president of the Association for the Study of Negro Life and History (founded by CARTER G. WOODSON [25]).

John Hope was born on June 2, 1868, in Augusta, Georgia, to James Hope (of Langholm, Scotland) and Mary Frances, the daughter of an emancipated slave mother, Alethea.

Hope graduated from the Augusta public schools in 1881 and worked in a restaurant as a clerk until he entered Worcester Academy in Massachusetts in 1886. After graduating in 1890, he enrolled at Brown University, receiving a B.A. in 1894. He taught at Roger Williams University in Nashville from 1894 to 1898. In 1898, he joined the faculty of Atlanta Baptist College, becoming its first black president in 1906. In 1929, he became the president of Atlanta University.

John Hope died on the campus of Spelman College on February 20, 1936, nearly six months before JESSE OWENS [56] won four gold medals at the Olympic Games.

59

Bayard Rustin

1910–1987

The Negro struggle has hardly run its course; and it will not stop moving until it has been utterly defeated or won substantial equality. But I fail to see how the movement can be victorious in the absence of radical programs for full employment, the abolition of slums, the reconstruction of our education system, new definitions of work and leisure. . . .

BAYARD RUSTIN

Bayard Rustin was the resident theoretician and practitioner of the modern civil rights movement. He was arrested at least twenty-three times in the struggle for equality in America. "By equality I do not mean 'separate but equal,'" Rustin said, "a phrase created by segregationists in order to prevent the attainment of equality. I mean equality based upon an integrated social order in which black people, proud of their race and their heritage, shall have no door closed to them."

Like one of his mentors, A. PHILIP RANDOLPH [31], Rustin believed in organizing the black masses to obtain power to bring about social reform through "hard work and programs." For over four decades Rustin reminded black leadership of the need to design, build, and institutionalize "programs for full employment, the abolition of slums, the reconstruction of our education system, [and] new definitions of work and leisure...."

Rustin's impact on the civil rights movement has been summarized by C. Vann Woodward: "Rustin has been reminding his people that the way out of their plight lies not through hairstyles and bizarre costumes...The real problems, from which all this is escape, are those of employment, wages, housing, health, education, and they are not to be solved by withdrawal and fantasy. They can only be solved in alliance with elements from the majority of the electorate, and the cement for such a coalition is not love but mutual interest. The way lies through nonviolence, integration, and coalition politics."

Bayard Rustin was born on March 17, 1910 in West Chester, Pennsylvania, where he was raised by his grandparents. His grandmother was a Quaker. He attended elementary and secondary schools in West Chester and then Cheyney State College in Pennsylvania and Wilberforce University in Ohio.

In 1936, Rustin joined the Young Communist League, organizing for two years and leaving in 1941 to join an antiwar group, Fellowship for Reconciliation, the forerunner of the Congress of Racial Equality (CORE). In 1941, he also joined A. PHILIP RANDOLPH [31] in planning the march to Washington that pressured President Franklin D. Roosevelt into ending discrimination by race or color in war industries. During World War II, Rustin served two and a half years in jail as a conscientious objector.

In 1947, as the field secretary of CORE, he led the first "freedom rides" in North Carolina, where he was jailed for twenty-two days and forced to work in a chain gang. In 1955, he helped DR. MARTIN LUTHER

KING, JR. [1] organize the Montgomery bus boycott. As a special aide to Dr. King for seven years, Rustin drafted the original plan for the Southern Christian Leadership Conference (SCLC), and with A. Philip Randolph and others provided the organizing genius for the 1963 March on Washington—the crossing of the Rubicon in the African-American quest for equality.

From 1964 until his death on August 24, 1987, Rustin headed the influential A. Philip Randolph Institute, in New York, which he used to bring about a new, radical social order. Rustin said, "The real radical is that person who has a vision of equality and is willing to do those things that will bring reality closer to that vision. . . . In such a social order there will no longer be walls, representing fear and insecurity, to separate people from one another. Such walls, whether constructed by whites or by blacks, are built to oppress and repress, but never to liberate. . . ."

60

T. Thomas Fortune

1856–1928

As the agitation which culminated in the abolition of African slavery in this country covered a period of fifty years, so may we expect that before the rights conferred upon us by the war amendments are fully conceded, a full century will have passed away. We have undertaken no child's play. We have undertaken a serious work which will tax and exhaust the best intelligence and energy of the race for the next century....

T. THOMAS FORTUNE

Timothy Thomas Fortune was one of the most prominent and influential of the post-Reconstruction black agitators and organizers. The "serious work which will tax and exhaust the best intelligence and energy of the race for the next century" was the ongoing struggle of black Americans to realize the "equal protection" of their civil rights (Fourteenth Amendment) and their right to vote (Fifteenth Amendment), which were being denied in a post-Reconstruction South dominated by white racist politicians, and which were undermined by decisions of a majority of the Supreme Court.

The above-mentioned words of Fortune were delivered at the founding of the National Afro-American League (NAAL) in Chicago in 1890, which was attended by 147 delegates from twenty-one states and the District of Columbia. The NAAL was but one of many examples of the African-American organization and active collaboration, according to Arthur Schomburg, "in the struggle for his own freedom and advancement." Other examples of black institutions and organizations created during this period were the Colored Men's Progressive and Co-Operative Union, 1875; State Convention of Rhode Island Negroes, 1882; State Convention of Colored Men of Texas, 1883; North Carolina State Teachers' Association, 1886; and the Convention of Colored Americans, 1890.

Fortune's leadership through the NAAL at the end of the nine-teenth century and his advocacy of the Fourteenth and Fifteenth Amendment rights of African-Americans justify his ranking here. The NAAL and its successor, the National Afro-American Council (NAAC, 1898), became the institutional progenitors of the Niagara Movement and its offshoot, the National Association for the Advancement of Colored People (NAACP), led by W. E. B. Du Bois [4].

Another measure of Fortune's impact on black and white America was his founding, in 1884, of a weekly newspaper, the *New York Freeman*. This newspaper, which was created to counter the negativity of the white press toward blacks, was renamed the *New York Age* in 1887. Fortune wrote: "The great newspapers, which should plead the cause of the oppressed and the downtrodden, which should be the palladiums of the people's rights, are all on the side of the oppressor, or by silence preserve a dignified but ignominious neutrality. Day after day they weave a false picture of facts—facts which must measurably influence the future historian of the times in the composition of impartial history. The wrongs of the masses are referred to sneeringly or apologetically."

From its inception until 1907, when it was sold, the *New York Age* had the reputation of being a militant and strident voice in pleading "the cause of the oppressed and downtrodden." However, the *Age* and Fortune's reputations would become even more controversial because of their association with and support of the most powerful black leader of the era, BOOKER T. WASHINGTON [3].

The *Age* and Fortune were often used by Washington and his "Tuskegee Machine" during this time to attack and counter W. E. B. DU BOIS [4], WILLIAM M. TROTTER [28], and others. For example, Fortune was a principal speaker supporting Washington and his policies at a 1903 church meeting in Boston, where Trotter was arrested for protesting and disrupting the meeting.

Fortune was born in Marianna, Florida, on October 3, 1856, six months after the birth of Booker T. Washington. At the time of his birth, his parents, Emanuel and Sarah Jane, were slaves. After the Emancipation Proclamation, Fortune's father became involved in politics and was elected to the Florida Legislature in 1868. His family moved from Marianna to Jacksonville when Fortune was a teenager because of threats made against his father by the Ku Klux Klan.

In Jacksonville, Fortune attended Freedman's Bureau schools and became a printer. He attended Howard University in 1876 briefly to study law but was forced to leave the school for economic reasons. Fortune subsequently worked for a black newspaper, the *People's Advocate*, and married Carrie C. Smiley.

Fortune moved to New York in 1879 and started working as a printer for the *Rumor*, later becoming a part-owner and its editor when it became the *Globe* in 1881. In 1884, he became the owner of the *New York Freeman* (subsequently the *New York Age*).

Also in 1884, Fortune published the polemical *Black and White: Land, Labor and Politics in the South*, utilizing Marxist language to call for the unification of black and white workers: "The hour is approaching when the laboring classes of our country, North, East, West, and South, will recognize that they have a *common cause*, a *common humanity*, and a *common enemy*; and that, therefore, if they would triumph over wrong and place the laurel wreath upon triumphant justice, without distinction of race or of previous condition, *they must unite!*"

From 1907 to 1919, Fortune was a writer for the *Norfolk Journal and Guide*. In 1923, he added another layer of controversy to his identity as a journalist and advocate of black causes by becoming the editor of MARCUS GARVEY's [21] *Negro World*. T. Thomas Fortune died in Philadelphia, on June 2, 1928.

61

Dorothy Height

1912–

Historically, black women built community organizations and welfare institutions.... Over and over again the defense of the family is seen as the primary concern of black women....

GERDA LERNER

Dorothy Irene Height, through the National Council of Negro Women (NCNW), now personifies "the defense of the [Black] family." Since her founding of the Black Family Reunion Celebration in 1986, she has encouraged millions of African-Americans to refocus on the black family and its positive role in the struggle for equality in American life.

Like other women in this book, Height represents the cultural and heritage sinews developed by black women and their organizations not only to defend the black family, but also to make the black community more viable in its ongoing struggle against racism and discrimination. Height and NCNW are a fulfillment of the vision and commitment expressed by Mrs. Booker T. Washington in 1915: "The home and the family are the starting point. Since the spirit of the age demands that the mother should have a wide knowledge of all matters pertaining to the moral, spiritual, and intellectual training of her children, we women must meet the demands by making our organizations avenues of help to the better way."

Height was born on March 24, 1912, in Richmond, Virginia, to James Edward and Fannie Height. When she was four years old the family moved to Rankin, Pennsylvania, where she attended elementary and secondary schools. After graduating from high school, Height applied to Barnard College, where she was told that they already had their quota of blacks (two) and that she would have to wait at least another semester before admission. Height then applied to New York University, where she earned B.S. and M.S. degrees.

Height taught at the Brownsville Community Center in Brooklyn, worked for the New York Department of Welfare, and traveled extensively as a representative of the United Christian Youth Movement. In 1937, she started working with the Young Women's Christian Association (YWCA) in Harlem; in the same year she met and began an association with MARY MCLEOD BETHUNE [35], the founder of the NCNW.

In 1939, Height moved to Washington, D.C., to become executive secretary of the YWCA's Phillis Wheatley Home. She joined the influential Delta Sigma Theta Sorority, becoming its national president in 1947. During her tenure as president, she globalized the organization's focus on the rights of black women in the United States and in developing countries by linking it to activities and programs of the United Nations Department of Information and the Political and Economic Committee on the Rights of Women. She also established a bookmobile program in the rural South and conducted national town meetings dealing with black issues.

In 1957, Height became the president of the NCNW, a coalition of some 240 local groups and 33 national organizations committed to equal rights for black women in particular, and blacks throughout the world. Although Height has influenced the black struggle for a more egalitarian America throughout her life, her greatest influence has been seen through her NCNW presidency as evidenced by her establishment of voter education and registration drives during the 1960s; her service on the influential Council for United Civil Rights Leadership; her role in shaping public welfare policy as a member of the Ad Hoc Committee on Public Welfare of the U.S. Department of Health; the founding of Operation Women Power, to help women of all races open their own businesses and receive needed vocational training; and the creation in 1986, of the Black Family Reunion Celebration, as a tool in revitalizing the black family and thereby the black community.

The Black Family Reunion Celebration is an annual series of events organized regionally by the NCNW to refocus the African-American community on positive aspects of the black family and community and to counter the pervasive negative image of the black family as "dysfunctional," as it often exists in public thought and is portrayed in mass media. Through weekend workshops, seminars, performances, and prayer breakfasts during the months of July through September, the NCNW has brought at least six million African-Americans together to rediscover and reassert venerable values, like kinship, the extended family, self-help, the importance of education, the work ethic, and spiritual beliefs.

Not since the publication of ALEX HALEY's [48] *Roots* have such great numbers of African-Americans begun to reaffirm the basic moral, spiritual, and intellectual values that have aided the black community in its quest for full equality. This fact supports Dorothy Irene Height's listing and ranking in this book.

Mary McLeod Bethune (left) and Dorothy Height during an awards ceremony at the Phyllis Wheatley YWCA.

62

Bill Cosby

1937–

The black man bringing gifts, and particularly the gift of laughter...is easily the most anomalous, the most inscrutable figure of the century.

JESSIE FAUSET

The gift of laughter to millions of Americans for the last three decades has made William Henry Cosby, Jr., a "most anomalous, a most inscrutable figure" to those who would attempt to determine his influence on the black struggle for freedom and equality in America.

The above observation by Jessie Fauset, in 1925, of the misconceptions held by both black and white Americans regarding the role of the black comic in conveying black aspirations, values, and demands can be associated more with comedian-actor Bill Cosby than any other African-American of the twentieth-century.

Cosby's emergence in the 1960s and 1970s as the Jackie Robinson of television, with his pioneering costarring role in "I Spy" with Robert Culp in 1965, and later, in 1969, with the sitcom "The Bill Cosby Show," would expose him to criticism from black and white America as being too mild an image of the black struggle in America. Robert Rosenberg has provided some instructive insights about Cosby, his times, and the efficacy of his humor in this regard:

> Cosby had begun working in the entertainment industry at a time when there were enormous barriers to black Americans. He had often been criticized by both blacks and whites who felt that his brand of gentle humor was an evasion, and that he should be more topical and race-oriented. Although he had used racial humor very early in his career, he had quickly abandoned it. Instead he chose to focus on that which unites people, not what separates them. This he considered a more universal language of humor, and the things he poked fun at were those that touched people of all backgrounds: childhood, marriage, family, the difficulties of raising children, and most recently, the effects of aging.

(The reader is encouraged to read about the role ALEX HALEY [48] played in using the mass media to convey black images and sentiment.)

Cosby's listing and ranking here recognize his impact in using the media to convey positive albeit controversial images of blacks to both black and nonblack America in the ongoing African-American struggle *to be*. Writer A. S. "Doc" Young has observed that: "Cosby would not be at his best as a professional civil rights leader, a Black Panther, or the head of a poverty program. But as Bill Cosby—comic, wit, humorist, and storyteller—he is making an important contribution to Afro-

Americans, to Americans as a whole. His contribution is not to be taken lightly."

Additional evidence that Cosby's contribution to the black experience is not to be taken lightly was his gift (with his wife, Camille) of $20 million to Spelman College in 1988. It was at that time the largest single gift ever to a historically black college and the largest single philanthropic gift by an African-American. While the gift received a great deal of media attention, it is rarely mentioned that the Cosbys have given millions of dollars to other black charities and colleges.

The Cosbys, through their philanthropy, have thus challenged African-Americans to emulate the sacrifices alluded to by Roscoe Conklin Bruce, a post–Civil War black soldier who "contributed a fund of over $6,000 to establish in Missouri a school where their children might enjoy the blessings of a useful education. Those Negro soldiers gave their savings to the same cause for which they had gladly offered their lives—the causes of freedom." The Cosbys' gift to Spelman also reminds one of Bruce's observation that "the quickening of Negro life must come more and more from within, the uplifting forces in Negro life must be more and more in the hands of Negroes."

William Henry Cosby was born on July 12, 1937, in Philadelphia to Anna and William Henry Cosby, Sr. He attended Wister Elementary School and Fitz-Simmons Junior High School. After attending Central High School for a year, he transferred to Germantown High School, where he dropped out after his sophomore year in 1952. For three years, Cosby worked at various odd jobs, from a shoe repairman to a laborer in an automobile muffler plant.

In 1956, he joined the U.S. Navy and became a medical corpsman. After leaving the navy, he received an athletic scholarship to Temple University in 1960, where he played on the football and track teams. During his second year at Temple, he worked part-time as a bartender and soon discovered his comedic talents when warming up audiences before the main acts in a Philadelphia nightclub, the Underground, where he earned five dollars a night.

In 1962, Cosby started performing at the Gaslight in New York City's Greenwich Village. That same year, he dropped out of Temple to become a full-time comedian. From 1962 to 1964, he performed throughout the United States and Canada. In 1964, he married Camille Hanks of Olney, Maryland.

In 1965 Cosby costarred with Robert Culp in what would become the highly rated "I Spy," for which he received three Emmy Awards before it was canceled in 1968. After starring in "The Bill Cosby Show" and several other projects, he launched "The Cosby Show," in September of 1984, which enjoyed one of the highest ratings of any sitcom in television history through its final season in 1992. Through his character, Dr. Heathcliff Huxtable, and the other Huxtable family members, Cosby created positive family images of blacks in a medium that has often distorted and negatively stereotyped them.

Another measure of Cosby's influence on black and nonblack America is seen in the reception of his "gift of laughter" best-selling books *Fatherhood* (1985), *Time Flies* (1987), and *Love and Marriage* (1989).

63

Jack Johnson

1878–1946

Most of what Jack Johnson [did] was condemned by America because of racist attitudes. Much of his persecution was rooted in the ugly soil of racism. . . . He was the first world symbol of black athletic achievement. . . .

GIL NOBLE

Jack Johnson became the "first world symbol of black athletic achievement" on December 26, 1908, in Rushcutter Bay, near Sydney, Australia, when he defeated the white heavyweight boxing champion of the world, Tommy Burns.

Boxing, like most aspects of American life, was "rooted in the ugly soil of racism." Johnson was the first African-American permitted to fight for *the* symbol of white male physical and macho supremacy: the heavyweight boxing championship of the world. White control of this title was yet another example of the racism which was promoted to keep blacks in their place, at the bottom of American life economically, socially, and politically.

The importance to all Americans of Johnson's capture of the title is evidenced by his first major defense of his title, in 1910, from former undefeated heavyweight champion Jim Jeffries, who came out of retirement to reclaim this symbol of white supremacy from a black man. The significance of the battle with Johnson was not lost on Jeffries. Before the fight, on July 4, 1910, in Reno, Nevada, Jeffries said: "I fully realize what depends upon me and won't disappoint the public. That portion of the white race which is looking to me to defend its athletic supremacy may feel assured that I am fit to do my very best. I'll win as quickly as I can."

Jack Johnson meets Tommy Burns in Sydney, Australia, in 1908.
(Date in photo is incorrect)

Johnson knocked Jeffries out in the fifteenth round. Many whites, upset with this outcome, started a series of race riots throughout the United States, resulting in the deaths of both blacks and whites. Many blacks, affected by racist attitudes about Jack Johnson's "white womanizing" and his other profligate habits and styles, thought the loss of black lives and the violence directed at black America after Johnson's victory over Jeffries were too severe a price to pay for a black champion. Author and educator William Pickens thought the contrary: "It was a good deal better for Johnson to win than for Johnson to have lost and all Negroes to have been killed in spirit by the preachments of inferiority from the combined white press."

Johnson's ranking acknowledges his impact on the psyche and spirit of black America at a time when the race problem was becoming nationalized by black migration from the South, and at a time when white America was becoming increasingly brutal and violent to keep blacks in a position, where, according to WALTER F. WHITE [32], they were "economically exploitable."

Like the listing and ranking of CRISPUS ATTUCKS [17], Johnson's ranking here owes more to his symbolic significance in the black struggle to throw off racist attitudes and images of black inferiority. This perspective on Johnson as heavyweight boxing champion of the world in a color-conscious and racist society should disavow the notion that he was merely a boxer. Surely, the same perspective on the black athlete as a symbol of the struggle for freedom and equality applies to JACKIE ROBINSON [42], JESSE OWENS [56], MUHAMMAD ALI [54], JOE LOUIS [71], ARTHUR ASHE [98], and HANK AARON [87].

In fact, Johnson was in many ways the precursor of outspoken athletes like Muhammad Ali and Jackie Robinson. He was unashamedly prosperous, famous, and flashy. He showed millions of black Americans that a black man not only could beat a white man in a boxing match but also could insist on living life as he saw fit in a society that claimed to be free and open. In this way, Johnson was a marvel of psychological as well as physical strength.

John Arthur Johnson was born in Galveston, Texas, in 1878, nearly a year after Rutherford B. Hayes compromised with Dixiecrats on the withdrawal of federal troops from the South so that he could become president of the United States. His father was a school janitor. Johnson left school after the fifth grade and, after leaving home at an early age, worked at a number of odd jobs, such as stableboy and dockworker. By the time he was seventeen, Johnson had built a reputation as a pugilist and started barnstorming his way through the United States. In 1897, he became a professional fighter, and during the following year he married Mary Austin, a childhood sweetheart.

In 1906, Johnson knocked out former heavyweight champion Bob Fitzsimmons and sought a championship fight with then-champion James Jeffries, who refused to fight him because he was black. Jeffries retired undefeated in 1905 and was succeeded by Tommy Burns. When Johnson defeated Burns on December 26, 1908, in Australia, he became the first black heavyweight boxing champion of the world.

Johnson lost his title to "White Hope" Jess Willard on April 15, 1915, in Havana, Cuba, by a controversial knockout in the twenty-sixth round. This loss occurred within months of the founding of the Universal Negro Improvement Association (UNIA) by MARCUS GARVEY [21].

Johnson died from injuries sustained while participating in one of his hobbies, car racing, on June 10, 1946, in a hospital in Raleigh, North Carolina.

64

Gwendolyn Brooks

1917–

At the nexus of Brooks's art lies a fundamental commitment to
both the modernist aesthetics of art and the common ideal of
social justice.

MARIA K. MOOTRY

Maria Mootry is correct in saying that the nexus of Gwendolyn
Brooks's art represents "a commitment to social justice" but less precise
in saying that it is "a commitment to modernist aesthetics." A commitment to modernist aesthetics would link Brooks's poetry to the likes of
Ezra Pound, T. S. Eliot, Wallace Stevens, E. E. Cummings, and others.

Because her art is linked to "the ideal of social justice" for African-Americans, Brooks is in the tradition of black artists like PAUL ROBESON [24], JAMES WELDON JOHNSON [26], LANGSTON HUGHES [34], ALAIN LOCKE [36], ZORA NEALE HURSTON [52], and others who have used black aesthetics or black culture to aid in the liberation of black people.

Brooks's influence as a black aesthetician has been cogently stated by Norris B. Clark: "Regardless of how one chooses to classify Brooks's poetry, if one must, her corpus remains as an undeniable statement about the condition humane. More precisely, it is a statement about the myriad black American experiences as it communicates the feeling of brotherhood and love. In each phase, arbitrarily defined or not, Brooks has clearly been committed to, as black aesthetic advocates desire, black people."

Brooks has often been quoted as saying that her poetry and style are intended to "appeal to black people in taverns, black people in gutters, schools, offices, factories, prisons, the consulate; I wish to reach black people in pulpits, black people in mines, on farms, on thrones." The extent to which Brooks has communicated to this black diversity is subject to debate and analysis beyond the scope of this book. One can conclude that Brooks's poetry has evolved over nearly five decades into one "committed to black people" and to their liberation.

Evidence of Brooks's use of black aesthetics over time to aid in the struggle for social justice has been summarized by Norris B. Clark:

> Critics suggest that Brooks's poetry, whether an extension of herself as an artist or as a black artist, can be divided into three groups: (1) *A Street in Bronzeville* [1945] and *Annie Allen* [1949], primarily devoted to craft and exhibit an "objective and exquisite detachment" from the lives or emotions of individuals; (2) *The Bean Eaters* [1960], *Selected Poems* [1963], and *In the Mecca* [1968], also devoted to craft but exhibit a strong awareness of black social concerns; and (3) *Riot* [1969], *Family Pictures* [1970], *Aloneness* [1971], and *Beckonings* [1975], less devoted to craft and more concerned about pronounced statements on a black mystique, the necessity of riot (violence), and black unity. Those categories can also be characterized in political language as traditional, pre-revolutionary and revolutionary; or in the language of sociologists as accommodationists, integrationist, and black nationalists; or in racial language as white, colored, and black....

Gwendolyn Brooks was born on June 7, 1917, in Topeka, Kansas, to David and Keziah Brooks—within one month of race riots in East St. Louis, Illinois, that resulted in the killings of both blacks and whites., Her paternal grandparents were slaves.

One month after her birth, the family moved to the South Side of Chicago, where Brooks attended Forestville Elementary School. After graduation in 1931, she attended Hyde Park High School briefly, transferring to Wendell Phillips High School for a short time, and finally transferring during the same school year of 1932 to Englewood High School, from which she graduated in 1934. In 1936, she graduated from Wilson Junior College in Chicago.

Brooks first exhibited her poetic talents at the age of seven, when she wrote a page filled with two-line verses. When she was thirteen, her poem "Eventide" was published in *American Childhood* magazine. She was encouraged to develop her talents in high school by JAMES WELDON JOHNSON [26] and LANGSTON HUGHES [34]. In 1934, she began making weekly contributions of her poetry to the *Chicago Defender*, the black newspaper published by ROBERT ABBOTT [41].

With the publication of her second volume of poetry, *Annie Allen*, in 1949, Brooks received the Pulitzer Prize for poetry, thus achieving recognition unique to a poet of African ancestry. Brooks demonstrated her commitment to the advocacy of social justice for those of African descent in America and throughout the world in additional volumes: *Primer for Blacks* (1980), *Mayor Harold Washington and Chicago, The I Will City* (1983), *The Near-Johannesburg Boys and Other Poems* (1986), *Blacks* (1987), and *Winnie* (1988).

One of Brooks's creative associates, Haki Madhubuti, has summed up Brooks's impact, through her art, on the ongoing black struggle:

> It is her vision—her ability to see truths rather than trends, to seek meaning and not fads, to question ideas rather than gossip—that endears her to us. Her uniqueness with language is common knowledge and few would argue with the fact that she has helped to set new standards for poetry in the twentieth century.... She has the stature of a Queen Mother, but is always accessible and giving. Ms. Brooks is a woman who cannot live without her art, but who has never put her art above or before the people she writes about.

65

Andrew Young

1932 –

The system that we enjoy in the United States is a system born
of struggle. Yes, it's also a system which was built on the
inhumanity of human slavery. But somehow those very slaves
who at one point in our history created the cheap labor force
which enabled that system to take off and thereby made
industrialization possible—those same slaves and their children's
children came back again in the fifties and sixties and
humanized that system.

ANDREW YOUNG

Andrew Jackson Young, Jr., is ranked here in recognition of his influential role as a civil-rights activist during the 1950s and 1960s in helping to humanize the American system or way of life. Young is also recognized for his impact as a politician in the 1970s and 1980s, for using the American political system—"a system born in struggle" because of its denial of basic rights and freedoms to blacks and the poor—to advocate the rights of blacks and whites in America and, also, to aid in the struggle for human rights throughout the world.

In the 1950s and 1960s, as a chief associate of DR. MARTIN LUTHER KING, JR. [1], Young through the Southern Christian Leadership Conference (SCLC, founded in 1957) played an important role in the boycotts, sit-ins, and marches throughout the North and South. He was also one of the key drafters of the 1964 Civil Rights Act, which acknowledged black rights in public accommodations and fair employment conditions, and the 1965 Voting Rights Bill, which did away with literacy tests and other capricious barriers to black voting. These legislative acts were the first fruits of the harvest of the 1950s and 1960s in the ongoing black struggle for full and fair participation in all aspects of American life.

Like Dr. King, Young believed in the philosophy and tactics of nonviolence. On this point of agreement with Dr. King, and King's influence on him and others, Young has said, "He was leery to condemn defensive violence in defense of the home. He never advocated violence. [He said] violence wouldn't solve our [collective] problems.... He thought of nonviolence as kind of a special calling, a method. He said we will either be nonviolent or—we'll be nonexistent."

Young's influence as a nonviolent tactician and strategist for Dr. King and other associates in the SCLC was evidenced in his directorship of the nonviolent demonstrations during the Birmingham Campaign. This campaign catapulted the civil rights movement into the minds of America and the world by exposing, through the media, the attacks of "Bull" Connor's policemen with man-eating dogs, and firemen with power hoses aimed at innocent school children and youth protesting racism and discrimination.

After Dr. King's assassination in April 1968, Young said, "There just comes a time when *any* social movement has to come off the street and enter politics." In 1970, he resigned from the SCLC as its executive vice president and ran for Congress in the Fifth Congressional District of Georgia and lost. In 1972, with a coalition of blacks and whites, he won a seat in the Fifth District, becoming the first black congressman from Georgia since Reconstruction. (Barbara Jordan was elected to Congress from Texas at the same time, becoming the first black elected from Texas since Reconstruction.)

Like HENRY M. TURNER [39] before him and BILL GRAY [83], his contemporary, Young as a minister and political activist used his public office to advance the rights of blacks and all Americans. While a congressman, Young supported major legislation to increase the minimum wage and benefits for the Medicaid and food stamp programs for the poor.

Yet Young's most significant impact on the struggle for human rights in America and throughout the world was demonstrated in his role as ambassador to the United Nations during the Carter administration from 1977 to 1979. With cabinet-level status, Young became the most influential African-American in Carter's cabinet. His often controversial views on racism did not prevent his bringing about better relations between the United States and African and Caribbean nations on human rights and economic development issues.

Andrew Jackson Young, Jr., was born in New Orleans on March 3, 1932, to Andrew Young, Sr., a dentist, and Daisy Fuller Young, a teacher. He grew up in a predominantly white neighborhood and due to the "separate but equal" practices of Louisiana attended a segregated elementary school. He attended Gilbert Academy, a private high school, graduating in 1947 at the age of fifteen. Because of his age, his parents felt it best that he attend a college close to home. For a year, he attended Dillard University in New Orleans. After leaving Dillard, he enrolled in Howard University as a premed student, graduating with a bachelor's degree in 1951.

After leaving Howard, he decided to go into the ministry instead of dentistry. He entered the Hartford Theological Seminary in Connecticut and graduated in 1955 with a bachelor of divinity degree. While at Hartford he embraced the philosophy and nonviolent tactics of Mohandas Gandhi. From 1955–1957 he pastored churches in Marion, Alabama, and Thomasville and Beachton, Georgia, emphasizing the role of the church in society by organizing voter registration programs.

In 1957, he moved to New York City to head a youth work program under the aegis of the National Council of Churches. In 1961, he moved to Atlanta, Georgia, to become director of a voter registration project for the United Churches of Christ, funded by the Field Foundation. Later that year he joined the SCLC and became one of its most prominent strategists and tacticians.

After the death of Dr. Martin Luther King, Jr., in April 1968, Young remained with SCLC. He resigned in early 1970 in order to run for Congress. After losing the first race, he was elected three times from the Fifth District, in 1972, 1974, and 1976. In 1976 he left Congress to become ambassador to the United Nations; he left the United Nations in 1979, after it was disclosed that he had had "unauthorized" meetings with members of the Palestine Liberation Organization.

In 1981, Young was elected mayor of Atlanta, and was reelected in 1985. He ran for governor of Georgia in 1990 and was defeated in the Democratic primary.

66

Ralph Abernathy

1926–1991

> If my life has any special meaning, it is because I was both a typical black growing up in the segregated South and because, unlike other typical blacks, I was privileged to be in "command headquarters"—in the earlier years as Martin Luther King's closest friend and "pastor" of the movement, and in later years as its leader.
>
> RALPH D. ABERNATHY

Indisputably, Ralph Abernathy, as the chief deputy to DR. MARTIN LUTHER KING, JR. [1], greatly influenced the modern civil rights movement. Abernathy's roles as strategist and as pastor in the "command headquarters" of the civil rights movement of the 1950s and 1960s justify his ranking here.

As Dr. King's closest friend and adviser, Abernathy is inextricably tied to the civil rights movement's successes and achievements such as the Twenty-fourth Amendment to the Constitution, which removed poll tax requirements for voting in federal elections; the 1964 Civil Rights Act, which acknowledged black rights to public accommodations and fair employment conditions; and the 1965 Voting Rights Act, which did away with literacy tests and other arbitrary barriers to black voting.

Like JESSE JACKSON [47], ANDREW YOUNG [65], ROY WILKINS [33], and A. PHILIP RANDOLPH [31], and tens of thousands of nameless laborers, professionals, and students, Abernathy showed through his contributions to the civil rights struggle that the eradication of institutional racism and prejudice went beyond a single person—Dr. King.

Ralph David Abernathy was born on March 11, 1926, to William and Lovivery Abernathy, farmers in Linden, Marengo County, Alabama. He and his eleven brothers and sisters were the grandchildren of slaves.

Abernathy attended segregated elementary and secondary schools in Linden, graduating from the all-black Linden Academy in 1943. In 1944, three weeks after his eighteenth birthday, he was drafted into the U.S. armed forces to serve in World War II, in a segregated black company. "The army that fought World War II was almost completely segregated," Abernathy said, "so all the enlisted men in my company were black, but our officers were white.... When World War II came along, the army perpetuated this bigotry when it structured the vast civilian army that was required to fight a global war...."

At the age of twenty-two in April of 1948, Abernathy was ordained a Baptist minister at the Hopewell Baptist Church in Linden. In 1950, he graduated from Alabama State College with a B.S. in mathematics. In fall 1950, he entered Atlanta University, from which he graduated in 1951 with an M.A. in sociology. Later that same year, he was appointed pastor of the First Baptist Church in Montgomery, Alabama.

In December 1955, when ROSA PARKS [100] refused to give her seat on a bus to a white man and was arrested, Abernathy helped to organize a citywide boycott of buses by blacks. Later, with Dr. King and others, Abernathy formed the Montgomery Improvement Association to guide the boycott, with Dr. King as president. The protests of the association led to the abolition of segregated busing and other segregated public facilities in December 1956.

In January 1957, Abernathy, King, Rev. Fred Shuttlesworth of Birmingham, Rev. Hosea Williams of Atlanta, and others founded the

Southern Christian Leadership Conference (SCLC) to combat racism and segregation in the South. Abernathy was in the "command headquarters" of the SCLC during all of its campaigns in the 1950s and 1960s. He was one of the key strategists for the March on Washington, a decisive moment in the African-American quest for equality in America.

After Dr. King's assassination in April 1968, Abernathy took over the leadership of the SCLC. What became apparent almost immediately during Abernathy's tenure as president was his inability to inspire and lead the organization that King had so successfully used to become the most renowned American civil rights leader of the twentieth century. In his autobiography, *And the Walls Came Tumbling Down* (1989), Abernathy acknowledged his leadership failings in the SCLC:

> What hurt was my growing awareness that I had failed the SCLC, an organization that I helped to found, that I had nurtured over the years, that had been left in my keeping by my dear friend, who had somehow known he would soon be dead. I have loved the organization from the very beginning, before it had even come into being, when its only existence was in my mind and Martin's, a shared dream waiting to be fully conceptualized.

Abernathy resigned as president of the SCLC in 1976, announcing his candidacy to fill the vacancy in the Fifth Congressional District of Georgia due to Andrew Young's resignation to become ambassador to the United Nations. Abernathy lost his bid for Congress.

In *And the Walls Came Tumbling Down*, Abernathy alleges that the evening before the assassination in Memphis on April 8, 1968, Dr. King spent time separately with two women and that he had a shoving match with a third woman who was angered that he had not spent time with her.

Many believed that these revelations were motivated by the hurt and resentment Abernathy felt due to his loss in the race for Congress, his failure to lead the SCLC after King's assassination, and the general lack of public awareness and appreciation for Abernathy's important role in the modern civil rights movement.

Abernathy died on April 17, 1990, in Atlanta.

67

Duke Ellington

1899–1974

But the strangest lack is that with all the great native musical endowment he is conceded to possess, the Negro has not in this most propitious time produced a single outstanding composer. ...It is a curious fact that the American Negro through his whole history has done more highly sustained and more fully recognized work in the composition of letters than in the composition of music. It is the most curious when we consider that music is so innately a characteristic method of expression for the Negro.

JAMES WELDON JOHNSON

The "most propitious time"—alluded to by JAMES WELDON JOHNSON [26]—was the Negro Renaissance of the twenties and thirties, when Johnson himself played a prominent role as a catalytic black culturalist. Johnson's observations, in a landmark essay in *Harper's Magazine* in 1925, about the "strangest lack" of a "single outstanding [black] composer" help provide the context for appreciating the rise of Duke Ellington as one of the most influential African-American composers of the twentieth century.

Ellington's ranking here is not intended to disparage the influence of older black composers and musicians, like Will Marion Cook, Will Vodery, W. C. Handy, James Reese Europe, Scott Joplin, and Eubie Blake, or his contemporaries like Daniel Louis "Satchmo" Armstrong

Duke Ellington plays at a recording session.

and William "Count" Basie, or younger musicians like Charlie Parker, Dizzy Gillespie, Quincy Jones, and Miles Davis, who used black aesthetics as tools in the struggle for a more egalitarian society. Ellington's ranking rests on the author's own criteria for influence on the black struggle.

Ellington recognized that the uniqueness of the American musical forms like jazz, blues, ragtime, swing, bop, originated in the creative soul of African-Americans, who never lost their cultural links to Africa (see JOHNSON [26] on this point). On the only original musical expressions from America, Ellington observed, "The common root, of course, comes out of Africa. That's the pulse. The African pulse. It's all the way back from what they first recognized as the old slave chants and up through the blues, the jazz, and up through the rock. And the avant-garde. And it's all got the African pulse."

Evidence of Ellington's use of the African pulse to influence and convey black meanings and values is seen in representative pieces like *Jump for Joy* (1941), *Black, Brown, and Beige Suite* (1943), *Liberian Suite* (1947), *The Tattooed Bride* (1948), *Manhattan Murals* (1948), *Harlem* (1950), and *New World a' Comin'* (1955). Ellington and his band performed in black-oriented movies such as *Black and Tan* (1927), *Check and Double Check* (1930), and *Cabin in the Sky* (1943). In the thirties he also produced records such as *Harlem Air Shaft*, *Portrait of Bert Williams*, and *Bojangles*.

Edward Kennedy Ellington was born in Washington, D.C., on April 20, 1899, to James Edward and Daisy Kennedy Ellington. He attended segregated elementary and secondary schools, dropping out of Armstrong High School in his senior year. As a young man, his friends started calling him Duke because of his impeccable style and manners.

After displaying musical and painting talent in high school, he formed his own band in 1918, the Washingtonians, which performed in local D.C. clubs. In 1923, his band moved to New York City to perform at the Barron's Club in Harlem and at the Kentucky Club in midtown Manhattan. That same year he wrote his first musical score, *Chocolate Kiddies*, which was performed in Europe.

Ellington gained his national reputation as a composer and big-band leader during a five-year stint, from 1927 to 1932, at Harlem's Cotton Club. These performances were often carried nationwide over CBS radio stations. During the sixties and seventies Ellington toured the Middle and Far East as musical ambassador for the U.S. State Department. He conducted his *Golden Broom and the Golden Apple* at

Lincoln Center (1965), conducted his inaugural religious concert at Grace Episcopal Cathedral in San Francisco (1965), and was elected to the National Institute of Arts and Letters (1970).

By his death, on May 24, 1974, in New York City, Ellington—nearly fifty years after Johnson's lament that not a "single outstanding [black] composer" existed among African-Americans—had been acknowledged to be one of the most influential African-American composers of the twentieth century and one of the most prolific American composers of all time, with vintage tunes like "Mood Indigo," "Satin Doll," "Sophisticated Lady," and nearly nine hundred other musical compositions.

68

Louis Armstrong

1900–1971

You see we colored people have our own music that is part of
us. It's a product of our souls. It's been created by the suffering
and miseries of our race. Some of the melodies made up by
slaves of the old days and others were handed down from the
days before we left Africa.

JAMES REESE EUROPE

The music that is a "product of our souls...created by the sufferings and miseries of our race" is jazz: the original musical form of America. Jazz pioneer James Europe—called the "King of Jazz" by renowned musician and composer Eubie Blake—got it right: jazz is rooted in the struggle of Americans of African descent for full equality.

Louis Armstrong's ranking here is justified by his vast success in making jazz integral to American culture and global culture during the twentieth century. Armstrong's efforts to help gain recognition for jazz throughout the world has resulted in cultural acceptance for blacks. This recognition is consistent with ALAIN LOCKE's [36] quest to destroy the notion of blacks as an anomaly in American life. In Locke's words such acceptance entails the "removal of wholesale social proscriptions and, therefore, the conscious scrapping of the mood and creed of 'white supremacy.'"

Much as PAUL ROBESON [24] used spirituals during the thirties through the fifties to enlighten and sensitize blacks and whites in America and throughout the world to the African-American struggle, so Armstrong, as the "Ambassador of Jazz" during the thirties through the seventies, reached more people with jazz as an expression of the black experience and "soul" than anyone except, perhaps, Duke Ellington. (The reader should note that Ellington didn't accept the label jazz musician. He once said, "I write Negro music. I don't write jazz." Further, it should be understood that Armstrong's ranking here, behind Ellington, is not an assessment of who was the *better* musician or artist. Ellington's higher ranking is based on the author's view that his role as the preeminent composer of "Negro music" had a relatively greater impact on blacks and nonblacks than did the life work of Louis Armstrong.)

Daniel Louis Armstrong was born on July 4, 1900, in a black ghetto in New Orleans, to Willie and Mary Ann Armstrong. His maternal grandparents were slaves. His father was a turpentine worker and his mother was a domestic worker.

Armstrong's parents separated when he was five. At the age of twelve, he was arrested for illegally firing a .38 pistol on New Year's Eve while celebrating with some boyhood friends. He was sent to the Waif's Home for Boys, where he stayed for over a year. It was there that he learned how to play the cornet—smaller in size and tone than a trumpet—and to read music under the tutelage of Peter Davis, the home's drill instructor and bandmaster.

After his release from the Waif's Home in 1915, Armstrong took cornet lessons from a popular local Dixieland jazz cornetist, Joe "King" Oliver. Oliver also taught him how to play the trumpet, and from 1915 to 1917 Armstrong played occasionally in Kid Ory's Band, which featured Oliver on cornet. In 1917, Oliver took a gig in Chicago, allowing Armstrong to replace him in Ory's Band. In 1919, he started playing on a Mississippi riverboat, *Dixie Belle*, with Fate Marable's Orchestra, further developing his talents as a cornetist.

In 1922, "King" Oliver asked Armstrong to join his Creole Jazz Band in Chicago. Armstrong agreed, and soon he and the "King" performed cornet duets that became the talk of the music world. In 1924, he joined Fletcher Henderson's Band in New York City, performing at the Roseland Ballroom. The next year he returned to Chicago to play trumpet with Erskine Tate's Orchestra. The trumpet became the instrument he would use, through his improvisational artistry, to revolutionize Dixieland jazz; from the collective ensemble the focus would turn to the virtuosity of the soloist.

Jazz expert Hugues Panassié said about Armstrong's role in revolutionizing jazz, "For invention, Louis is incomparable. In all his solos of all periods he constantly creates, and his inventiveness is so genuine that Louis seems the very incarnation of jazz music.... The whole of jazz music was transformed by Louis, overthrown by his genius. In Louis Armstrong's music is the New Orleans style at its peak, and also the basis of almost all styles that were derived from it, directly or indirectly...."

In the 1930s, Armstrong with his bands and ensembles toured such countries as Norway, Sweden, Holland, France, Belgium, Italy, Scotland, and England. It was while performing in England in 1932 at the London Palladium that he acquired the nickname "Satchelmouth," later abridged to "Satchmo." It was also during this time that Armstrong gained international acclaim as a jazz vocalist, using improvisational techniques and inventive lyrics to enhance his distinct, small scratchy voice.

Panassié further summarized Armstrong's identification with the black experience and his influence on jazz and jazz trumpeters in particular:

> His music identifies with the soul of the black. No wonder, therefore, that all blacks and so many whites opened their hearts to all that Louis Armstrong had to say.

Jazz musicians are unanimous in recognizing Louis' genius and influence. To quote but one, Roy Eldridge once declared that nobody will exercise the influence Louis Armstrong had on trumpet style; that his tone, his phrasing, and his power had never been equalled, and that Louis was the first modern jazzman. Coming from the musician who had the biggest subsequent influence on trumpet players after Louis himself, such a statement means a lot.

Daniel Louis "Satchmo" Armstrong died on July 6, 1971, in New York City of kidney failure—eight days after the U.S. Supreme Court overturned the draft-evasion conviction of MUHAMMAD ALI [54].

69

Shirley Chisholm

1924–

When I decided to run for Congress, I knew I would encounter both antiblack and antifeminist sentiments. What surprised me was the much greater virulence of the sex discrimination....I was constantly bombarded by both men and women exclaiming that I should return to teaching, a woman's vocation, and leave politics to the men.

SHIRLEY CHISHOLM

As a progeny of strong black suffragists like Sojourner Truth [15], Ida B. Wells–Barnett [29], Mary Church Terrell [45], and Mary McLeod Bethune [35], Shirley Chisholm refused to "leave politics to the men." In 1969, she became the first black woman to be elected to Congress. Her election made her a symbol of modern black female resistance to and victory over "antiblack and antifeminist sentiments" in America. She became the latter-day incarnation of her idol, Mary McLeod Bethune, who symbolized the quest of black women for full and equal participation in American society.

Chisholm, as a political activist and feminist, helped to end the practices of a male-dominated, racist, and antifeminist society. As she observed:

> Although women in this country, for the most part, have been the envelope stuffers, have been the ones who have given the card parties to raise the monies in order that the gentlemen can go to different political offices, have gathered the petitions, have been the speechwriters for many of the gentlemen, very few women in this country have actually been the standard-bearers for political parties.

Chisholm was the precursor in Congress of a cadre of black women who were elected in 1972, like Yvonne Braithwaite Burke of California, Barbara Jordan of Texas, and Cardiss Collins of Illinois. In 1972, raising the ceiling on the expectation of women as the "standard-bearers for political parties," Chisholm sought to become the first African-American woman nominee for president of the United States from the Democratic party. Although she lost the nomination to Senator George S. McGovern, her quest for the presidency would later influence expectations and views of black and white voters during Jesse Jackson's campaigns for the same nomination backed by his Rainbow Coalition in 1984 and 1988 (see [47]).

Chisholm was born on November 30, 1924, in Brooklyn, New York, to Charles and Ruby Seale St. Hill. Her father was born in Guyana and her mother was born in Barbados. For economic reasons, she was sent at the age of three to live in Barbados with her maternal grandmother, Emmeline Seale. Her father was a laborer in a burlap bag factory and her mother was a domestic worker and a seamstress.

After returning to New York City from Barbados in 1934, Chisholm attended integrated elementary schools. She graduated from Junior High School 78 in June 1939, and entered Girls High School in Brooklyn that fall. In 1942, she enrolled in Brooklyn College, graduating with a B.A. cum laude, in 1946. She completed graduate work in elementary education at Columbia University in 1949 and later that year, she married Conrad Chisholm, a detective for a private security firm in New York City.

Chisholm's elective political career began in 1964 when she became the first black woman assembly member from Brooklyn. She was reelected to the assembly in 1965 and 1966. In 1968, after winning the Democratic primary for the newly created Twelfth Congressional District of New York (consisting of 70 percent blacks and Puerto Ricans), Chisholm faced black civil-rights activist James Farmer, a founder of the Congress of Racial Equality (CORE).

Ironically, it was Farmer who injected antifeminist sentiments into the general campaign by calling for his election as a "strong male image" over that of Chisholm's as a "mere" black woman who had been a schoolteacher and an assembly member. By organizing and convincing her black and Puerto Rican constituents, consisting of a hard core of at least ten thousand women, Chisholm beat Farmer 34,885 votes to 13,777, a two-and-a-half-to-one margin.

In 1972, she lost the Democratic nomination for president to George McGovern but retained her congressional seat. Chisholm continued to advocate the causes of blacks and feminists. She supported the Office of Economic Opportunity (OEO), which served to distribute federal funds for self-help, food, and antipoverty programs in large urban centers; supported increased funding for the Minimum Wage Bill, designed to provide decent wages for poor blacks and whites, especially domestic workers who were disproportionately female; supported increased funding for Medicare and Medicaid, designed to provide basic medical care and services to the poor and needy; and supported, as honorary president, the controversial National Association for the Repeal of Abortion Laws (NARAL), which placed her at the vortex of the feminist movement. Chisholm also cosponsored Public Law 91–277, which authorized the erection of a memorial to MARY MCLEOD BETHUNE [35] in the District of Columbia—the first time federal dollars had gone to a memorial honoring a black.

Shirley Chisholm resigned her seat from the Twelfth Congressional District of New York in 1982.

70

Ralph Bunche

1904–1971

Among the many defects which have been pointed out in the federal constitution, it is much to be lamented that no person has taken notice of its total silence upon the subject of an office of the utmost importance to the welfare of the United States, that is, an office for promoting and preserving perpetual peace in our country.

Let a Secretary of Peace be appointed to preside in this office....

Let a large room, adjoining the Federal Hall, be appointed for transacting the business and preserving all the records of this office. Over the door of this room, let there be a sign, on which the figures of a Lamb, a Dove, and an Olive Branch should be painted, together with the following inscription in letters of gold: PEACE ON EARTH—GOOD WILL TO MAN. AH! WHY WILL MEN FORGET THAT THEY ARE BRETHREN?

BENJAMIN BANNEKER

The remarkable words of a visionary, BENJAMIN BANNEKER [16], calling for a permanent Department of Peace, headed by a secretary of peace, were proffered nearly 150 years before the founding of the United Nations. Among the influential blacks in attendance at the founding of the United Nations were: MARY MCLEOD BETHUNE [35], W. E. B. DU BOIS [4], WALTER F. WHITE [32] and Ralph Bunche, all latter-day African-American visionaries for peace among blacks and nonblacks in America and throughout the world.

To be sure, the African-American peacemakers who were present have been in large measure included in this book because of their significant contributions to the black struggle for equality and peace. Bunche's ranking here is in recognition of his continuing this legacy as a preeminent peacemaker at the United Nations during the first twenty-five years of the organization's existence. Although Banneker's proposals for peace were not acted on by the United States government, Bunche became the symbol of Banneker's vision of a "Secretary of Peace" in ameliorating racial conflicts throughout the world.

Bunche saw his peace role and that of the United Nations as being inseparably tied to the welfare of blacks and humankind:

[The UN's role] is very important, highly significant, and very vital to all of us of whatever race, creed, or color because this concerns the future of mankind... the question of whether or not there is to be peace or nuclear war or survival on this planet. That is why I say it is of a deep concern to every individual of whatever race in Mississippi as in the rest of the world. Nuclear weapons, the death and destruction of war, are color-blind, and in that context, there is complete equality among the races. The entire world will be living on borrowed time until peace is finally made secure, and if that is to be accomplished, it will be only the UN that can do it.

Ralph Johnson Bunche was born in Detroit on August 7, 1904, nearly two months before Mary McLeod Bethune founded the Daytona Normal and Industrial School for Negro Girls. His father, Fred, was a barber, and his mother, Olive, was a musician. Both of Bunche's parents died when he was twelve, leaving him to be reared by his maternal grandmother, Lucy Johnson, in Los Angeles, California.

Bunche attended elementary and secondary schools in Los Angeles, graduating from Jefferson High School in 1922. He attended the University of California, graduating summa cum laude and Phi Beta Kappa in 1927, with a B.A. in international relations. He received an M.A. in government from Harvard University in 1928.

That same year, he joined the faculty of the political science department of Howard University, during the presidency of MORDECAI W. JOHNSON [40]. Bunche was Johnson's assistant from 1931 to 1932. After teaching at Howard he started doctoral work at Harvard. He received a Ph.D. in 1934, winning the Toppan Prize for the outstanding dissertation in the social sciences. He did postdoctoral work with the Social Science Research Council (1934–1936), at Northwestern University (1936), and at the London School of Economics (1937).

During World War II, Bunche worked as a senior social science analyst for the Office of Strategic Services (OSS), serving the Joint Chiefs of Staff on matters relating to colonial peoples. After a series of other positions with the OSS, in 1944 he was appointed the assistant divisional head for colonial problems in the State Department, where he participated in the planning conferences that lead to the formation of the United Nations in 1945.

In 1946, Bunche began his permanent relationship with the United Nations by becoming director of the Trusteeship Division. In this position, he served on the UN Special Committee on Palestine, and dealt with the Arab-Jewish conflicts in partitioning this area. In 1948, he became UN mediator in Palestine and shepherded the plan to partition Palestine into Galilee as a Jewish state, the Negev desert into an Arab area, and Jerusalem into a city under the supervision of the United Nations.

Bunche acted as mediator during the ensuing Arab-Israeli conflicts and successfully brought about a truce in October of 1949. In recognition of his accomplishments as a peacemaker and skilled mediator he was awarded the Noble Peace Prize in 1950, the first African-American ever to receive it.

In 1955, Bunche was appointed UN Undersecretary for Special Political Affairs; he used this position not only to help keep peace in the world, but to assist people of African descent in countries like the Congo (Zaire) and South Africa in attaining full rights and freedoms. In 1963 Bunche played an important role in persuading the General Assembly—it had 111 members at the time—to overwhelmingly (106 votes) denounce apartheid in South Africa and to call for the release of all its political prisoners.

Until his resignation from the United Nations in October 1971, Bunche utilized the auspices of the UN to bring moral persuasion on the United States to live up to its promises of full rights and freedoms for all Americans, irrespective of color:

> There is no doubt that overwhelmingly the sympathy of the members of the UN, from all sections of the world and people of all colors, is for the American Negro in his heroic struggle for justice. The eyes of the world are focused on this problem, on what happens in the United States. This has a tremendous effect on the United States' image abroad. I have always been confident that the Negro will win this struggle, but it is not the Negro, really, but the nation that must win it. There are still many obstacles and much trouble ahead which will require ever greater effort, persistence, courage, and sacrifice. . . .
>
> The impatience of the Negro about the lack of *decisive* and *immediate* progress—and that is the *only* kind of progress that can now have meaning in the removal of racial shackles— is increasing and will continue to increase until all of the racial shackles are removed. . .

Bunche died on December 9, 1971, in New York City, within a week of the founding, by JESSE JACKSON [47], of the People United to Save Humanity (PUSH).

71

Joe Louis

1914–1981

Unconsciously they had imputed to the brawny image of Joe
Louis all the balked dreams of revenge, all the secretly
visualized moments of retaliation, *and he had won!* Good Gawd
Almighty! Yes, by Jesus, it could be done! Didn't Joe do it? You
see, Joe was the consciously-felt symbol. Joe was the
concentrated essence of black triumph over white.

RICHARD WRIGHT

In describing the reactions of thousands of black Chicagoans to Joe
Louis's defeat of former heavyweight champion Max Baer in September
1935, RICHARD WRIGHT [50] insightfully described Louis as "the

consciously felt symbol...of black triumph over white." Like JACKIE ROBINSON [42], JACK JOHNSON [63], JESSE OWENS [56], HANK AARON [87], ARTHUR ASHE [98], and other black athletic achievers, Louis became a potent symbol to the masses of African-Americans from the thirties through the fifties of the determination, ability, and resolve of blacks to overcome racist attitudes and practices that were designed to relegate them to inferior status in America.

Millions of blacks would have an even greater vicarious victory over a symbol of white domination and supremacy, the heavyweight boxing title, when Louis, on June 22, 1937, defeated James Braddock to become heavyweight champion of the world.

Louis's ranking here is more an acknowledgment of his extraordinary psychological and cultural significance than his political significance to the black struggle for equality. More specifically, for nearly twelve years after winning the heavyweight title, Louis made a conscious political decision not to use his title directly to further the civil rights cause of blacks, unlike MUHAMMAD ALI [54] some twenty-seven years later. Louis saw himself more as the champion of all Americans and not simply the champion of blacks. However, his views did not significantly prevent blacks who were living in a color-conscious, racist society from projecting through him their pent-up frustrations and rage at whites who would deny them their rights and freedom.

Athlete and activist Arthur Ashe has astutely summarized the impact of Joe Louis on blacks and nonblacks during the period before the emergence of the modern civil rights era, especially as he became a symbol in contrast to that of Jack Johnson as persona non grata:

> Joe was the first black American of any discipline or endeavor to enjoy the overwhelming good feeling, sometimes bordering on idolatry, of all Americans regardless of color. And he was schooled for this, particularly as a result of Jack Johnson's legacy. Joe Louis was told in no uncertain terms, "You're not supposed to gloat after your victories. Never take a photograph alone with a white woman." He was taught how to use a knife and fork correctly. He was given elocution and very simple English lessons. He was told to be kind and generous to people.

In conveying these perspectives on the influence of Louis, the author does not take a value position on his decision vis-à-vis the social and political demands of blacks. His ranking here is in recognition of the influence his athletic achievements had beyond boxing on the quest of blacks *to be*, at a time when a racist society was continuing to deny them basic rights and freedoms. (See BOOKER T. WASHINGTON [3], PAUL LAURENCE DUNBAR [18], and PHILLIS WHEATLEY [19] for other examples of blacks who strongly affected white America while at the same time influencing blacks.)

Joe Louis versus Max Schmeling (1938).

Joseph Louis Barrow was born on May 13, 1914, near Lexington, Alabama, to Monroe and Lillie Barrow, sharecroppers. His father died when he was four, and his mother remarried when he was seven to Patrick Brooks. Brooks moved the family to Detroit in the early 1920s, where Louis dropped out of Duffield Grammar School in the seventh grade to help support his family.

At the age of sixteen he started boxing at Brewster's East Side Gymnasium in Detroit. From 1930 to 1934 Louis boxed as an amateur while working full time at Ford Motor Company, eventually winning the National Amateur Athletic Union light-heavyweight title in St. Louis in 1934. In June of that year, he became a professional boxer and changed his name to Joe Louis. After winning his first twenty-three professional fights, he fought and defeated former heavyweight champion Max Baer, in September 1935.

In his twenty-eighth bout, in the summer of 1936, Louis fought and lost to a symbol of Aryan supremacy, Max Schmeling. This was the same summer in which JESSE OWENS [56] would destroy Aryan notions of supremacy by winning four gold medals at the Berlin Olympic Games while Adolf Hitler looked on.

Louis won the heavyweight title from James J. Braddock on June 22, 1937, by a knockout in the eighth round. He held the title for nearly twelve years, and successfully defended his championship twenty-five times before his retirement from boxing in March 1949.

After an unsuccessful return to boxing in 1950 to challenge Ezzard Charles for the world title, Louis finally retired from boxing in 1951, after being knocked out by Rocky Marciano. From his final retirement to his death, he was rendered penniless by unsuccessful business ventures and a series of legal battles with the Internal Revenue Service. At the time of his death, he was employed by Caesar's Palace in Las Vegas as the "host in residence" for boxing.

Louis died on April 12, 1981, in Las Vegas, nearly six months before ANDREW YOUNG [65] was elected mayor of Atlanta.

72

Lerone Bennett, Jr.

1928–

Black history is American history with the accent and emphasis
on the point of view, attitude, and spirit of Afro-Americans, as
well as on the events in which they have been either the actors
or the objects of action. . . .
The central theme of black history is the quest of Afro-
Americans for freedom, equality, and manhood.

EARL G. THORPE

Lerone Bennett's ranking here is in acknowledgment of his influence
in popularizing for both blacks and nonblacks "black history [as]
American history with the accent and emphasis on the point of view,
attitude, and spirit of Afro-Americans."

Although he was not university trained as a historian, like CARTER G. WOODSON [25] or JOHN HOPE FRANKLIN [74], Bennett's scholarship and readable writing style, as in his *Before the Mayflower: A History of the Negro in America* (1962), have made him arguably the best-known and most influential black historian of the last three decades of the twentieth century. (Two other prominent black historians of the twentieth century who were not university trained are J. A. Rogers, 1880–1966, and John Henrik Clarke, b. 1915.)

Buttressing Bennett's influence as a populist historian has been his association with *Ebony* magazine. As senior editor with the largest black-oriented publication—*Ebony* has a circulation of nearly two million—he has been able to reach blacks with timely and readable historic articles and features that illuminate the ongoing "quest of Afro-Americans for freedom, equality, and manhood."

Bennett's unusual ability to communicate the central theme of the black quest to a reader appears in the following excerpt from *Before the Mayflower,* in which he describes with poignancy and lyrical qualities the "attitude and spirit" of African-Americans during the nightmare of the advent of Jim Crow in America—the "separate but equal" era—following Reconstruction (see P. B. S. PINCHBACK [20], for further discussion):

> For the average black, life was a shadowy nightmare of dirt and danger and humiliation. So violent was the assault on his nervous system, so intense and overwhelming was the oppression to which he was subjected, so forsaken by government and man did he feel, and so overwhelmed by the shape and size of the forces that battered him, that he had neither the space nor the time to formulate alternatives. To work from sunup to sundown for a whole year and to end up owing "the man" for the privilege of working; to do this year after year and to sink deeper and deeper into debt; to be chained to the land by violence and bills at the plantation store; to be conditioned by dirt and fear and shame and signs; to become a part of these signs and to feel them in the deepest recess of the spirit; to be powerless and to curse one's self for cowardice; to be knocked down in the streets for failing to call a shiftless hillbilly "mister"; to be a plaything of judges and courts and policemen; to be black in a white fire and to believe finally in one's own unworthiness to be without books

and words and pretty pictures; to be without newspapers and radios; to be without understanding, without the rationalizations of psychology and sociology, without Freud and E. Franklin Frazier and *Jet*; to give in finally; to bow, to scrape, to grin; and to hate one's self for one's servility and weakness and blackness—all this was a Kafkaesque nightmare that continued for days and nights and years.

Bennett was born on October 17, 1928, in Clarksdale, Mississippi, within a month of the election of Oscar DePriest to the United States Congress from Illinois—the first black congressman since Reconstruction. He attended segregated elementary and secondary public schools in Jackson, Mississippi, where he developed his journalistic skills by working on the school paper and later by editing a local black newspaper, the *Mississippi Enterprise*.

Bennett graduated from Morehouse College in 1949 with a bachelor's degree, during the tenure of BENJAMIN E. MAYS [53]. After graduation, he became a reporter for the *Atlanta Daily World* (1949–52) and later city editor for the same (1952–53). In 1953, he joined the Johnson Publishing Company as an associate editor for *Jet* magazine. He became an associate editor in 1954 for the then nine-year-old *Ebony* and a senior editor in 1958. Bennett's highly acclaimed and widely read book, *Before the Mayflower*, was the outgrowth of a series of articles originally published in *Ebony*, the most visible and influential organ of the black community and its values, aspirations, and accomplishments for nearly the last fifty years.

Other important works by Bennett illuminating the black quest for "freedom, equality, and manhood" are *The Negro Mood and Other Essays* (1964), *What Manner of Man* (1964), *Confrontation, Black and White* (1965), *Black Power, U.S.A., The Human Side of Reconstruction 1867–1877* (1967), *Pioneers in Protest* (1968), *The Challenge of Blackness* (1972), *The Shaping of Black America* (1974), and *Wade in the Water: Great Moments in Black History* (1979).

In 1982, Bennett combined salient perspectives and insights of the black experience from many of the above volumes into a revision of *Before the Mayflower*, which has been reprinted many times since.

73

Toni Morrison
1931–

I want to participate in developing a canon of black
work...where black people are talking to black people.
TONI MORRISON

Beginning with *The Bluest Eye* (novel, 1969) and *Sula* (novel, 1973), Toni Morrison has made a singular contribution to an expansive "canon of black work" committed to the liberation of blacks in America and throughout the world. The influence of Morrison as a female black artist in focusing on, in particular, the experiences of African-American women to get "black people...talking to black people" warrants her ranking here. Her works add to the "canon of black work" by black artists like JAMES WELDON JOHNSON [26], LANGSTON HUGHES [34], ALAIN LOCKE [36], ZORA NEALE HURSTON [52], GWENDOLYN BROOKS [64], and others.

Morrison is without peer in her use of African-American women as metaphors, through elaborate symbols, when portraying their rich and diverse personal and communal experiences—from the days of slavery to modern times—in order to illuminate the larger ethos of African-Americans in their struggle against racism and discrimination. As to the why of her focus on black women, Morrison has said, "It was inevitable I would focus on black women, not out of ignorance of any other kind of people, but because they are of compelling interest to me."

Morrison has become a most important literary provocateur in causing black and nonblack Americans to reexamine the effects of racism and other negative factors on the dream of an egalitarian society. "My work requires me," Morrison said, "to think about how free I can be as an African-American woman writer in my genderized, sexualized, wholly racialized world."

In addition to her previously cited works, the nexus of Morrison's perspectives as a black woman writer and her use of the African-American woman's experience to aid in the liberation of blacks and nonblacks are seen in her novels: *Tar Baby* (1981), *Beloved* (1987, for which she won the Pulitzer Prize for Literature), and *Jazz* (1992) and *Song of Solomon* (1977), which both predominate with male metaphors and images in portraying the ongoing black quest *to be.*

The extent of Morrison's influence as an African-American writer in shaping how black and nonblack Americans view themselves in a color-conscious, racist society has been observed by critic and author Wendy Steiner: "Toni Morrison is both a great novelist and the closest thing the country has to a national writer. The fact that she speaks as a woman and a black only enhances her ability to speak as an American, for the path to a common voice nowadays runs through the partisan."

Toni Morrison's "partisan" view of self and the black ethos began at her birth as Chloe Anthony Wofford on February 18, 1931, in Lorain, Ohio, nearly one month before WALTER F. WHITE [32] became secretary of the NAACP. She was the second of four children of George and Ramah Wofford. Like most blacks reared during the Great Depression, she and her family were exposed to conditions of poverty and economic exploitation of blacks, that were intended to crush both psyche and spirit.

Morrison attended integrated elementary and secondary schools in Lorain. After graduating from high school in 1949, she entered Howard University, graduating with a B.A. in 1953. She did graduate work in English at Cornell University, earning an M.A. in 1955. She taught at Texas Southern University (1955–1957) and at Howard University (1957–1964). While at Howard, she started writing short stories and other pieces and took the name by which she is popularly known, Toni Morrison.

In 1964, she became a textbook editor for Random House, eventually becoming a senior editor. While at Random House she wrote her first novel, *The Bluest Eye* (1969), in her spare time, launching her career as a major literary voice in the black struggle for equality.

In *Playing in the Dark: Whiteness and the Literary Imagination* (lectures, 1992), Morrison again signaled her importance as an African-American woman writer, literary provocateur, and "national writer" by calling for a thorough examination of the "impact of notions of racial hierarchy, racial exclusion, and racial vulnerability and availability on nonblacks who held, resisted, explored, or altered those notions. The scholarship that looks into the mind, imagination, and behavior of slaves is valuable. But equally valuable is a serious intellectual effort to see what racial ideology does to the mind, imagination, and behavior of masters. Urgently needed is... attention [to be] paid to the literature of the western country [the United States] that has one of the most resilient Africanist populations in the world—a population that has always had a curiously intimate and unhingingly separate existence within the dominant one...."

74

John Hope Franklin

1915–

History must restore what slavery took away, for it is the social damage of slavery that the present generations must repair and offset....

Certain chapters of American history will have to be reopened. Just as black men were influential factors in the campaign against the slave trade, so they were among the earliest instigators of the abolition movement. Indeed, there was a dangerous calm between the agitation for the suppression of the slave trade and the beginning of the campaign for emancipation. During that interval colored men were very influential in arousing the attention of public men who in turn aroused the conscience of the country.

ARTHUR A. SCHOMBURG

Using many of the scientific methods and procedures pioneered by CARTER G. WOODSON [25], W. E. B. DU BOIS [3] and preeminent Africanist historian William Leo Hansberry, John Hope Franklin has helped, for nearly the last six decades, to "restore what slavery took away" through full and accurate historical views of the role of blacks in the ongoing struggle for full equality.

Franklin's influence in reopening "certain chapters of American history" to reveal these roles justifies his ranking here. Franklin viewed the process of this reopening of American history:

> As much a part of the Negro revolt as the demand for equality in other areas. It is as though Negro Americans were saying that the past injustices done them in recounting the history of the country are part and parcel of injustices they have suffered in other areas. If the house is to be set in order, one cannot begin with the present; he must begin with the past.

Evidence of Franklin's scholarly documentation of blacks as influential factors in American history, from the beginning of slavery to the Emancipation Proclamation, can be seen in his books: *The Free Negro in North Carolina, 1790–1860* (1943), *From Slavery to Freedom: A History of American Negroes* (1947), *The Militant South* (1956), and *The Emancipation Proclamation* (1963). His influence in causing both blacks and whites to reexamine the roles of blacks during Reconstruction is evidenced in *Reconstruction After the Civil War* (1961).

Although many critics have viewed Franklin's writings as formidable undertakings for the average reader, this does not detract from the impact of his works in aiding the black struggle "to repair and offset" the damage of racism and discrimination in America and throughout the world. (A more popular and readable modern black historian is LERONE BENNETT [72].)

Franklin was born on January 2, 1915, in Rentiesville, Oklahoma, to Buck and Mollie Franklin, almost one year before the publication of the *Journal of Negro History*, founded by Carter G. Woodson. His father was an eminent attorney whose office was burned down in the summer of 1921 during the Tulsa race riots, in which twenty-one whites and sixty blacks were killed.

Franklin attended elementary and secondary schools in Tulsa, graduating from Booker T. Washington High School in 1931. He attended Fisk University in Nashville as a history major, graduating Phi Beta Kappa and magna cum laude in 1935. He obtained an M.A. in history from Harvard in 1936. Returning to teach at Fisk from 1937 to 1938, he subsequently decided to return to Harvard to finish his Ph.D. in history, graduating in 1941.

After a series of teaching positions and research projects during the early forties, he became a full professor at Howard University in 1947 during the presidency of MORDECAI W. JOHNSON [40] and the tenure of prominent Africanist and historian William Leo Hansberry of Howard's history department which was then headed by the outstanding historian and scholar, Rayford W. Logan. While at Howard, Franklin made a significant contribution to an accurate historic perspective into the economic and social factors undermining the black experience in America, in the legal brief submitted by the National Association for the Advancement of Colored People in the momentous United States Supreme Court decision of 1954, *Brown* v. *Board of Education*. During this time Franklin also served on the editorial board of the seminal *Journal of Negro History*, established by Carter Woodson in January 1916.

Designated by the National Endowment for the Humanities as Jefferson Lecturer in 1976, Franklin in the last of a trilogy of lectures had this to say about the vitalness of making equality a condition of life for all Americans: "Americans of every race, creed, economic rank, and social position need to recognize that equality is indeed indivisible.... On the basis of our experience we are now faced with the grim choice of declaring that we shall adhere to a position that equality has no place in our society and sink into a state of general degradation characteristic of other decaying societies or concede that equality is a principle so essential to the shaping of our future and the future of any civilized community that we must abandon the futile policy of seeking to divide it and adhere to the principle of sharing it."

75

Fannie Lou Hamer

1917–1977

Women were the spine of our movement. It was women going
door-to-door, speaking with their neighbors, meeting in voter
registration classes together, organizing through their churches,
that gave the vital momentum and energy to the movement.
Mrs. Hamer was special but she was also representative....

ANDREW YOUNG

As a self-described "grass-root" person, Fannie Lou Hamer came to
symbolize the black woman as the venerable "spine" of the ongoing
black struggle for freedom and equality in the 1960s and 1970s. As this

book has already documented, black women, past and present, lettered and unlettered, renowned and nameless, have been integral to the continuum of black resistance to white racism and discrimination. Hamer's listing and ranking here acknowledges that, like her spiritual soul mates HARRIET TUBMAN [12], SOJOURNER TRUTH [15], IDA B. WELLS–BARNETT [29], and countless other black women, she courageously exposed her body and soul to the violence and indignities of being black in a racist society in order to liberate blacks and all people.

Although ANDREW YOUNG, JR. [65] didn't intend to portray black women's involvement and actions as only going "from door-to-door, speaking with their neighbors, meeting in voter registration classes, organizing through their churches" during the most recent civil rights movement, his observations unwittingly feed some popular stereotypes of the roles of black women during this era. These stereotypes included the belief that black women played "safe" and "behind-the-scenes" roles, not life-threatening and endangering ones, even though, ironically, it was ROSA PARKS [100] who "midwifed" the modern civil rights movement by refusing to give her seat on a bus to a white male, for which she was arrested in December 1955 in Montgomery, Alabama, setting in motion the modern struggle.

Hamer came to represent her own words of the role of black women—common and ordinary black women—in the black struggle *to be* in America: "We are here to work side by side with the black man in trying to bring liberation to all people." Proof of how close she and other black women came to this goal and commitment is seen in her plain, yet poignant, words describing how she was beaten under the command of white police officials in 1963, after being arrested and jailed in Greenwood, Mississippi, when she returned from a voter registration drive in the deep South:

> Black people know what white people mean when they say law and order....
>
> And he [police officer] asked me where I was from. And I told him I was from Ruleville. He said, we are going to check that. So they left the room and finally they come back. And he said, you are from Ruleville and he called me an awful name. And he said, get up fatso and we're going to make you wish you was dead. And I was led out of that cell into another cell where they had two black prisoners. The [police officer] gave the first black prisoner a blackjack and it

was loaded with some kind of metal and he ordered me to lay
down on my face.... The prisoner asked him, say do you
want me to beat this woman with this. And he told him, say
you damn right. If you don't beat her, you know what we'll do
for you. So the first prisoner, you know started beatin'. And I
was really beaten because he had to do what they told him to
do because he didn't have anything but the blackjack. But it
was three white men in there with guns. So he didn't have
any other choice. And he beat me until he was exhausted and
I was very tired. My hands at that time had become blue,
very blue. I couldn't bend even the first joints in my fingers.

Hamer goes on to describe how the second black male prisoner
beat her until "I just couldn't believe that I could be beat any more. So I
know what law and order is. I know what law and order is about."

Fannie Lou Hamer was born on October 6, 1917, in Ruleville,
Mississippi, to Jim and Lou Ella Townsend. She was the last of twenty
children. Her parents were sharecroppers, and the children of former
slaves. She dropped out of a segregated elementary school at an early
age and started to work full time to help her family by cutting
cornstalks, though she had been working since the age of six picking
cotton.

In 1944, she married Perry Hamer, a sharecropper, and joined him
and other sharecroppers at work on a former plantation in Ruleville,
where she rose to the position of plantation timekeeper, tracking time of
workers and sharecroppers. In response to voter registration drives of
the Southern Christian Leadership Conference (SCLC) and the Student
Nonviolent Coordinating Committee (SNCC) in the early sixties, she
decided to register to vote and after doing so was fired from her job,
which she described as follows: "I will begin from the first beginning,
August 31, in 1962. I traveled twenty-six miles to the county courthouse
to try to register to become a first-class citizen. I was fired the 31st of
August in 1962 from a plantation where I had worked as a timekeeper
and a sharecropper for eighteen years.... I was fired that day and haven't
had a job since...."

Unemployed, Hamer now began her mission to "work side by side
with the black men in trying to bring liberation to all people." She
organized and led a voter registration drive in Mississippi which evolved
into one of the most successful and influential political organizations
from the deep South during the modern civil rights era, the Mississippi

Freedom Democratic Party (MFDP). Evidence of the impact of the MFDP on the politics of Mississippi and the nation came in 1964, when it unsuccessfully challenged the legitimacy of the all-white Mississippi delegation to the National Democratic Convention in Atlantic City on the grounds that it adhered to rules and practices that deliberately excluded blacks.

The significance of Hamer's challenge to party politics and the body politic of America has been summarized by author and activist Anna Hedgeman: "[MFDP] challenged the national committee to know that they had to begin to look much more realistically at the delegations which came in to be sure they represented the whole population and not just a portion of it. So that was a challenge really to the whole white South where there had not been adequate participation in the political process and a challenge to the party itself and a challenge to the American people in a way that had not been challenged as directly and in as dramatic a fashion for a very long time."

Another measure of Hamer's impact on changing the whole political process in America with that of civil rights leaders like MARTIN L. KING, JR. [1], ANDREW YOUNG [65], RALPH ABERNATHY [66], and others, is seen in the passage of the 1965 Voting Rights Act, which did away with the literacy tests and other arbitrary barriers used initially to keep blacks from voting.

Fannie Lou Hamer died on March 14, 1977. Gil Noble commented on Hamer as being "special" and a symbol of black women's involvement in the continuing black struggle *to be*: "If there is to be a continuum of our struggle for justice, we must tell our children about such great forerunners. Black women fought side by side with black men in that movement. Without black women's contributions, the movement could not have occurred. Mrs. Hamer is the best example of that point."

76

Kenneth B. Clark

1914–

The "nuclear" irony of American history and the American social, political and economic system is that the destiny of the enslaved and disadvantaged Negro determines the destiny of the nation...

The Negro remains the constant, and at times irritating reality that is America. He remains the essential psychological reality with which America must continuously seek to come to terms—and in so doing is formed by.

KENNETH B. CLARK

Kenneth Clark built the sociological theories and explanations of how best to understand black behaviors vis-à-vis nonblacks that were pioneered by E. FRANKLIN FRAZIER [38] and others. During the 1950s through the 1970s he shaped the interpretations of the "essential psychological reality" of America, as the nation struggled with the dilemma of how to deal with the demands of blacks for equal rights. Clark believed that the quality and the extent of the resolution of this dilemma would determine the "destiny of the nation."

Clark's signal influence on the resolution of the "'nuclear' irony of America history," the black struggle for freedom and equality, came in 1954, when he synthesized the scientific findings of black and white social scientists—psychologists, sociologists, historians, and anthropologists—to show the adverse impact of racially segregated schools on the psyches of children. His findings were used by the legal team of the National Association for the Advancement of Colored People (NAACP), headed by THURGOOD MARSHALL [22], to convince the U.S. Supreme Court that the doctrine and practices of "separate but equal" as expressed in *Plessy* v. *Ferguson* violated the Constitution by not providing equal educational opportunities for black children.

In May 1954, Chief Justice Earl Warren, speaking for a unanimous court in *Brown* v. *Board of Education*, indicated the extent to which the court had been convinced by Clark's compendium of scientific findings that racially segregated schools adversely affected children, especially black children: "Does segregation of children in public schools solely on the basis of race, even though the physical facilities and other tangible factors may be equal, deprive the children of the minority of equal educational opportunities? We believe it does." Clark's ranking here is in recognition of his prominent influence in *Brown* v. *Board of Education*, which brought about what Thurgood Marshall called a "momentous social transformation of our system of constitutional government."

Kenneth Bancroft Clark was born on July 24, 1914, in the Panama Canal Zone, where his father worked for the United Fruit Company. When he was five years old, he and his mother moved to Harlem, leaving his father in Panama.

Clark attended integrated elementary and junior high schools in Harlem. While in Junior High School 139, Clark was influenced by what he called "clear and visible heroes," like poet Countee Cullen, who was a member of the faculty, and by prominent bibliophile and

Africanist collector ARTHUR SCHOMBURG [55], whom Clark knew when Schomburg was curator of the Division of Negro Literature, History, and Prints at the 135th Street Branch of the New York Public Library.

In the early twenties, Clark's mother was a follower of MARCUS GARVEY [21] whose black-identity philosophy and programs impressed on Clark the need for a positive self-concept and identity, especially among black children in terms of how toys and playthings like dolls shaped images of self and others. "The first time I remember caring anything about black dolls," Clark said, "[was] because Marcus Garvey insisted that young Negroes should have black dolls and I think my mother went out and paid probably more than she should have for a black doll for my sister." Clark would later use his insights into images and emotions conveyed by dolls in his research for *Brown v. Board of Education*, which showed that black children in Harlem, when asked to express preferences among a group of dolls—white, Japanese, and black—almost invariably preferred the black doll least.

Clark graduated from George Washington High School in Harlem, after which he attended Howard University, where he received an A.B. in 1935 and an M.S. in 1936. In 1940, he received a Ph.D. in experimental psychology from Columbia University. He taught at Hampton Institute (1940–41) and in 1942, began teaching at City College of New York, where in 1960 he became the first African-American to receive a permanent appointment as a full professor.

Significant writings by Clark that have aided both black and white Americans in better understanding blacks as the "essential psychological reality" of America are *Desegregation: An Appraisal of the Evidence* (1953), *Prejudice and Your Child* (1953), and *Dark Ghetto* (1965).

Clark also played an influential role in the fifties and sixties in helping to clarify the proper response of blacks—or any group—to white hate and violence. In expressing these thoughts, Clark compared nonviolent activists, like DR. MARTIN LUTHER KING, JR. [1], to confrontational activists, like MALCOM X [23]:

> On the surface, King's philosophy [nonviolence] appears to reflect health and stability, while the black nationalists [like Malcolm X] betray pathology and instability.... It is questionable whether the *masses* of an oppressed group can in fact "love" their oppressor. The natural reactions to injustice, oppression, and humiliation are bitterness and resent-

ment.... Any demand that the victims of oppression be required to love those who oppress them places an additional and probably intolerable psychological burden upon these victims.

The reader should note that these insights corroborate those E. Franklin Frazier posited some forty years earlier.

77

Lorraine Hansberry

1930–1965

I'm not talking about Black racism. Let's keep in mind what we're talking about. We're talking about oppressed peoples who are saying that they must assert themselves in the world....

Let's not equalize the oppressed with the oppressor and saying that when people stand up and say that we don't want any more of this that they are now talking about a new kind of racism. My position is that we have a great deal to be angry about, furious about. You know it's 1959 and they are still lynching [killing] Negroes in America. And I feel, as our African friends do, that we need all ideologies which point toward the total liberation of the African peoples all over the world.

Lorraine Hansberry

During the 1950s and until her untimely death in 1965, Lorraine Hansberry was a prominent voice crying for the "total liberation of African peoples all over the world," especially the liberation of African-Americans in their protracted struggle for freedom and equality.

Hansberry's influence as an artist and activist is best understood by examining the social, political, and historic contexts through which she sought to convey the experiences of oppressed people who were determined to "assert themselves in the world." MALCOLM X [23] described this period as "a time when there's a revolution going on, a worldwide revolution." Hansberry herself corroborated Malcolm's views by saying, "For me this is one of the most affirmative periods in history. I am very pleased that those peoples in the world whom I feel closest to, the colonial peoples, the African people, the Asian peoples, are in an insurgent mood and are in the process of transforming the world and I think for the better. I can't quite understand pessimism at this moment unless of course one is wedded to things that are dying out which should die out like colonialism, like racism."

It was in this global context of change that Hansberry's controversial play, *A Raisin in the Sun* (1959), signaled a new era for the role of the black artist in the American civil rights struggle, a post–*Brown v. Board of Education* period in which there was a vortex of direct actions and protests by blacks against racism and discrimination in American life. This was also a time that saw the emergence of diverse civil rights organizations and leaders, often with different and competitive ideologies, tactics, and agendas for black liberation throughout the world. Examples of these organizations and individuals are the Southern Christian Leadership Conference (SCLC) and Dr. Martin Luther King, Jr.; the Student Nonviolent Coordinating Committee (SNCC) and Stokely Carmichael, Rap Brown, Malcolm X and others. (See ROY WILKINS [33], for more discussion of this period.)

Hansberry's listing recognizes the impact of her ideals and work, especially in the play *A Raisin in the Sun*, in conveying to black and white society the singlemindedness and persistence of blacks *to be*—to overcome white racism and oppression.

Measures of the impact of *A Raisin in the Sun* go beyond it being the first play on Broadway by a black female playwright. One must also mention the play's lengthy run of 538 performances which indicated its acceptance by white society, the patrons of Broadway theater; Hansberry's New York Drama Critics Circle Award for Best Play of the Year in

1959; and the opportunities provided for black artists, like Sidney Poitier, Ruby Dee, Lou Gossett, and black director, Lloyd Richards, and others to display their considerable talents on Broadway. At the same time, *A Raisin in the Sun* opened the doors for other blacks to the economic potential of a multibillion dollar entertainment complex (Broadway and Off-Broadway), which would witness an unprecedented rise in black theatre during the 1960s, 1970s and 1980s.

Lorraine Vivian Hansberry was born on May 19, 1930, in Chicago, to Carl, a successful real estate broker, and Nannie, a schoolteacher. Her maternal grandparents were slaves. Both her parents were active politically, her mother as a ward committeeperson and her father as a member of the National Association for the Advancement of Colored People (NAACP) and the Urban League, as a United States marshal, and as an unsuccessful candidate for the United States Congress.

Hansberry attended public elementary schools on the southeast side of Chicago. While in the third grade, her family moved into an all-white neighborhood on the South Side of Chicago, where they were taunted, harassed, and forced to leave the neighborhood by a lower court ruling that upheld restrictive housing covenants in Chicago, which barred blacks from moving into white areas. Her father challenged this ruling all the way to the United States Supreme Court and, in 1940, the Court, in *Hansberry* v. *Lee*, struck down restrictive covenants. This struggle against discrimination in housing and other areas would later become the theme of *A Raisin in the Sun* and other works.

Hansberry graduated from Englewood High School in Chicago in 1948—also the alma mater of GWENDOLYN BROOKS [64]. She then attended the University of Wisconsin, where she developed her interests in theatre. Leaving Wisconsin after two years, she studied painting at several schools, including the Art Institute of Chicago.

In 1950, she moved to New York City, studying briefly at the New School for Social Research. During that year, she also met PAUL ROBESON [24] and started working as a reporter for his newspaper, *Freedom*, becoming an associate editor in 1952. During her association with Robeson and others, like W. E. B. DuBois [4] and her uncle, renowned Africanist historian William Leo Hansberry, she developed a global view of the struggle of all oppressed peoples—black and nonblack.

In 1953, she married Robert Nemiroff, a writer, composer, and Communist activist. By this time Hansberry had started writing essays and plays. In 1957, inspired by her childhood experiences with racism and discrimination, she wrote the first version of *A Raisin in the Sun*. The title was adapted from a line of Langston Hughes's famous poem, "Harlem," in which he prophesied the dire consequences of "a dream deferred," drying up "like a raisin in the sun" and festering and exploding like the dynamite of "frustrated hopes and pent-up folk consciousness." RICHARD WRIGHT [50] and others saw and felt that frustration during the four decades preceding the *Brown* v. *Board of Education* era.

After successful runs of *A Raisin in the Sun* in New Haven, Philadelphia, and other cities, it opened on Broadway at the Ethel Barrymore Theatre on March 11, 1959, the first significant black play on Broadway since Langston Hughes's *Mulatto*, in 1938. Hansberry saw *A Raisin in the Sun* as unambiguously portraying the "fact of racial oppression.... The reason these people are in the ghetto in America is because they are Negroes."

Other significant works by Hansberry illuminating the black struggle against racial oppression are *The Movement: Documentary of a Struggle for Racial Equality in the USA* (1964); *The Sign in Sidney Brustein's Window* (1965); *To Be Young, Gifted, and Black: Lorraine Hansberry in Her Own Words* [adapted by Nemiroff, 1969]; and *Les Blancs: The Collected Last Plays of Lorraine Hansberry* (edited by Nemiroff, 1972).

Lorraine Hansberry died of cancer on January 12, 1965, in New York City. Another measure of her impact on African-Americans can be seen by the attendance of PAUL ROBESON [24], OSSIE DAVIS [91] and MALCOLM X [23] among the hundreds of mourners at her funeral on January 16, 1965, at Church of the Master on 122nd Street in Harlem, nearly one month before the assassination of Malcolm X at the Audubon Ballroom in Harlem.

78

Benjamin Hooks

1925–

For the first time since Woodrow Wilson, we have a national
administration that can be rightly characterized as anti-Negro.
This is the first time since 1920 that the national administration
has made it a matter of calculated policy to work against the
needs and aspirations of the largest minority of its citizens.

BISHOP STEPHEN G. SPOTTSWOOD

The above words were spoken by Bishop Stephen G. Spottswood,
then chairman of the National Association for the Advancement of
Colored Peoples (NAACP) board of directors, at its annual convention in
June 1970, characterizing the Richard M. Nixon administration as

having "anti-Negro" policies. In February 1992, Benjamin Hooks, executive director of the NAACP for fifteen years, announced his retirement at the organization's board of directors meeting by saying, "I have enjoyed immensely the privilege of serving you through one of the most tortuous periods in our people's history. We have kept the organization alive and growing against seemingly insurmountable odds. We have maintained the integrity of this organization and kept our name out front and on the minds of those who would turn back the clock."

These two events bookend the "most tortuous periods in our people's history" and serve to show the influence of Hooks on the struggle of African-Americans for full equality through his leadership at the NAACP in thwarting those who "would turn back the clock."

Spottswood in his speech went on to detail the "anti-Negro" policies of the Nixon administration: its retreat on school desegregation; its attempts to weaken the 1965 Voting Rights Act; its support of the view of "benign neglect" of black interests and demands; and its nominations of political conservatives disguised as "strict construction-ists" of the United States Constitution to the United States Supreme Court. All of these policies and actions demonstrated to the NAACP and other Americans—black and nonblack—a clear shift of the nation's administration away from supporting policies and programs that were created in the Kennedy and Johnson administrations, or the so-called Great Society era from 1961 to 1968.

The significance of these social and political realities to Hooks is that when he became the fourth black secretary of the NAACP in 1977, he had a different challenge than his predecessors in keeping the NAACP alive as a viable organization in the ongoing black struggle for liberation. Hooks's view that he resisted those who would "turn back the clock" is accurate when "they" are understood to be the Reagan and Bush administrations, with their latter-day antiblack policies, which prevailed for eleven of Hooks's fifteen years as executive secretary of the NAACP. (The only respite from the Nixon-Reagan-Bush policies oc-curred during the administration of Jimmy Carter from 1977 to 1980.)

The Reagan-Bush administrations attacked or retreated from programs such as the 1964 Civil Rights Act, the 1964 Public Accom-modations Act, the 1964 Food Stamp Program, the 1965 Federal Aid to Higher Education Act, the 1965 Voting Rights Act, and the 1965 Medicare and Medicaid Acts—all designed to improve the quality of life and opportunities for all Americans—black and nonblack.

Hooks's ranking is warranted by his successful use of the NAACP's resources and those of concerned Americans who supported the goals of an egalitarian society by lobbying and through direct protests for the last twenty-five years of this century. Examples of this are: lobbying for the passage of the D.C. Home Rule Bill, the Humphrey-Hawkins Full Employment Bill, and the 1991 Civil Rights Act; lobbying to defeat the Mott Anti-Busing Amendment; and establishing the Fair-Share Economic Development Program to provide blacks with greater entrepreneurial opportunities in the private sector with support from corporations such as Wendy's International, Anheuser-Busch, Walt Disney, Time Warner, and Exxon Corporation. His efforts against the forces that would "turn back the clock" were in the legacy or tradition of the NAACP as described by Spottswood in his speech of 1970:

> We have worked too long and too hard, made too many sacrifices, spent too much money, shed too much blood, lost too many lives fighting to vindicate our manhood as full participants in the American system, to allow our victories to be nullified by phony liberals, die-hard racists, discouraged and demoralized Negroes and power-seeking politicians.

Hooks was born on January 31, 1925, in Memphis, Tennessee, to Robert and Bessie Hooks. He attended segregated elementary and secondary schools in Memphis. After graduating from high school, he attended Lemoyne College in Memphis from 1941 to 1943 and Howard University from 1943 to 1944, from which he received a B.A. In 1948, he received a law degree from DePaul University in Chicago.

After practicing law from 1949 to 1965, during which time he also served as the first black public defender in Memphis, Hooks was appointed a judge in the Shelby County Criminal Courts in 1965–68, becoming the first black to serve as a jurist in the South since Reconstruction. In 1972, he became the first African-American to serve on the Federal Communications Commission, where he influenced public policy to increase employment opportunities and ownership for blacks in the television and radio industries.

In 1977, Hooks was unanimously elected executive secretary of the NAACP, succeeding ROY WILKINS [33] who had successfully transformed the NAACP into an influential collaborator with other black organizations and labor leaders during the maelstrom of the civil rights struggle of the 1950s and 1960s.

79

Leon Sullivan

1922–

In the first place, we need to attain economic independence. You may talk about rights and all that sort of thing. The people who own this country will rule this country. They always have done so and they always will. The people who control the coal and iron, the banks, the stock markets, and all that sort of thing, those are the people who will dictate exactly what shall be done for every group in this land. More than that, liberty is to come to the Negro, not as a bequest, but as a conquest. When I speak of it as a conquest, I mean that the Negro must contribute something to the good of his race, something to the good of his country, and something to the honor and glory of God. Economic independence is the first step in that direction.

CARTER G. WOODSON

The above words of CARTER G. WOODSON [25] written in 1922—the year Leon Sullivan was born—emphasized that "economic independence" is the only way for African-Americans to protect their political, social, and cultural interest in America and throughout the world. Although Leon Howard Sullivan described himself as "just a simple pastor," he has come to symbolize, for nearly the last thirty years, the "black theologian-activist" as architect and builder of economic programs and institutions which provide the "economic independence" necessary to ensure blacks their full rights in America. In 1964, Sullivan founded the Opportunities Industrialization Centers of America (OIC). OIC is the prototypical black self-help program in which blacks provide job training for blacks on a massive scale, as well as encouraging them to become entrepreneurs.

Sullivan's listing and ranking here acknowledge his singular role in conceptualizing and building OIC and its economic affiliates into arguably the most viable black self-help economic institution since MARCUS GARVEY's [21] Universal Negro Improvement Association (UNIA). Yet notably, Sullivan has accomplished this without adopting Garvey's racially divisive and separatist theories. Ideologically, Sullivan is more a kindred spirit with black theologian-activists like Revs. RICHARD ALLEN [6], DR. MARTIN LUTHER KING, JR. [1], BILL GRAY [83], JESSE JACKSON [47], and ADAM CLAYTON POWELL, JR. [43], who was one of Sullivan's mentors in civil rights protests during the forties and fifties.

Leon Howard Sullivan was born on October 16, 1922, in Charleston, West Virginia, nearly seven months before Marcus Garvey was convicted of fraud and sentenced to five years in prison, bringing his UNIA and "Back to Africa" movements to a halt. Sullivan attended segregated elementary and secondary schools in Charleston.

His first palpable experience with discrimination and racism came at the age of ten. He remarked about this incident: "One day I got myself a nickel and went across the road to a place with a Coca-Cola sign. . . . I went and sat down, with my nickel in my hand. A man came over and I said, 'I want a Coca-Cola' and I put my nickel down. He said, 'Stand on your feet, black boy, you can't sit down.' And his eyes were blazing, this white, red-haired, vicious type of man. And I said to myself, 'I'm going to fight against this kind of thing for the rest of my life.'"

In 1939, while still in high school, Sullivan was ordained a Baptist minister. He received an athletic scholarship in 1940 to attend West Virginia State College from which he received a B.A. in 1943. While at West Virginia State College he met the Rev. Adam Clayton Powell, Jr., who encouraged him to continue his studies in theology and sociology at Union Theological Seminary and Columbia University, respectively.

While studying in New York, Sullivan joined Powell's influential community-oriented Abyssinian Baptist Church in Harlem as an assistant and worked in Powell's initial campaign for Congress. During this time, he learned the philosophy and tactics of mass boycotts and protests of businesses that discriminated against blacks, under the credo: "Don't buy where you can't work."

After receiving an M.A. in sociology from Columbia in 1947, he became pastor of the First Baptist Church of South Orange, New Jersey, leaving in 1950 to become the pastor of the Zion Baptist Church in North Philadelphia. At Zion, his congregation grew from 600 to over 5,000 as a result of his linking theology with what he called "evangelistic materialism."

Sullivan's model for black economic independence was born during the 1959 protests of Philadelphia businesses that refused to hire blacks. Joining four hundred other black ministers, he led boycotts that emulated Adam Clayton Powell's successful boycotts in the 1930s of New York area white businesses. By 1962, Sullivan's boycotts had achieved the goals of getting almost three thousand more blacks hired.

Also that year, reports of the efficacy of Sullivan's "selective buying" boycotts came to the attention of Dr. Martin Luther King, Jr., of the SCLC, who persuaded Sullivan and his associates to share information with them on their success. This exchange led to SCLC's formation of its economic arm, Operation Breadbasket, in 1967, headed by Jesse Jackson. Jackson used Sullivan's tactics to gain thousands of jobs and business opportunities for blacks in major cities throughout America during the late sixties and early seventies.

Although the boycotts were successful in getting more jobs for blacks and poor nonblacks, Sullivan observed that: "Integration without preparation only leads to frustration. Our people were getting jobs, but it was more and more difficult to find people to fill these jobs. Black people had been denied an opportunity to acquire the necessary experience and had not been sufficiently motivated or had adequate access to training in fields where there was the greatest demand."

In 1964, with capital raised mainly from his congregation, donations from private sector businesses, and a grant of funds and a gift of an abandoned jailhouse from the city of Philadelphia, Sullivan founded the centerpiece of his self-help economic program, the OIC, to help blacks train unskilled, unemployed, and underemployed blacks and nonblacks for jobs in a postindustrial, high-tech era.

Measures of the impact of OIC on the quest of blacks for economic independence are seen in the following: OIC has grown since its inception in Philadelphia to over one hundred training centers throughout the United States; OIC International, which was started in 1963, has established training centers in twelve African countries, and several centers in the Philippines and Eastern Europe; OIC has trained more than one million American men and women, with over 800,000 finding employment, and generated about $15 billion in annual income in the United States, with an additional 25,000 men and women having been trained through its international arm.

Yet Sullivan's influence on the economic empowerment of blacks didn't end with providing jobs. "Our people must be able to add to the economy of their community," he has asserted, "not just by work but by production. We're going to have to develop literally thousands of entrepreneurs who know business for business's sake." Evidence of Sullivan's ability to make these words a reality is seen in his founding, in 1962, the black venture capital group, Zion Investment Associates, Inc. By selling shares to members of his congregation, Sullivan enabled black entrepreneurs to form and grow, notably Progress Plaza, Inc., the first black-owned and operated shopping plaza in the United States; Progress Garment Manufacturing Co.; Zion Gardens, Inc., an apartment complex; and Progress Aerospace Enterprises, Inc., one of the first black-owned and operated aerospace businesses.

Other indicators of Sullivan's impact on the American economy and throughout the world are his appointment, in 1971, to the board of directors of General Motors Corporation, where he influenced the policies and practices for expanding black dealerships and employment opportunities, and his impact in getting General Motors and other American and multinational corporations to use their economic power in South Africa to help change that country's policies and practices of apartheid. In 1977, Sullivan promulgated the "Sullivan Principles" for United States companies doing business in South Africa with the intent of destroying apartheid, by integrating their personnel and providing parity in salaries and work conditions. Sullivan believed that there was "no greater moral issue in the world today than apartheid."

The Sullivan Principles aided the withdrawal of international businesses from South Africa and the boycott of South African businesses, as well as the creation of international sanctions against the South African government. This has led to the dismantling of apartheid through the legalization of black trade unions, the release of black political prisoners (the most notable being Nelson Mandela), and a white-majority-approved referendum in the spring of 1992, calling for a new South African constitution that will recognize the political, social, and economic rights of a black majority.

80

Louis Farrakhan

1933–

I believe that it would be almost impossible to find anywhere in America a black man who has lived further down in the mud of human society than I have; or a black man who has been any more ignorant than I have been; or a black man who has suffered more anguish during his life than I have.

MALCOLM X

He [Elijah Muhammad] went down in the mud and got the brother that nobody else wanted. He got the brother from prison, the brother from the alley, the brother from the poolroom, the sister from the corner and he polished us up.

LOUIS FARRAKHAN

ELIJAH MUHAMMAD [51] went down into the "mud of human society" to bring his nonorthodox Islamic teachings about a Nation of Islam (NOI) to the masses of blacks as the only viable way for them to realize full economic, political, spiritual, and social equality. One of those whom Elijah Muhammad rescued from that "mud" was MALCOLM X [23], who became the most influential and effective spokesperson for the Nation of Islam and in later years for his own black-oriented and human rights causes.

After Muhammad's death in 1975, his son Wallace D. Muhammad (Warith Deen Muhammad, as he is now called) succeeded him. Wallace repudiated his father's teachings of black supremacy, racial separation, and a separate nation for blacks. He also rejected the deity of the founder of the Nation of Islam (1930), W. Farad Muhammad, who allegedly was born in Mecca, Saudi Arabia, in 1877 and was called by Allah, the God of Islam, to redeem the original race of humankind—the black race. In the late 1970s, Warith Deen Muhammad moved his followers toward "orthodox" Islam, changing the name of the NOI to "the American Muslim Mission," later to the "World Community of Islam," and finally to the "Community of Al Islam in the West," which permitted whites to join.

The second most prominent and influential of Elijah Muhammad's converts from the "mud" to be "polished up" was Louis Farrakhan. Farrakhan's listing and ranking here acknowledge his influence in revitalizing, during the seventies and eighties, the basic tenets and beliefs of the Nation of Islam as espoused by Muhammad among significant numbers of the masses of black Americans—both poor and middle-class—who still view Christianity and white Western values as tools for excluding blacks from the benefits of American life.

Also supporting Farrakhan's ranking here is his skillful manipulation of the mass media to communicate to the black masses the imperative of economic empowerment as a vital prerequisite for their full equality.

Farrakhan was born Louis Eugene Walcott on May 11, 1933, in New York City. Both of his parents were born in the Caribbean, his father in Jamaica and his mother in the Bahamas.

Shortly after the death of his father, when Louis was three years old, his family moved to Boston, where he attended public elementary and secondary schools. He graduated from Boston English High School, where he exhibited intellectual, musical, and athletic skills. He played the violin in the school orchestra, ran track on the 1950 state championship team, and graduated with honors. Also while in high school, he demonstrated considerable talent as a vocalist, especially as a calypso singer.

After high school, Farrakhan attended Winston-Salem State Teachers College in North Carolina, dropping out after two and a half years to support himself and his pregnant wife, Betsy. Returning to Boston, he became a professional calypso singer, and was known as "Calypso Gene" and "The Charmer." While performing in Boston in 1952, he met Malcolm X, who was fast becoming second only to Elijah Muhammad as spokesperson for the Nation of Islam. In 1955, while performing in Chicago, Farrakhan took time out of his schedule to attend the NOI's Savior's Day Service conducted by Elijah Muhammad. He was rescued from the "mud" when he converted to the message and teachings of Muhammad.

After his conversion, Farrakhan returned to Boston and took the name Louis X, becoming one of the most prominent of the Boston Temple's members. He was described during this time by Malcolm X in his *Autobiography*: "The Boston Temple's outstanding young Minister Louis X, previously a well-known and rising popular singer called "The Charmer," has written our Nation's popular first song, titled 'White Man's Heaven Is Black Man's Hell.' Minister Louis X has authored our first play, 'Orgena' ('A Negro' spelled backwards)."

Louis X became minister of the Boston Temple in 1956 and remained there until 1965. He left to become the minister of Temple Seven in New York City, after Malcolm X resigned from the Nation of Islam and repudiated Elijah Muhammad to form his own Muslim Mosque, Inc., and Afro-American Unity, Inc., in order to further his orthodox Muslim beliefs.

After Muhammad's death in 1975, Farrakhan worked for two years with Wallace D. Muhammad. Dissatisfied with Wallace D. Muhammad's reforms of the NOI, including its name change to the American Muslim Mission, Farrakhan decided to quit the organization in 1977. He contemplated a return to a professional career as a musical entertainer but in 1978 decided to revive the original teachings, beliefs, tenets, and organization of the NOI and Elijah Muhammad, declaring himself as the "National Representative of Elijah Muhammad and the NOI" and formally changing his name to Louis Farrakhan.

Measures of Louis Farrakhan's impact on the ongoing black struggle are his appeal to tens of thousands of poor and middle-class blacks with the original teachings of Elijah Muhammad, some forty years after Muhammad had shaken the foundation of the Negro Christian community; his establishment and reestablishment of scores of temples and learning centers across the United States and the Caribbean to propagate the NOI's teachings; and his use of the mass media and stirring speeches to large groups to proselytize for his faith—for example, from 1984 to 1990 over 700 articles have been written about Farrakhan and the Nation of Islam in major dailies and periodicals. He has also appeared on every major television network's news program. George Curry, of *Emerge* magazine, has summarized Farrakhan's appeal to and impact on today's blacks: "Farrakhan continues to draw sell-out crowds everywhere he speaks. He is glorified on the records of Public Enemy, the popular rap group, and was the subject of a skit on the Fox television comedy program *In Living Color....* Blacks, for the most part, are attracted to Farrakhan, the most outspoken person in America, because of his emphasis on black pride and insistence on blacks empowering themselves economically by supporting black businesses."

With this last message of economic empowerment, Farrakhan joins other black influential religious activists, like Revs. HENRY H. GARNET [14] and RICHARD ALLEN [6], and more modern religious activists such as ADAM C. POWELL, JR. [43], MARTIN LUTHER KING, JR. [1], JESSE JACKSON [47], and LEON SULLIVAN [79] in calling for the institutionalization of CARTER WOODSON's [25] belief that economic independence is the first step to real freedom and equality for blacks in America.

In 1985, while speaking to a capacity crowd at Madison Square Garden, Farrakhan revealed his economic Power Program—with simple, ordinary, everyday examples—as an appeal to his followers and other blacks to:

> Marshal some of our purchasing power and start producing some of the things we are already spending money for. You spent $400 million last year just for toothpaste. You spent nearly $800 for mouthwash. God knows what you spent on toilet paper and the sisters, sanitary napkins. But we don't make none of this. But since you got to use these things, why shouldn't we produce it, and we use it. Now look, if all of us use our own toothpaste, our own mouthwash, our own toilet paper, our own soap, our own sanitary napkins, look how much money is coming into our own coffers. Then before you

know it, you'll be strong enough to put your money in your
own national banking system. And then you put your money
in your own bank. Nearly 30 billion dollars poor people
threw away on foolishness. Don't you think we ought to be a
little more wise with the money we have and using it to build
black people up?

Ultimately, the true measure of Farrakhan's impact on the black
struggle *to be*—whether viewed through a Muslim or a non-Muslim
agenda—will be his ability to build concrete economic institutions like
those of the REV. LEON HOWARD SULLIVAN [79], whose ranking above
Farrakhan in this book reflects the author's view that Sullivan has taken
the rhetoric of economic empowerment of blacks and made it a
significant institutional reality.

81

Oscar Micheaux

1884–1951

Motion pictures are one of the most influential means of
communication ever developed—a potentially powerful medium
of propaganda. Hollywood['s]...depiction of black people on the
screen has not only reinforced and sharpened some of the
prejudices of the white majority, but it has also to a great extent
shaped the often negative images blacks have had of themselves.

GARY NULL

The release of *The Birth of a Nation* in 1915 signaled the nadir of white
racist Hollywood's use of film as a "powerful medium of propaganda" to
depict negatively black people in America so as to reinforce and sharpen

"some of the prejudices of the white majority." The film was based on the bestselling novel *The Clansman* (1905) by racist Thomas Dixon, Jr., which extolled the virtues of the Ku Klux Klan and portrayed blacks as inferior, degenerate, and brutish.

The film's release led to widespread protests and demonstrations by blacks across the country, including the National Association for the Advancement of Colored People (NAACP) and its most prominent member, W. E. B. DU BOIS [4], and the militant activist and publisher WILLIAM M. TROTTER [28], who was arrested and jailed in Boston in 1915 for attempting to shut down a screening.

Film expert Gary Null summarized the tradition of Hollywood in the negative portrayal of blacks in films before and after *The Birth of a Nation:*

> In film after film, the same Negro stereotypes appear—the foolish and irresponsible citizen, the grinning bellhop or flapjack cook, the hymn-singing churchgoer, the song-and-dance man, the devoted servant or contented slave, the barefoot watermelon eater, the corrupt politician, the hardened criminal, and the African savage. Thus emerge two broad categories into which the Negro can be fitted—the clown and the black brute.

African-Americans not only protested and demonstrated against the virulent racist stereotypes spread by *The Birth of a Nation* and scores of other racist films, but, consistent with the aphorism of ARTHUR SCHOMBURG [55], they also became "an active collaborator, and...a pioneer in the struggle for [their] own freedom and advancement" by producing and directing their own films to aid in this protracted struggle.

The most prominent and influential of these black filmmakers during the 1920s and 1930s was Oscar Micheaux, who with other blacks and sensitized whites tried to counter the blatantly racist nature of Hollywood films. Micheaux's ranking here is warranted by his extraordinary influence in helping to develop a black underground of filmmakers committed to destroying the "prejudices of the white majority [and] negative images blacks have had of themselves."

Film expert Donald Bogle has recounted the pioneering challenges, difficulties, and successes encountered and realized by Micheaux and other black filmmakers in redirecting this medium to aid in the struggle of blacks *to be:*

The truth is that black Americans have made their films for many years. While the mainstream of Hollywood filmmakers demeaned and ridiculed the American Negro, an underground movement gave rise to a group of independent black filmmakers who flourished in the late 1920s and 1930s. They tried to present realistic portraits of black Americans.... And always they were plagued by financial, technical, and distributing problems. Yet some came up with remarkable achievements that survive today. A host of black writers, directors, producers, and technicians gained valuable experience from working on these films. In fact, had it not been for such underground features, many blacks would never have worked in films at all.

There are few exact details about the early life of Oscar Micheaux, who was born in 1884 on a farm near Cairo, Illinois, the same year T. THOMAS FORTUNE [60] started publishing the *New York Freeman* (changed later to *New York Age*) to counter the negativity of the white press towards blacks.

Micheaux's parents were former slaves. One of thirteen children, he left home in his early teens to work at a variety of jobs, eventually becoming a Pullman porter and traveling extensively to the far western United States. He became enamored of the West and in 1904, bought a homestead in South Dakota. He quit his job as a porter, formed his own publishing company, and started writing about the adventures and opportunities of blacks in the West.

Beginning in 1913 with his novel *The Conquest: The Story of a Negro Pioneer*, Micheaux would eventually write ten novels, among them: *The Forged Note: A Romance of the Darker Races* (1915) and *Homesteader* (1917), the basis for his first film. Micheaux self-promoted all of his novels in inimitable style (cowboy garb and western flair), traveling to black communities throughout the country, where he sold his works directly to diverse groups of blacks—from doctors and lawyers to farmers and teachers and common folk—and also attempted to persuade them to take advantage of the opportunities and lifestyle offered in the West.

In 1918 Micheaux was approached by a black-owned underground film company, the Lincoln Motion Picture Company of Lincoln, Nebraska, to make a film of his novel *The Homesteader*. When he insisted that he direct the movie, his offer was rejected, and he decided to form his own film company in New York City, the Oscar Micheaux Corporation, to change the "negative images blacks have had of themselves" through white-produced and directed films.

Beginning with his first film, *Homesteader* (1919), to his last, *Betrayal* (1948)—about thirty-five films altogether—Micheaux was independently the most influential black image-maker, using the medium of film to change how both blacks and nonblacks viewed African-Americans. Among Micheaux's significant films are: *Within Our Gates, The Brute, Symbol of the Unconquered* (1920), *Son of Satan* (1922), *Birthright, Body and Soul* (1924, which starred Paul Robeson), *Millionaire* (1927), *Veiled Aristocrats, Black Magic* (1932), *Harlem After Midnight* (1934), and *God's Stepchildren* (1937).

Although Micheaux has been criticized by blacks and nonblacks for using black middle-class or black bourgeoisie images and themes to counter those of white Hollywood's in his films, this does not detract from his significance as the most influential of all black filmmakers in shaping how blacks and nonblacks viewed the black quest for a better life for nearly thirty years. (These criticisms of Micheaux are much like those leveled at BILL COSBY [62], who would use high-tech mass-media television to convey controversial black images and values during the 1960s through the 1990s.)

Oscar Micheaux died in Charlotte, North Carolina, while promoting his films. Donald Bogle has insightfully summarized the controversy about what he represented and conveyed in his films and works about blacks:

> What remains Oscar Micheaux's greatest contribution (and somewhat revealed explicitly in *God's Stepchildren*) is often viewed by contemporary black audiences as his severest short-coming. That his films reflected the interests and outlooks of the black bourgeoisie will no doubt always be held against him. His films never centered on the ghetto; they seldom dealt with racial misery and decay. Instead they concentrated on the problems of "passing" or the difficulties facing "professional people." But to appreciate Micheaux's films one must understand that he was moving as far as possible away from Hollywood's jesters and servants. He wanted to give his audience something to further the race, not hinder it.

82

Carl Rowan

1925–

The great newspapers, which should plead the cause of the oppressed and the down-trodden, which should be the palladiums of the people's rights, are all on the side of the oppressor, or by silence preserve a dignified but ignominious neutrality. Day after day they weave a false picture of facts— facts which must measurably influence the future historian of the times in the composition of impartial history.

T. THOMAS FORTUNE

The above words of T. THOMAS FORTUNE [60] were written in 1887 to indicate the obligation of and justification for his founding a black weekly newspaper, the *New York Freeman* (later changed to the *New York Age*), in order to combat the negativity of the white press toward blacks.

Fortune's *New York Age,* like many other black publications,* was in the tradition of the first black newspaper in America, *Freedom's Journal,* founded by SAMUEL CORNISH and JOHN RUSSWURM [8] on March 16, 1827 to provide black perspectives on African-Americans and their struggle for equality in America.

Although Carl Rowan did not establish a separate black publication like those previously cited to plead the cause of the oppressed and downtrodden, he has arguably been the most prominent and influential African-American journalist for the last four decades of this century in utilizing the "great [white] newspapers" of America and other media to "weave a [true] picture of facts" about the ongoing quest of blacks *to be* in America and throughout the world. These facts support his listing and ranking here.

Carl Thomas Rowan was born on August 11, 1925, in Ravenscroft, Tennessee, to dirt-poor parents, Thomas David and Johnnie Rowan, nearly three months after MALCOLM X [23] was born in Omaha, Nebraska. At an early age, he and his brother and three sisters moved to McMinnville, Tennessee, where during the Depression they—like most blacks—were exposed to poverty, discrimination, and economic exploitation, which he later described: "My parents never expected an economic calamity that would make life miserable for most people everywhere, especially black people in brutally racist communities, which is what McMinnville was. But they lapsed into poverty that was so bad that my children wince when I talk about it. It is as though they cannot believe that in that rat-infested house we had not a single clock or watch. We told time by the arrival of the train from Tullahoma to Sparta, and if it was late then I was late for school. We had no electricity, no running water, and, for most of the time, no toothbrushes...."

---

*Thomas Hamilton's *The Anglo-African Magazine* (founded 1859); William Monroe Trotter's Boston *Guardian* (founded 1901); Robert Abbott's *Chicago Defender* (founded 1905); NAACP's *Crisis* (founded 1910 by W. E. B. Du Bois); A. Philip Randolph's *The Messenger* (founded 1917); Leon Washington's *Los Angeles Sentinel* (founded 1933); and John Johnson's *Negro Digest* (founded 1942).

Rowan attended segregated public elementary and secondary schools, graduating in 1942 from Bernard High School as class president and valedictorian. That same year, he moved in with his grandparents in Nashville and entered Tennessee State University. In 1943, he left Tennessee State to pursue a commission in the U.S. Navy, attending Washburn University in Kansas, Oberlin College in Ohio, and the Naval Reserve Midshipmen School in Fort Schuyler, New York, obtaining his commission in 1944.

After serving as a naval officer on two vessels in the Atlantic, he returned to Oberlin College in 1946. The following year he received a B.A. in mathematics. While at Oberlin, he worked as a freelance writer for the black newspaper, the *Baltimore Afro-American.* Interested in journalism as a career, he enrolled in the Graduate School of Journalism at the University of Minnesota, from which he graduated with an M.A. in 1948. During this time he also wrote for two black newspapers, the *Minneapolis Spokesman* and the *St. Paul Recorder.*

In 1950, Rowan began a singular and anomalous role as a voice for "the cause of the oppressed and the downtrodden," by joining the all-white *Minneapolis Tribune* as a copy editor, from 1948 to 1950 and as its first black staff reporter, from 1950 to 1961. Rowan's impact in painting true pictures of the facts, realities, and experiences of black Americans in their struggle against racism and discrimination is evinced by a series of award-winning articles written during the tumultuous fifties: "How Far From Slavery" (1951, articles examining the effects of "separate but equal" Jim Crow laws on blacks in thirteen Southern states); "Jim Crow's Last Stand" (1953, articles on the court cases involved in the landmark *Brown* v. *Board of Education* decision of 1954); and "Dixie Divided" (1955, articles covering the emergent Montgomery bus boycotts led by Dr. Martin Luther King, Jr., and others, set in motion by Rosa Park's [100] refusal to give up her bus seat to a white man).

By the late 1950s, Rowan was the most prominent black journalist in America and was lashing out at those who were, in his words, "compromising away the freedom of America's black people." Other significant writings by Rowan that illuminate the black struggle for equality are *South of Freedom* (1952); *The Pitiful and the Proud* (1956, based on travels to India and Southeast Asia in which he described their political and social conditions); *Go South to Sorrow* (1957); *Wait Till Next Year: The Life Story of Jackie Robinson* (1960); *Just Between Us Blacks* (1974); *Race War in Rhodesia* (1978); and *Breaking Barriers: A Memoir* (1991, autobiography).

Other indicators of Rowan's impact on black and nonblack America came when President John F. Kennedy appointed him deputy assistant secretary for public affairs in the Department of State (1961–63) and again when Kennedy named him ambassador to Finland (1963–64). During Lyndon Johnson's administration, Rowan was appointed director of the United States Information Agency (1964–65), responsible for the worldwide communication network, including the Voice of America.

In 1965, Rowan returned to journalism as a nationally syndicated columnist for the powerful Field Newspaper Syndicate, where he has continued his role as one of the most influential black journalists in America over the last twenty-five years.

Rowan has incisively and poignantly observed the state of black America in the 1990s: "I think the greatest tragedy within black America is that we lost a sense of direction. KING [1], ABERNATHY [66], YOUNG [65], WILKINS [33], MARSHALL [22], and the other towering figures of the fifties and sixties had it easy in the sense that black people and their white friends were driven toward one goal: the elimination of legally sanctioned racism in America. Every black person could understand the hatred of having to ride in the back of the bus. But once the legal basis for racial separation was wiped out, a lot of blacks walked into fogs of confusion about what the next goals ought to be."

Rowan, through his influential nationally syndicated column and syndicated television and radio shows, continues to remove the "fogs of confusion" and helps to clarify what "the next goals ought to be."

83

Bill Gray

1941–

In the Congress, I surely had opportunities to influence
national legislation and policy. But it does not take very long to
understand the sociology of this particular moment in history
and the importance of educating more minorities.... Nothing is
more powerful and liberating than knowledge, and nothing is
more important than educating our young people. Knowledge is
the basic requirement; it is absolutely essential for individuals
to have it in order to gain the full advantage of their rights to
both freedom and opportunity. This is the philosophical vision
around which I intend to craft my ambitions at the United
Negro College Fund.

WILLIAM H. GRAY, III

Indisputably, William Herbert Gray III was the most influential, most powerful black congressman since ADAM CLAYTON POWELL, JR. [43]. That is why his announcement, in June 1991, that he would be leaving the Congress and his powerful post as House majority whip (the third ranking position in the Democratic Party-controlled Congress) to become the president and chief executive officer of the United Negro College Fund (UNCF) sent shock waves throughout America. The UNCF is a group of forty-one historically black colleges and universities educating nearly 51,000 predominantly black students.

Gray's views of the "importance of educating more minorities" and of "knowledge [as] essential for individuals to have... in order to gain the full advantage of their rights to both freedom and opportunity" are consistent with a venerated value and an immemorial belief held by African-Americans that quality higher education is a potent means to freedom and to "uplift" blacks throughout the world.

Gray's decision to leave a life of influence on national legislation and policy to head the UNCF is in the finest tradition of other black theologian-activists such as HENRY H. GARNET [14], MORDECAI W. JOHNSON [40], HENRY MCNEAL TURNER [39], BENJAMIN E. MAYS [53], and his own father, Dr. William H. Gray, II. Like Gray, each of these men, at critical junctures in their careers, opted to head black colleges or universities as a means of aiding the liberation of blacks and furthering the "advantage of mankind," as Mordecai Johnson once said.

Bill Gray's ranking here acknowledges his impact as a congressman on shaping national legislation and policies that affected the quality of life of blacks and nonblacks, and his courage and vision in taking his fame, visibility, and influence—at a time when his political star was rising—to seize "the sociology of this particular moment in history" to strengthen and expand the role of historically black colleges and universities. Gray's decision came at a critical time, when black America faced the scandalizing and sobering fact that more college-age black males are in prison, jail, or on probation than in institutions of higher learning!

William Herbert Gray, III was born August 20, 1941, in Baton Rouge, Louisiana, to William H. and Hazel Gray, nearly two months after A. PHILIP RANDOLPH [31] called off his threatened march on Washington to protest discrimination against blacks in war industries. His father was a renowned clergyman and educator who served as president of the historically black colleges Florida Normal and Industrial College in St. Augustine (1941–44) and Florida A&M College in Tallahassee (1944–49). His mother was a high school teacher.

When Gray was eight, his family moved to Philadelphia, where his father became pastor of the Bright Hope Baptist Church, succeeding Gray's grandfather, William H. Gray, I, after his death. Gray attended public elementary and secondary schools in Philadelphia and graduated from Simon Gratz High School in 1959. He received a B.A. from Franklin and Marshall College in 1963, and a master of divinity degree from Drew Technological Seminary in 1966. While at Drew, he was appointed assistant pastor of the Union Baptist Church in Montclair, New Jersey. Two years after finishing at Drew, he became the senior pastor of Union Baptist at a service officiated by Dr. Martin Luther King, Jr. In 1970, Gray received a master of theology degree from Princeton Theological Seminary. In 1972, after his father's death, he became the third generation of his family to serve as pastor of the Bright Hope Baptist Church in Philadelphia.

As a black theologian-activist, much like ADAM CLAYTON POWELL, JR. [43] and LEON SULLIVAN [79], Gray involved his church in the black struggle by organizing nonprofit housing corporations for the poor in Philadelphia, and by running, in 1976, for the Second Congressional District against incumbent black Congressman Robert Nix, for whom he had once paged while an undergraduate student. Gray lost. He ran again in 1978 and won, and went on to win six consecutive two-year terms until his resignation.

The magnitude of Gray's power and influence in the Congress was felt in 1985 when he became the first black to chair the powerful House Budget Committee. He described the importance of this committee as follows: "The function of the chairman is to run the committee, chair its meetings, supervise its staff and set the tone and the direction of the committee and help to build a consensus among the members of the committee as to what should be the budget of the United States of America. The budget is then put forth, if it is passed out of committee, it is the chairman's budget." The trillion-dollar-plus budgets of the United States bore his imprimatur from 1985 to 1988, during which time he used his influence and power to protect domestic programs designed to benefit the needy, such as the Urban Development Action Grants and the Appalachian Development Program, from cutbacks or outright elimination by the Reagan administration.

Leveraging his position as chairman of the Budget Committee with his membership on the Subcommittee on Foreign Operations,

Gray became a prominent spokesperson on African policy. An example of his attempts to improve conditions for Africans was evinced by his authorship of the Anti-Apartheid Acts of 1985 and 1986, which sought to end economic support to the government of South Africa. These sanctions, along with the Sullivan Principles, have greatly contributed to the dismantling of apartheid.

Another measure of Gray's impact on furthering the African-American struggle for economic empowerment came in 1983, when he authored legislation to set aside money for minority and women business owners, historically black colleges, and other minority agencies to get their fair share of funds from the United States Agency for Internal Development, which has provided almost $1 billion in such set-asides since its inception.

In 1989, Gray was elected majority whip of the Democratic Party in the Congress. In 1991, he announced to the world that his visibility and remaining influence would be used as president and CEO of the UNCF to affect "the sociology of this particular moment in history," a moment described by him as one of "substance abuse, alcohol abuse, and spousal and child abuse. . . . Of infant mortality, teenage pregnancy, black-on-black crime, the tragedy we call AIDS, and black male incarceration. . . . We are living in an age without morals . . . community without conscience . . . children without heroes . . . schools without discipline. In our presence is a culture that is out of control. Education is the cure." Bill Gray continues to work tirelessly toward achieving that cure for all African-Americans.

84

Katherine Dunham

1909–

If you read the history of Africa, the history of your ancestors—
people of whom you should feel proud—you will realize that
they have a history that is worth while. They have traditions
that have value of which you can boast and upon which you can
base a claim for right to share in the blessings of democracy.
    . . . We are going back to that beautiful history and it is
going to inspire us to greater achievements.

CARTER G. WOODSON

Katherine Dunham was born in Glen Ellyn, Illinois, on June 22, 1909, to Albert and Fanny June Dunham, almost four months after the National Association for the Advancement of Colored People (NAACP) was founded. At twenty-five, she was the recipient of a $2,400 Julius Rosenwald Foundation travel fellowship to study the African origins of Caribbean dance in order to learn, in the exhortation of CARTER G. WOODSON [25], the "history of Africa, the history of your ancestors—people of whom you should feel proud."

In her study of the African origins of Caribbean dance, Katherine Dunham was inspired to "greater achievements." As an anthropologist, dancer, and choreographer, she pioneered the introduction of African dance throughout the world during the thirties, forties, and fifties. Much as LOUIS ARMSTRONG [68] helped jazz gain recognition and appreciation as the original musical form of America, Dunham popularized dance of African origin, using it as a vehicle to convey the richness and diversity of African-American culture and as an aid in the struggle of blacks "to share in the blessings of democracy." These facts justify her listing and ranking here.

Dunham's mother died when she was three years old. She and her brother, Albert, Jr., were moved by their father to the South Side of Chicago, where they lived with an aunt while he was away for long periods as a traveling salesman. Shortly after arriving in Chicago, a stepsister took Katherine and Albert from their aunt's care, winning a court order for their custody, with the condition that if their father proved he was able to take care of them, he could have custody. The father proved this by the time Katherine was five, and moved her and Albert, Jr., with a new wife, Annette Poindexter, a former schoolteacher from Iowa, to Joliet, Illinois, where he opened a dry-cleaning business.

Dunham attended public elementary and secondary schools in Joliet. While in elementary school, she took private dancing and piano lessons. In high school, she joined the dance club and showed athletic skills as a member of the girls' basketball team. As a result she became president of the Girls' Athletic Association. After completing two years at Joliet Township Junior College, she transferred to the University of Chicago, where she studied ethnology and cultural anthropology under Dr. Robert Redfield.

While a student in Chicago, she and two other dancers, Mark Turbyfill and Ruth Page, formed a dance group named Ballet Nègre, specializing in African dance. Their debut at the Chicago Beaux Arts

Ball in 1931, *Negro Rhapsody,* launched Dunham's career as one of the most influential black dancer-choreographers of the twentieth century.

In 1933, while still a student at the University of Chicago, Dunham earned a reputation as an exponent of African dance. She was chosen to select and teach 150 young blacks to dance for the Chicago Century of Progress Exposition. That same year, she decided to major in anthropology, with an emphasis on the African origins of Caribbean dance. In 1935, she used the Rosenwald travel fellowship to study dance in Jamaica, Martinique, Trinidad, and Haiti. There she documented that dances and rituals of African origin were the bases of Caribbean dances and were also integral to the social and cultural structures of the Caribbean.

Katherine Dunham in production of "Tropical Revue."

In 1936, Dunham received a B.A. from the University of Chicago. She later earned a master's degree from the University of Chicago and a doctorate from Northwestern University, under Melville Herskovits, the world-renowned anthropologist. (Herskovits had contributed an important essay, "The Negro's Americanism," to Alain Locke's *New Negro* (1925), the landmark volume that signaled the beginning of the Harlem Renaissance.)

Changing the Ballet Nègre to the Negro Dance Group in 1937, Katherine Dunham took the art form of African and Caribbean dance to nearly sixty countries throughout the world. Some of her important works which have conveyed the richness and diversity of black culture and the black quest *to be* are: *Ballet Fedre* (1938), *Tropics and Le Jazz Hot* (1940), *Tropical Review* (1943), *Bal Nègre* (1946), *Caribbean Rhapsody* (1950), and *Bamboche* (1962). She and the Negro Dance Group also appeared in black-oriented movies such as *Stormy Weather* (1943).

Among Dunham's important writings documenting that "beautiful history" of African-Americans and those of African descent throughout the world are *Journey to Accompong* (1946, about her studies and experiences among the Maroons of Jamaica, descendants of the Koromantee tribe of West Africa); *Les Danses d'Haiti* (1950, research on Haitian dance), and *A Touch of Innocence* (1959, autobiography).

Having retired from the stage in the 1960s, Dunham moved to East St. Louis, Illinois—one of the most poverty-stricken cities in America—and founded the Katherine Dunham Center in order to continue training new generations of youth in African dance and other aspects of African culture. She also maintained a home in Haiti, which she purchased in the late 1940s.

Her ongoing commitment to the struggle of peoples of African descent for justice and equality is seen in her 1992 hunger strike, at the age of eighty-two, against the mistreatment of Haitians fleeing to America, who were denied political asylum by the Bush administration after the deposing of populist Haitian President Jean-Bertrand Aristide in 1991. She saw her fast as one last expressive tool for dramatizing to the world the fact that "this isn't just about Haiti. It's about America. This country doesn't feel that Haitians are human. And America treats East St. Louis the way it does Haitians."

85

Maya Angelou

1928–

All my work, my life, everything is about survival. All my work
is meant to say, "You may encounter many defeats, but you
must not be defeated." In fact, the encountering may be the
very experience which creates the vitality and the power to
endure.

MAYA ANGELOU

Maya Angelou's ranking here is warranted by her signal impact in using the genre of the autobiography to illuminate her courage and strength as a black woman to survive and "not be defeated" in a racist society, while at the same time illuminating and portraying the "survival" and struggle of all blacks against racism and discrimination.

Angelou's life, as portrayed in her work, has made her a pithy symbol and metaphor of the ongoing black quest *to be*. Like HARRIET TUBMAN [12], the highest-ranked black woman in this book, Angelou through her work, especially her autobiographies, has come to represent the indomitable spirit of blacks in their unending quest for full economic, political, and social equality.

The five autobiographical works by Angelou that represent her struggle *to be* during various stages of her life, and the larger or more collective struggle of African-Americans, are *I Know Why the Caged Bird Sings* (1970, on her childhood and youth in the South and in California), *Gather Together in My Name* (1974, describes the period after her son's birth and her difficulties as a single parent), *Singin' and Swingin' and Gettin' Merry Like Christians* (1976, on her theatrical career up to her international tour with *Porgy and Bess*), *The Heart of Woman* (1981, on her maturation as an artist), and *All God's Children Need Traveling Shoes* (1986, describes her experiences in Africa in the early 1960s through her return to America in the late 1960s).

Angelou has commented on the focus on herself in *I Know Why the Caged Bird Sings* as a metaphor and symbol of blacks in their struggle: "When I wrote *I Know Why the Caged Bird Sings*, I wasn't thinking so much about my own life or identity. I was thinking about a particular time in which I lived and the influences of that time on a number of people. I kept thinking, what about that time? What were the people around young Maya doing? I used the central figure— myself—as a focus to show how one person can make it through those times." She used this same rationale and technique in her four remaining autobiographies.

Angelou was born on April 4, 1928, as Marguerite Johnson, in St. Louis, Missouri, four months to the day after MARCUS GARVEY [21] had his sentence for mail fraud commuted by President Coolidge. She was the younger of two children of Bailey and Vivian Johnson. Her parents divorced when she was four, and she and her brother, Bailey, Jr., were sent to Stamps, Arkansas, to live with their paternal grandmother,

Annie Henderson. Angelou attended the all-black Lafayette Training School in Stamps, graduating from the eighth grade there in 1940.

After finishing Lafayette, she and her brother moved to San Francisco to live with their mother, who had settled there from St. Louis. She attended George Washington High School during this period and took dance and drama lessons at the California Labor School. When she was sixteen, she became pregnant and had a son out of wedlock, which forced her as a black, single, female parent to "survive" and endure the realities of racism and her own proclivities, choices, faults, and weaknesses as a human being. All the stages of her life, from young adulthood to womanhood to a world-renowned artist, are detailed in her vivid and didactic autobiographies. Her name Maya was given to her by her brother, Bailey, and Angelou was her married name from a two-and-a-half-year marriage to a former sailor, Tosh Angelos or Angelou.

An example of the pain borne by Angelou that helped shape her view of self, blacks, men, and the world came when she was raped at the age of eight by her mother's boyfriend, Mr. Freeman, while she was living with her mother in St. Louis. Here is her description of the rape from *I Know Why the Caged Bird Sings:*

> He released me enough to snatch down my bloomers, and then he dragged me closer to him. Turning the radio up loud, too loud, he said, "If you scream, I'm gonna kill you. And if you tell, I'm gonna kill Bailey." I could tell he meant what he said, I couldn't understand why he wanted to kill my brother. Neither of us had done anything to him. And then.
>
> Then there was the pain. A breaking and entering when even the senses are torn apart. The act of rape on an eight-year-old body is a matter of the needle giving because the camel can't. The child gives, because the body can, and the mind of the violator cannot.

Mr. Freeman was put on trial and convicted but didn't live to serve his sentence of one year and a day—he was kicked to death by a mob of outraged blacks. Tragically, the young Angelou blamed herself for his death and continued to traumatize herself by not speaking to anyone for five years.

Other important works by Angelou are her volumes of poetry: *Just*

Give Me a Cool Drink of Water 'Fore I Die (1971); *Oh Pray My Wings Are Gonna Fit Me Well* (1975); *Still I Rise* (1978); *Shaker, Why Don't You Sing* (1983); *Poems: Maya Angelou* (1986); *Now Sheba Sings the Song* (1987); and *I Shall Not Be Moved* (1990). *I Know Why the Caged Bird Sings* was made into a television movie in 1979, for which she wrote the script and music. Her *Georgia, Georgia* (1972) was the first screenplay produced by a black woman.

Through her life experiences, Angelou has shown the "vitality and the power to endure." Through her exceptional talents as an artist committed to the struggle of blacks, she has become griot among African-Americans, attesting to the "vitality and the power" of them to do likewise.

86

Earl Graves

1935–

The Negro is at last developing a middle class, and its main center is in Durham. As we read the lives of the men in Durham who have established the enterprises there, we find stories paralleling the most amazing accounts of the building of American fortunes....

The greatest achievement of the Durham group and no doubt the greatest monument to Negroes' business enterprises in America [is]—the North Carolina Mutual Life Insurance Company. The first organization of this company in 1898 consisted of seven men who paid in fifty dollars each to meet immediate expenses.... Today it has $42,000,000 of insurance in force and assets amounting to over $2,000,000.

E. Franklin Frazier

E. FRANKLIN FRAZIER'S [38] interpretation in 1925 of the significance of black middle-class entrepreneurial activities in Durham, North Carolina, as signaling the growth of a black middle class in America and his opinion of the North Carolina Mutual Life Insurance Company as representing the "greatest monument to Negroes' business enterprise in America" provide an historic benchmark for looking at the significance and influence of Earl Graves on the black struggle *to be*. Since his founding of the monthly magazine *Black Enterprise* in 1970, Graves has become a most prominent leader among African-American publishers in documenting the growth of black enterprises and in advocating black entrepreneurship as a means of ensuring the full rights and freedoms of African-Americans.

BE's annual listing and ranking of the top 100 black businesses in America has become *the* compilation of and report on the health and progress of black businesses. For example, the twentieth anniversary issue of the *BE 100* in 1992 updated Frazier's report on the North Carolina Mutual Life Insurance Company as follows: $8.8 billion of insurance in force, assets of $214 million, and still the largest black-owned insurance company in America. (Arguably, North Carolina Mutual is still "the greatest monument to Negroes' business enterprise." It is not, however, the largest black-owned corporation in America in terms of gross sales—that distinction presently belongs to TLC Beatrice International Holding Inc., with sales of over $1.5 billion.)

Graves has established *BE,* with a circulation of nearly 250,000, and his monthly publisher's column as primary sources on the importance and need of black economic empowerment through entrepreneurship, with blacks as the vendors, suppliers, and producers. Graves's espousal and practice of entrepreneurship as a necessary economic foundation for political and social equality in America warrant his listing and ranking here.

Earl Gilbert Graves was born in 1935 in Brooklyn, New York, to Earl Godwin and Winifred Graves. He attended public elementary and secondary schools in Brooklyn and received a B.A. in economics from Morgan State College in 1958.

Upon graduation Graves joined the army and rose to the rank of first lieutenant. After leaving the army in the early 1960s, he worked at an assortment of jobs, from narcotics agent with the Justice Department to selling real estate in the Bedford-Stuyvesant area of Brooklyn, New

York. In 1965, he became an administrative assistant to Senator Robert F. Kennedy. After Kennedy's assassination in 1968, Graves decided to create his own management consulting firm. In 1969, he received a grant from the Ford Foundation to study black-owned businesses in the Caribbean, sparking his interests in establishing a black-oriented business magazine.

In 1970, with a $150,000 loan from Chase Manhattan Bank, he founded *Black Enterprise* as a how-to publication for black entrepreneurs. Its initial annual revenues were $900,000; today it has a circulation of nearly 250,000 and revenues of over $17 million.

Another measure of Graves's impact on the black struggle for total equality has been his ability not only to "talk" economic development or empowerment for blacks for the last twenty years but also to make black economic development palpable through the establishment and growth of the following corporations: Earl G. Graves Publishing Co.; EGG Dallas Broadcasting, Inc.; Earl G. Graves Marketing and Research Co.; B.C.I. Marketing; and Pepsi-Cola of Washington, D.C., L.P., which he owns with Earvin "Magic" Johnson, and which grosses nearly $60 million in sales annually.

In a typically insightful publisher's column dedicated to his late father in the twentieth anniversary issue of *Black Enterprise*, Graves had this to say about the state of black businesses in America and about some of the forces against which blacks still must struggle, as did his father's generation:

> The progress made by black business is about more than just numbers. It is a story of men and women who are benefiting from the entrepreneurial legacy of men and women of your generation.... Larger societal issues also persist in our "brave new world." Racism is alive and well; many of its practitioners are graduates of the same Ivy League schools as many of the best and brightest of your grandsons' generation of African-Americans. Black children, in general, still do not have equal access to a quality education. And health issues continue to disproportionately threaten our communities— too often striking significant contributors to African-American progress.

As a successful entrepreneur leading the way toward economic empowerment, Graves has contributed significantly to eradicating the pernicious effects of racism on a generation of African-Americans.

87

Hank Aaron

1934–

Look, I don't have the vision or the voice of Martin Luther King or James Baldwin or Jesse Jackson or even of Jackie Robinson. I'm just an old ballplayer. But I learned a lot as a ballplayer. Among other things, I learned that if you manage to make a name for yourself—and if you're black, believe me, it has to be a big name—then people will start listening to what you have to say. That was why it was so important for me to break the home run record. . . . I had to break that record. I had to do it for Jackie and my people and myself and for everybody who ever called me a nigger.

HANK AARON

JACK JOHNSON [63] became the first world symbol of black athletic achievement when he won *the* symbol of white male physical and macho supremacy, the heavyweight boxing championship of the world, on December 26, 1908. On April 8, 1974, nearly sixty-six years after Johnson's feat, Hank Aaron became yet another significant symbol of black athletic achievement by surpassing the most inveterate of white male symbols of athletic achievement: Babe Ruth's home-run record of 714. Like JACKIE ROBINSON [42], MUHAMMAD ALI [54], JESSE OWENS [56], JACK JOHNSON [63], JOE LOUIS [71], and ARTHUR ASHE [98], Aaron won fame in a color-conscious, racist society. Though "just an old ballplayer," he transcended the national sport of baseball and made himself a potent symbol of the black struggle for freedom and equality in America.

Aaron's decision to use the home-run record of major league baseball to further the causes of freedom and equality for African-Americans (much as Muhammad Ali used the heavyweight boxing title) counters his self-effacing observations of not having the "vision or the voice of Martin Luther King, Jr., or James Baldwin or Jesse Jackson or even of Jackie Robinson." His vision, ability, and courage to "break that record... for Jackie and my people and myself and for everybody who ever called me a nigger" have contributed significantly to a nearly mystical phenomenon of projecting pent-up frustrations, rage, and resolve through athletes against racist conditions, attitudes, and institutions that would deny blacks their rights and freedom in America.

This phenomenon is better appreciated when one understands the link of major league baseball to a racist American society as its national sport, and the sport's institution of traditionally white male competitive attitudes. Baseball from its origins mirrored the enduring and pervasive American lie: a declaration of equal rights for all Americans and the simultaneous denial of those rights to people of African descent. Not until Jackie Robinson broke the color barrier of major league baseball in 1947 were blacks permitted to play in this exclusive white league; a game born in the racial intolerance of a post-Reconstruction era that midwifed the doctrine and practices of "separate but equal" in *Plessy* v. *Ferguson* and Jim Crow. Racism throughout America forced blacks to form their own Negro Baseball Leagues.

Ruth's record of 714 home runs was set nearly thirteen years before Jackie Robinson broke the color barrier. Whites projected notions and images of white male athletic superiority on Ruth and made his home-run record a standard of excellence for justifying the exclusion of blacks from baseball and therefore symbolized a justification for most whites to continue to exclude blacks from the benefits and freedom of American life. Aaron's 715th home run on April 8, 1974, shattered this myth for millions of blacks and again exposed the American lie. Aaron knew that blacks were imputing their "dreams of revenge and retaliation" on him as voiced nearly forty years earlier by RICHARD WRIGHT [50].

Henry Louis Aaron was born February 5, 1934, in Mobile, Alabama, to Herbert and Estella Aaron. He was the third of eight children. The family lived in an all-black area of Mobile called "Down the Bay" until he was eight, then moved to Toulminville, where he attended segregated elementary and secondary schools. Aaron's father worked as a boilermaker's assistant for the Alabama Dry Dock and Shipbuilding Company and his mother worked occasionally as a domestic.

Aaron decided at an early age to become a baseball player. In 1945, when Toulminville was annexed to Mobile, he gained the opportunity to play baseball when the city built a baseball field near his home. In 1952, while still attending Central High School in Toulminville, he received an offer to play for the Indianapolis Clowns of the Negro League for $200 a month. That same year his contract was bought by the Milwaukee Braves of the National League. After an outstanding year with one of the Braves' minor league clubs, Aaron was brought up to the parent club in 1954. In his first season he played right field and batted .280, with 13 home runs and 69 runs batted in.

By the time Aaron's twenty-two-year major league baseball career ended, he had a lifetime batting average of .302, with 755 home runs and 2,297 runs batted in, both major league records.

Aaron retired as a player in 1976 and became an executive with the Atlanta Braves. He continued to use his visibility to get more blacks into the management and ownership of America's "national pastime," a multibillion-dollar business. Aaron was inducted into the Baseball Hall of Fame in 1982.

After Bowie Kuhn retired as commissioner of baseball in 1984, Aaron applied for the job. Evidence of how baseball continues to reflect the pervasive racism in American life can be seen in the way Aaron's application was treated by the all-white owners of the game and the white male dominated media:

I was the only one who stepped forward publicly as a candidate to replace Kuhn. But I was never a serious candidate in the committee's eyes, or in the media's. A lot of people seemed to be amused by the thought of me as commissioner. I didn't happen to think it was so outrageous. . . .

It struck me as ironic that baseball was always saying blacks didn't have the experience for front-office jobs, and yet they hired consecutive commissioners who had no background in baseball.

I never heard back from the search committee after my interview.

88

Dick Gregory

1932–

Personally, I've never seen much difference between the South and the North. Down South white folks don't care how close I get as long as I don't get too big. Up North white folks don't care how big I get as long as I don't get too close.

DICK GREGORY

Just as LANGSTON HUGHES [34] and ZORA NEALE HURSTON [52] used the rich and diverse experiences of common black people—as revealed in their folktales and folklore—to convey the black struggle for freedom and equality, Dick Gregory for the last three decades has used humor drawn from the black experience in America (so-called "racial" humor) as a weapon in the struggle of African-Americans against racism and discrimination.

Gregory's ranking here is justified by his lifelong impact as a civil and human rights activist in the liberation of people of African descent throughout the world. To accomplish these goals, he has made good use of his gift as a black humorist and comedian to reveal that there is not "much difference between the North and the South" in the way that white America deals with blacks.

By fusing his art with the demands and aims of the black struggle *to be*, Gregory has come to personify Langston Hughes's belief in the authentic link of the black artist's work with the "eternal tom-tom beating in the Negro soul—the tom-tom of revolt against weariness in a white world, a world of subway trains, and work, work, work; the tom-tom of joy and laughter, and pain swallowed in a smile."

Richard Gregory was born on October 12, 1932, in St. Louis, Missouri, the second of six children of Presley and Lucille Gregory. His father abandoned the family when Richard was very young, leaving his mother to raise the children during the nadir of the Great Depression. To support her children, she worked as a domestic in St. Louis suburbs for two dollars a day and carfare.

Gregory attended segregated public elementary and secondary schools. He started working to support his family before he entered the first grade by carrying packages and hauling groceries. By the time he was seven, he was a shoeshine boy in a pool hall that catered to white patrons. He credits his mother's "pain swallowed in a smile" for his sense of humor about being black and proud. "When there was no fatback to go with the beans, no socks to go with the shoes, no hope to go with tomorrow," he has said, "she'd smile and say: 'We ain't poor, we're just broke.'"

At Sumner High School, he distinguished himself as a track star, winning the Missouri state mile championship in 1951 and becoming class president in his senior year. After graduating, he chose to attend Southern Illinois University from among the twelve athletic scholarships he had been offered. At Southern Illinois, he was exposed to virulent institutional racism. On this point he observed, "In high school I was fighting being broke and on relief.... But in college I was fighting being Negro." His consciousness of "being Negro" gave him a perspective on the black struggle in America that would characterize and leaven his "black humor" for the rest of his life.

It was while at Southern Illinois that he discovered his comedic talents. He left the university in 1953 and was drafted into the army, serving for two years. While in the army, he honed his comedic skills by entertaining at GI shows in the Special Services Division. After leaving the army in 1956, he returned to Southern to finish a degree in business, but dropped out permanently to pursue a full-time career as a comedian.

From 1956 to 1958, Gregory worked at assorted jobs in Chicago, from postal clerk to car washer, while appearing part-time as a comedian in various black nightclubs. In 1958 he opened his own club, The Apex. After some initial success, he had to close it later the same year. In 1959, he became the main comedian at a popular black club, Roberts Show Club, where part of his act was filmed by ABC television and shown in the documentary, *Cast the First Stone*, which was viewed by nearly sixty million Americans.

His biggest break came at the Playboy Club in 1961: substituting for the resident white comedian, Gregory impressed management with the positive reception accorded his "racial humor" by a predominantly white Southern-conventioneer audience. As a result, the Playboy Club signed him to a two-month contract. He later performed in nightclubs throughout the United States, and received a bigger boost to his career when he appeared on television on the popular late-night Jack Paar show.

Gregory used his growing visibility, fame, and fortune during the turbulent 1960s and 1970s to support black protests and demonstrations. Evidence of this can be seen in the use of his nationally popular nightclub act to satirize racism and discrimination; his participation in and financial support of every major civil rights march or protest during the sixties and seventies, including the March on Washington and the Selma March; and his many arrests and jailings for protesting racism and discrimination. He was shot in 1965 while trying to help restore order during the Watts uprisings.

Some important writings by Gregory in which he uses his humor as a tool to attack racism in America are *From the Back of the Bus* (1962), *Nigger: An Autobiography* (1964), *The Shadow That Scares Me* (1968), *Write Me In* (1968), *No More Lies: The Myth and Reality of American History* (1972), *Dick Gregory's Political Primer* (1972), and *Up From Nigger* (1976).

In the 1970s, Gregory started using his visibility and prominence as a civil and human rights activist and comedian, to influence black and nonblack Americans to change their diets, in order to be physically and mentally healthier. His *Natural Diet for Folks Who Eat: Cookin' With Mother Nature* (1973) signaled his impact in the seventies and eighties in getting more Americans to eat right and think right. A measure of his effectiveness in helping people throughout the world change to a healthier diet is evidenced by the international sales of his *Slim Safe Bahamian Diet* Program, which grosses millions of dollars annually.

89

Oprah Winfrey

1954–

I would hope that Spelman students will not only graduate to
become great surgeons or corporate executives, but that they
will also be among the core of folk who are seeking solutions
to such issues as homelessness in America. . . . there is a saying
that solutions to problems are often found by people who can
see out of more than one eye. And it is black women who are
able to see out of their blackness, out of their womanness,
often out of their poverty and sometimes out of their privilege.
So I believe that it is going to be black women who will find
the answers to many of the problems we face today.

JOHNNETTA COLE

Although not an alumna of Spelman, Oprah Winfrey has emerged in the eighties and nineties as an influential black woman "able to see out of [her] blackness, out of [her] womanness, often out of [her] poverty and sometimes out of [her] privilege" the questions and answers to problems facing both black and non-black America.

Her sense of responsibility of service, derived from her "black womanness," to both black and non-black Americans has made her a most influential solution giver to a generation facing the problems, opportunities, and challenges of moving into the third millennium. In fact, she has become such a visible and pervasive image in the medium of television that she is the one-name icon, *Oprah*. This *Oprah* phenomenon is seen by Oprah Winfrey as something deeply rooted in her "black womanness":

> The fact that I was created a black woman in this lifetime, everything in my life is built around honoring that. I feel a sense of reverence to that. I hold it sacred. And so I am always asking the question, "What do I owe in service having been created a black woman: to change people's lives for the better."

Like BILL COSBY [62], Oprah has used the powerful, influential medium of television in *The Oprah Winfrey Show*, the highest rated talk-show in history, to shape the thoughts, opinions, and consciousness of black and non-black Americans on issues from racism to sexism to sexual abuse to homelessness to images and sentiments about blacks in a color-conscious American society. In doing so, she has become the quintessential example of the talk-show genre; thus her ranking here.

Oprah Winfrey was born January 29, 1954, to unwed parents Vernita Lee and Vernon Winfrey, in Kosciusko, Mississippi. Oprah's mother moved to Milwaukee shortly after her birth, leaving her to be brought up under humble circumstances on her paternal grandmother's farm in Kosciusko. At the age of six she began to have her "blackness" shaped out of the poverty of living with her mother in Milwaukee, who worked as a domestic and was on welfare.

After nearly two years of living with her mother, Oprah was sent to Nashville, Tennessee, to live with her father and his wife. After about a year of living with her father, she went back to Milwaukee to live with her mother, who had married a man with two children. During the next five years of living with her mother, Oprah had a set of experiences that gave shape to her views of self, blacks, "womanness," the world, and men. It especially shaped her view of men and her sexual identity in that she was sexually abused by a cousin and other male relatives until she left Milwaukee at fourteen, going live with her father again. Her traumas from these experiences had much in common with MAYA ANGELOU'S [85] as told in her *I Know Why the Caged Bird Sings* (*See* p. 311).

Oprah read Angelou's *I Know Why the Caged Bird Sings* when she was sixteen. Reading the book had a life-altering affect on Oprah: "I read it over and over. I had never read a book that validated my own existence." As the full-blown *Oprah*, Angelou has become her mentor and mother figure and the greatest influence on her life as a living metaphor and symbol of the black woman's quest for full economic, political, and social equality in America.

Oprah spent her high school and college years with her father in Nashville, attending Tennessee State University, working for a local radio station while in high school, and for a local TV station while in college. Leaving college before graduating in 1976, Oprah took a job as a TV reporter in Baltimore, Maryland. After TV successes in Baltimore, Oprah moved to Chicago, ultimately hosting *The Oprah Winfrey Show*, which now reaches 20 million viewers daily.

Oprah has used her popularity, visibility and influence from the medium of TV to portray black images and values in the medium of film. In 1985 she appeared in Alice Walker's *The Color Purple*, for which she earned an Academy Award nomination. Oprah formed Harpo Productions in 1988 with her "privilege" and wealth to portray aspects of black culture—with its values and history—beginning with the TV miniseries *The Women of Brewster Place*, based on Gloria Naylor's novel. Her understanding of and commitment to illuminating the larger ethos of African Americans through the experiences of African American women are seen in her 1988 production—during Black History Month—of a multigenerational miniseries based on Dorothy West's *The Wedding*, her October 1998 production of a full-length film of TONI MORRISON'S [73] *Beloved*, and her intention to produce a full-length film of ZORA NEALE HURSTON'S [52] *Their Eyes Were Watching God*.

A dramatic example of Oprah's influence on both black and non-black America's understanding of hopes, issues, problems, and solutions that affect us all is her use of Oprah's Book Club, which started in 1996 and appears monthly on *The Oprah Winfrey Show*. Every book she has recommended to her viewers has become a *New York Times* bestseller overnight. Oprah has also used the Book Club to give visibility to black artists like TONI MORRISON [73], MAYA ANGELOU [85], and Ernest Gaines (*A Lesson Before Dying*) and non-black writers like Francine Nolan (*The Deep End of the Ocean*), Sheri Reynolds (*The Rapture of Canaan*), Wally Lamb (*She's Come Undone*), and others. Since the Book Club's inception, over 12 million copies of recommended books have been bought by Oprah's fans.

90

Ron Karenga

1941–

Black Power may not be the ideal slogan to describe this new self-image that the black American is developing... to frustrated blacks, however, it symbolizes unity and a newly found pride in the blackness with which the Creator endowed us and which we realize must always be our mark of identification. Heretofore this blackness has been a stigma, a curse with which we were born. Black Power means that henceforth this curse will be a badge of pride rather than of scorn.

ROBERT S. BROWNE

The above quote by educator and activist Robert S. Browne from a speech in June 1968, has been cited for two reasons: first, to show his views and that of a larger number of black Americans during the 1960s and 1970s of the significance of the slogan "Black Power" as symbolizing "unity and a newly found pride in the blackness with which the Creator endowed us," and, second, to suggest that such views of Black Power's "newness" reflect the pervasive ignorance among too many Americans about the immemorial struggle of Americans of African descent throughout the world.

"Black Power" as a slogan was made popular by Stokely Carmichael in a speech in May 1966 at a demonstration in Jackson, Mississippi. The intimation by Browne and others that African-Americans developed a "new self-image" which repudiated the stigmas of "blackness" slights the continuum of struggle of those of African descent. "A struggle that Africans had waged in Africa," according to Leonard Jeffries, "a struggle waged as they crossed in the Middle Passage." A struggle that this book has documented continued to be waged by all those listed in *The Black 100* and millions not listed. The Black Power assertion of the sixties and seventies is properly understood as a recent part of the continuum of the African-American struggle (see BLACK POWER [99]).

Among the most prominent of the advocates of Black Power—with its many different definitions and meanings—during the sixties and seventies was Maulana Ron Karenga. His listing and ranking here acknowledges his influence as a black aesthetician and activist in institutionalizing the celebration of Kwanzaa as a means of bringing about unity, positive images, and values among those of African descent in their ongoing struggle for equality. Arguably, Karenga, by institutionalizing the celebration of Kwanzaa among millions of African-Americans, has become the "first" among the Black Power advocates such as H. Rap Brown, Eldridge Cleaver, Stokely Carmichael, Huey Newton, and James Forman to produce the salutary results hoped for by former Gary, Indiana, mayor Richard Hatcher in 1968:

> The Black Power advocates have fostered a sense of oneness and completeness. They have made "Black is beautiful, Baby" a meaningful slogan of pride. They have tapped the same resources which Africans, under the leadership of Senghor and Kenyatta, call *Négritude*. They have helped our young find themselves.

(The reader should note that in-depth discussion of the Black Power Movement is beyond the scope and intent of this book. Black Power is only alluded to here to help show the relative impact of Maulana Karenga and others on the black struggle.)

Kwanzaa is an African-American celebration focusing on the family, community, and culture, much like the "Black Family Reunion Celebration" founded by DOROTHY HEIGHT [61], to refocus African-Americans on the positive aspects of the black family and community and to counter widespread negativity associated with blackness. However, unlike "Family Reunion," Kwanzaa focuses more on the *Négritude* of the African past, by using a seven-day celebration, which begins on December 26 and runs through January 1, as a means "to rescue and reconstruct African history and culture." According to Karenga, "Kwanzaa is a time for [black] people to come together to reaffirm these bonds, to be rooted in your culture and return to your history."

In celebrating Kwanzaa (a Swahili word meaning "first fruits") over seven days, seven principles are observed through prescribed rituals and ceremonies: *Umoja* (unity), *Kujichagulia* (self-determination), *Ujima* (collective work and responsibility), *Ujamaa* (cooperative economics), *Nia* (purpose), *Kuumba* (creativity), and *Imani* (faith).

A measure of Karenga's impact in institutionalizing Kwanzaa, as a nonreligious, cultural reaffirmation among blacks is seen in its celebration by millions of people in the United States, Canada, the Caribbean, parts of Europe, and Africa.

Karenga was born Ronald Everett on July 14, 1941, in Parsonsburg, Maryland. He moved to Los Angeles, California, in the late 1950s to attend Los Angeles City College. After the Watts uprising in 1965, he founded US, which he said, "was born in 1965 out of the fires of the August revolt in Watts. It was created as a social and culture change organization." US became the fastest-growing black nationalist and culturalist group on the West Coast, with Maulana (Swahili for "master-teacher") convincing his followers to adopt Swahili names and African dress and to follow his philosophy and doctrines of cultural nationalism embodied in the seven principles of blackness called *Kawaida*, which are used in the celebration of Kwanzaa.

Some important works by Karenga are *The African-American Holiday of Kwanzaa* (1988), *Introduction to Black Studies* (1982), and *Kwanzaa: Origin, Concepts and Practice* (1977).

91

Ruby Dee

1924–

Ossie Davis

1917–

[Ruby] Dee and [Ossie] Davis...have a deep-rooted commitment to African-American performance and cultural traditions. Their sober allegiance to a proud African oral tradition and a rich African-American folklore is what they agree on, what they have in common as a support and a cause. In probing the whats and whys of African-American people in history, they embody the characters of our ancestry.

W. CALVIN ANDERSON

Ruby Dee and Ossie Davis have each distinguished themselves as both artists and activists; however, it is their "deep-rooted commitment to African–American performance and cultural traditions" that link them as influentials to the protracted struggle of blacks *to be*. Dee and Davis, by fusing their artistic talents with their historic perspectives of, and commitments to the black struggle for freedom and equality, have come to "embody the characters of our ancestry" like few others in media over the last four and a half decades.

Dee and Davis are progenies of the likes of W. E. B. DU BOIS [4] and ALAIN LOCKE [36], who both played influential roles in the black cultural renaissance of the twenties and thirties. Dee and Davis's ties to Du Bois can be seen in Du Bois's pioneering role in establishing the Krigwa Players' Little Negro Theatre in Harlem in 1926 as an artistic offshoot of the NAACP's *Crisis* magazine, which encouraged black community theatre to be:

> 1. *About Us.* That is, they must have plots that reveal Negro life as it is. 2. *By Us.* That is they must be written by Negro authors who undrstand from birth and continued association just what it means to be a Negro today. 3. *For Us.* That is the Negro theatre must cater primarily to Negro audiences and be supported by their entertainment and approval. 4. *Near Us.* The theatre must be in a neighborhood near the mass of Negro people. (See AUGUST WILSON [96] on this point.)

The Krigwa Players became the model for black theatre groups throughout the country during the twenties and thirties, including the Negro People's Theatre in Harlem which was organized by Richard Campbell and Rose McClendon in 1935 (later called the Rose McClendon Players). Davis's link to Alain Locke was forged in his undergraduate days at Howard University, where Locke as a professor and a prominent black aesthetician and scholar encouraged him to make the theatre his career.

Dee was born Ruby Ann Wallace on October 27, 1924, in Cleveland, Ohio, to Marshall Edward and Emma Wallace. Her father was a porter and waiter for the Pennsylvania Railroad and her mother was a schoolteacher. Her family moved to Harlem when she was an infant, where she later attended public elementary and secondary schools. While attending Hunter High School, she decided to become an actress.

After graduating from high school in 1941, she attended Hunter College, obtaining a B.A. in 1945. While at Hunter, she joined the American Negro Theatre as an apprentice, which had among its members Sidney Poitier and HARRY BELAFONTE [92] and at that time had a close working association with the Rose McClendon Players, through whom she met Ossie Davis.

Davis was born on December 18, 1917, in Cogdell, Georgia, to Kince Charles and Laura Davis. He was reared in Waycross, Georgia, where he attended segregated elementary and secondary schools. After graduating from high school, Davis enrolled at Howard University, where he met Alain Locke.

He left Howard during his junior year in 1941 to pursue an acting and writing career in New York. It was there that he joined the Rose McClendon Players. In 1942 he was drafted into the army, serving most of his time in Liberia, West Africa, as a surgical technician and later as a member of the Special Services Unit, writing and producing shows for service personnel. After leaving the military, he returned to New York and to the Rose McClendon Players, performing in several of their community productions. In 1946, he appeared with Dee in the Broadway play *Jeb Turner*, which addressed the readjustments of a black war hero to racist America. Two years later, he and Dee were married.

Dee and Davis's "deep-rooted commitment to African performance and cultural traditions" are evinced in the following collaborative works: *No Way Out* (film, 1950); *Alice in Wonder* (play, 1952); *Purlie Victorious* (play, 1961); *Gone Are the Days* (film version of *Purlie*, 1963); *The History of Negro People* (nine-part series for National Educational television, 1965); *The Poetry of Langston Hughes* (record, 1964); "The Ruby Dee/Ossie Davis Story Hour" (television show on sixty National Black Network stations, 1974); *Do the Right Thing* (film, 1989); and *Jungle Fever* (film, 1991).

Like other black artists, Dee and Davis view their work as inseparable from the black struggle *to be*. Evidence of their political commitment is seen in their affiliations with the missions and causes of the National Association for the Advancement of Colored People (NAACP), the Student Nonviolent Coordinating Committee (SNCC), the Southern Christian Leadership Conference (SCLC), and the Congress of Racial Equality (CORE). Examples of their involvement with these organizations and other causes beyond the necessary and vital donation of money and time are: Davis's service as master of ceremony at the historic March on Washington in 1963 and Dee's establishment of the Ruby Dee Scholarship in Dramatic Arts, to encourage and support young black women in the arts.

In the 1980s and 1990s both Dee and Davis have expressed a concern about the extent to which the modern cadre of black media artists, especially producers and directors of film and television, understand the rich and proud history of Americans of African descent in their use of these powerful media. Davis, speaking for both on this issue, has said:

> What I think is happening is that more of the young people are self-generated. They come into the arena sort of fresh and new. This is both good and bad. They don't bring baggage, they don't bring history, they just bring an appetite—a raw appetite for sensation. That can give you energy and color and rhythm and a whole lot of exciting things. What it cannot give you is depth, continuity and an understanding of the human condition, which is what art should also be about. The young directors are very lucky and gifted in the initial energy they are capable of bringing—the youth, the raw hunger for experience—but they're highly unfortunate in that they have no sense of history.

Dee and Davis, by having probed and expressed the rich and proud history of Americans of African descent, truly "embody the characters of our ancestry."

92

Harry Belafonte
1 9 2 7 –

I just want to say how much we are indebted to my dear and
abiding friend, Harry Belafonte, and to all the distinguished
and famous artists and entertainers who have taken the time out
from their prestigious schedules to be with us here in
Montgomery, Alabama, as we march on the state capital
tomorrow morning. I know that our thanks will go out to them
and will abide them for years to come.

MARTIN LUTHER KING, JR.

The above words were spoken by DR. MARTIN LUTHER KING, JR. [1] on the eve of what would be the culminating rally at the Alabama Capitol, after the historic five-day march from Selma to Montgomery, in March 1965, protesting racism and discrimination in the Deep South. As revealing as King's words were in describing Harry Belafonte as "my dear and abiding friend," they don't begin to reveal the influence of Belafonte as an entertainer and activist in bringing together "all the distinguished and famous artists and entertainers" from around the nation and the world to attend the rally in Montgomery and other marches, protests, and nonviolent demonstrations during the 1950s and 1960s.

As special as Belafonte's friendship might have been to King, who became the symbol of the modern-day black struggle for freedom and equality, this would not in my view be enough to list and rank him here. Belafonte's contribution as an entertainer and activist to the ongoing struggle of blacks *to be* warrants his inclusion here, beginning with his influential role as organizer and fundraiser, with King and the Southern Christian Leadership Conference (SCLC) and his current involvement with human rights issues throughout the world.

Belafonte once described what he did in bringing influential actors and entertainers together such as Sidney Poitier, Sammy Davis, Jr., Lena Horne, Marlon Brando, Steve Allen, Shelley Winters, and Julie Harris at strategic times to support the struggle for justice and equality in America:

> I organized the group and I had taken care of funding. . . . A couple of Broadway shows closed down at night to let some of the artists come as they had done also at the March on Washington. And that was because I had prevailed upon some producers who responded very supportively. That was a big part of my activity. That was to define the movement for people who had public, who had a constituency who were in the public eye. I was very proud of us, many of us black and white who did that. As a matter of fact it created a political consciousness among a lot of people who have since stayed on with it.

Recent examples of Belafonte's ability to raise the "political consciousness" among artists with significant constituencies are: his pivotal role in organizing a massive reception for the symbol of post-apartheid South Africa and its black majority, Nelson Mandela, in the summer of 1990; and his participation with heads of state and other celebrities in celebrating the Universal Declaration of the Human Rights of the Child at the United Nations in the fall of 1990.

Harold George Belafonte was born on March 1, 1927, in New York, to Harold George and Melvine Belafonte. His father was born in Martinique and his mother was born in Jamaica. His family returned to Jamaica to live when he was eight, and there he attended elementary school. Returning to New York after five years, he attended St. Thomas the Apostle School and then George Washington High in Harlem for two years, leaving to join the navy in 1944.

After leaving the navy, he worked as a janitor at an apartment complex, where one day a tenant gave him tickets to an American Negro Theatre Production of *Home Is the Hunter*, sparking his interest in drama. He studied acting at the Dramatic Workshop of the New School for Social Research in New York. While studying acting, he developed an interest in singing. During a dramatic workshop production he was heard singing a song he had written called "Recognition" and was signed to a contract by one of the owners of the Royal Roost, a jazz club. His singing career was launched. From 1948 to 1950, Belafonte toured the United States, singing popular songs in nightclubs.

Dissatisfied with his career, Belafonte decided to quit his tour to study African-inspired Caribbean folk music. The music, he discovered, "was more than pulp and fodder and superficial statements of unrequited love, not just about moon-tune. It was about pain and anguish and social oppression and political oppression. And...about man's inhumanity to man." By 1952, after an extensive engagement at the Village Vanguard in New York, Belafonte had established himself as a major exponent of African-inspired Caribbean folk music and a musical hybrid called calypso, from the same African roots. During the fifties and sixties Belafonte popularized African-inspired Caribbean folk music and calypso throughout the world, much as LOUIS ARMSTRONG [68] did for jazz and KATHERINE DUNHAM [84] did for Caribbean dance.

From the 1950s through the 1970s, Belafonte appeared in a number of black-oriented movies, among them *Bright Road* (1953), *Carmen Jones* (1954), *The World, the Flesh, and the Devil* (1959), *Odds Against Tomorrow* (1959), *Buck and the Preacher* (1972), and *Uptown Saturday Night* (1974).

Belafonte met Dr. Martin Luther King, Jr., in New York City, after

King had begun his Montgomery bus boycott campaign and after he had founded SCLC in 1957. Through his commitment to the struggle for a more egalitarian society Belafonte emerged as one of the most prominent of the entertainers and activists of the 1950s and 1960s. Belafonte has reflected on his involvement in the ongoing black struggle and the inspiration of those who came before him:

> Great and noble people...preceded me. I am by no means exclusive. I may have had some significance in my time because of the boundaries that I had crossed that had not been crossed before. But had there been no Paul Robeson, I would never have had a platform to be able to say what I was saying. If there had been no Billie Holiday, if there had been no Harriet Tubman, if there had been no history before me, so I do not see myself as any great innovator. I may have picked up the standard that was laid down by the standard bearers before and just moved on with it a little further.... [When] political activitists in the political arena sought my support, it was evident that they knew that I represented a constituency that is very serious and that I had some influence with.

93

Marian Wright Edelman

1939–

I am not fighting just for myself and my people in the South, when I fight for freedom and equality. I realize now that I fight for the moral and political health of America as a whole and for her position in the world at large.

MARIAN WRIGHT EDELMAN

Marian Wright Edelman is listed and ranked here in recognition of her outstanding contributions to the "fight for freedom and equality" for blacks and nonblacks as a civil rights activist and for her "fight for the moral and political health of America" as the most prominent advocate for America's neediest children, among whom a disproportionate number are black and poor.

Edelman's fight for herself and "my people in the South" during the 1950s and 1960s was evidenced by her participation in student sit-ins in the South, in which she was arrested and jailed; her involvement in voter registration drives in Mississippi with the Student Nonviolent Coordinating Committee (SNCC); and her internship with the Mississippi NAACP Legal Defense and Educational Fund as an attorney and later as its head from 1964 to 1968. (In 1965, she became the first black woman to pass the Mississippi State Bar.)

In 1973, Edelman's "fight for the moral and political health of America" was institutionalized with her founding of the Children's Defense Fund (CDF), which under her leadership has become the most influential lobbying group for a gamut of children's and family issues: teenage pregnancy, school dropouts, miseducation, child health care, child abuse, youth unemployment, intergenerational poverty, and others. Through CDF, Edelman has, over the last twenty years, become the most powerful and visible spokesperson for needy children and their families. At the same time, she is an influential voice in encouraging all Americans to invest in children as a way of protecting America's competitive position in a world increasingly being recognized and experienced as a "global village."

Marian Wright was born on June 6, 1939, to Arthur Jerome and Maggie Leola Wright, in Bennettsville, South Carolina. She was named after MARIAN ANDERSON [94]. Her father was a minister and social activist, who with her mother in the early forties established the Wright Home for the Aged, which her mother operated.

Edelman attended segregated elementary and secondary schools, graduating at seventeen from the Marlboro Training High School in Bennettsville. She entered Spelman College in 1956, where during her third year she won a Charles Merrill yearlong grant to study in Europe at the Sorbonne University in Paris and the University of Geneva in Switzerland.

Upon returning to Spelman for her senior year in 1959, she

became involved in the burgeoning civil-rights movement in the deep South, participating in student sit-ins and protests. It was at this time that she decided to become a civil rights lawyer. After graduating from Spelman as valedictorian in 1960, she applied to Yale University Law School and was accepted as a John Jay Whitney Fellow. While at Yale, she remained involved in the struggle in the South during her study breaks, involving herself in voter registration drives conducted by SNCC in Mississippi.

In 1963 she graduated from Yale Law School. After one year of legal training in New York, she went to Jackson, Mississippi, to join the NAACP Legal Defense and Education Fund as an intern, assisting civil rights workers who, like herself, were being arrested, jailed, and harassed by those whites committed to denying blacks their full rights and freedom. In late 1964, she was appointed to head the Fund and remained there until 1968.

After receiving a grant in 1968 from the Field Foundation to study the impact of the legal system and public policy on the poor, Edelman moved to Washington, D.C. That same year, she established the Washington Research Project to facilitate her studies of the poor.

By 1973, her studies at the project revealed the vulnerability of America's children to a myriad of destructive societal forces that, if not ameliorated, would not only destroy them but also "the moral and political health of America." It was out of this context of concern and urgency for children that Edelman founded the Children Defense Fund (CDF) in 1973. In one of its first reports, CDF identified the kinds of children "pushed" out of the public schools throughout the nation, for whom CDF would advocate: "If a child is not white, or white but not middle class, does not speak English, is poor, needs special help with seeing, hearing, walking, reading, learning, adjusting, growing up, is pregnant, or married at age fifteen, is not smart enough, or is too smart, then in too many places school officials decided school is not the place for that child."

Important writings by Edelman that further explore the policies and practices of American school personnel and others in dealing with these kinds of children are *Children Out of School in America* (1974), *School Suspensions: Are They Helping Children* (1975), *Portrait of Inequality: Black and White Children in America* (1980), *Families in Peril: An Agenda for Social Change* (1987), and *The Measure of Our Success* (1992).

From the mid-seventies through the eighties, Edelman became one of the foremost educational leaders in America through her association with Spelman College, first as a board member, and then as its first black woman chairperson, in 1980. Edelman's vision and efforts made Spelman into one of the top liberal arts colleges in America for African-American women.

94

Marian Anderson

1897–1993

To put it even more bluntly, in many areas of this country, a
white paroled murderer would be welcomed in places which
would at the same time exclude such people as Ralph Bunche,
Marian Anderson, Jackie Robinson, and many others.
Constitutionally protected individual rights have been
effectively destroyed by outmoded theories of racial or group
inferiority.

THURGOOD MARSHALL

One would find it difficult to prove Thurgood Marshall's assertion that "a white paroled murderer" would have been more welcome in 1939 to use Constitution Hall in Washington, D.C., for a concert. However, the fact is that Marian Anderson, recognized by blacks and nonblacks as one of the greatest singers of the twentieth century, was kept by the Daughters of the American Revolution (DAR)—which owned the Hall—from performing there because she was black.

This event, and those that followed, metamorphosed Marian Anderson into a symbol for African-Americans in their struggle against discrimination and racism, against "outmoded theories of racial or group inferiority."

Just as athletic achievers JACKIE ROBINSON [42], MUHAMMAD ALI [54], JACK JOHNSON [63], JESSE OWENS [56], JOE LOUIS [71], ARTHUR ASHE [98], and HANK AARON [87] were used by blacks to project their hopes, frustrations, and rage against symbols of white superiority in sports, Marian Anderson was used by millions of blacks as a potent symbol and metaphor of the black struggle for freedom and equality in the arts. The significance of this struggle was made clear by JAMES WELDON JOHNSON [26], who observed that "through artistic achievement the Negro has found a means of getting at the very core of the prejudice against him, by challenging the nordic superiority complex." These facts justify her listing and ranking here.

By February 1939, Marian Anderson had studied with master voice teachers like Giuseppe Boghetti and Raimund Von Zur Muhlen; received a Rosenwald grant to study with Michael Raucheisen; performed extensively throughout Europe, where in Salzburg in 1935, Maestro Arturo Toscanini described her voice as: "what I heard today one is privileged to hear only in a hundred years"; and performed at Town Hall and Carnegie Hall in New York City. Yet when Howard University sought to bring her to perform at Constitution Hall, the DAR refused permission because she was black. The swell of protest among black and nonblack Washingtonians included Eleanor Roosevelt, who sat on the board of the DAR. After resigning from DAR over this controversy, Mrs. Roosevelt arranged, through Secretary of the Interior Harold Ickes, a concert for Anderson on April 9, 1939, at the Lincoln Memorial. Seventy-five thousand people attended.

It is the popular view that whites such as Roosevelt and Ickes, outraged over the egregious act of bias by the DAR, used their influence to schedule Anderson's concert at the Lincoln Memorial,

Marian Anderson performing at the Lincoln Memorial on April 9, 1939.

which became a symbol of triumph over discrimination in the arts. Although Roosevelt and Ickes played commendable and pivotal roles in these events, appreciating the roles that blacks also played reveals Anderson's significance as a symbol and metaphor to the black struggle for freedom and equality. John Lovell, Jr., then field secretary of the NAACP in Washington, D.C., detailed the role of black Washingtonians in advocating and collaborating with others to correct this injustice, as blacks had done on a continuum of struggle, immemorially, including their protest of the same treatment by the DAR of renowned black singer Roland Hayes thirteen years earlier:

In February, March and April, Marian Anderson was insulted by the local DAR.... Such an insult had been visited upon Roland Hayes thirteen years ago—denial of the same Constitution Hall which was denied Miss Anderson—and Washington Negroes had responded with some spirit. But the spirit they showed this year was beyond the recollection of the oldest old-timer. They flooded the newspaper with letters, bitterly and skillfully written. They got their friends from outside to shower Congressmen with petitions....

Eleanor Roosevelt awarding the Spingarn medal to Marian Anderson.

They demanded a picket line against the DAR national Convention.... Sixty-five Negro organizations, of every description and social status, joined thirty-two white and mixed ones in one of the most brilliant displays of mass action this nation has seen. The national press put the credit for the furor upon Mrs. Roosevelt and Secretary Ickes; but it was the Marian Anderson Citizens Committee which first notified Mrs. Roosevelt and which got her first response. It was the same Committee which asked for an expression from Secretary Ickes nearly two months before he granted Lincoln Memorial. The 600 newspaper clippings from Singapore to London would never have been possible if the Marian Anderson Citizens Committee had not set off the explosion....

The 75,000 who heard Miss Anderson Easter Sunday were a tribute to fighting Negroes in the District of Columbia as much as to democracy and the preservation of art.

Lovell goes on to describe how the "Marian Anderson Struggle" inspired blacks and nonblacks to challenge racist institutions and practices in Washington, concluding that "the fighting on all fronts is going to go on!"

Anderson was born in Philadelphia, on February 27, 1897, to John and Anna Anderson. Her father sold ice and coal, and her mother was a former teacher, who after Marian was born did laundry to supplement the family's income.

Anderson's interest in singing developed early because of the talents displayed by her mother and father in the home and at church. She joined the junior choir of the Union Baptist Church in Philadelphia, where her father was an officer. It became apparent by the time she was eight that she had an exceptional voice.

Anderson's talent for music was developed and nurtured while attending elementary and secondary schools in South Philadelphia. During her high school days, she sang with the all-black Philadelphia Choral Society, performing often in schools and churches throughout the Philadelphia area. She graduated from South Philadelphia High School for Girls in 1921.

After high school, Anderson sought formal training to develop her voice and applied to an all-white music school in Philadelphia, where she was rejected because she was black. With the encouragement and support of her mother, church, and friends, she continued to study with world-famous voice teacher Giuseppe Boghetti, with whom she had first taken lessons in her senior year in high school. He remained her teacher and adviser until his death.

After an artistic and financially unsuccessful concert at Town Hall in New York City in 1924, Anderson under the guidance of Boghetti and others began to study with European masters to perfect her contralto voice.

Anderson gave many successful concerts and performances in America and throughout the world before the DAR incident at Constitution Hall in 1939. She once commented poignantly on what the DAR incident and her subsequent performance at the Lincoln Memorial meant to blacks and America: "I could see that my significance as an individual was small in this affair. I had become whether I liked it or not, a symbol representing my people. I had to appear."

In September, nearly four months after the landmark *Brown* v. *Board of Education* decision outlawing segregated schools, Anderson again used her art to fight for equal rights; she became the first black to join the Metropolitan Opera in New York. She successfully challenged "outmoded theories of racial or group inferiority" by pioneering the opening of the Metropolitan Opera to a new generation of black divas, like Leontyne Price, who made her debut with the Metropolitan Opera in January 1961.

Marian Anderson died in Portland, Oregon on April 8, 1993, nearly fifty-four years to the day of her 1939 Easter concert at the Lincoln Memorial.

95

Colin Powell

1937–

And when the next war comes, I want to know whose war and why. . . . And what about a voice in who's running this country and why—before I even think about crossing the water and fighting again? Who said I want to go to war? If I do, it ain't the same war the President wants to go to. No, sir, I been hanging on a rope in Alabama too long.

LANGSTON HUGHES

Surely, LANGSTON HUGHES [34] could not have imagined when he spoke the above words in 1934, criticizing the mistreatment of black Americans by white racists in war and peace, that nearly a half-century later an African-American, Colin Powell, as chairman of the Joint Chiefs of Staff, would represent "a voice in who's running this country" and would have emerged as the most influential military adviser to a President in whose war (Operation Desert Storm) a disproportionate number of African-Americans would serve.

Powell's ranking here is owed to his service as chairman of the Joint Chief of Staff and as national security adviser to the president. As one of the most influential policy makers in the world, he has been a most potent symbol of the black struggle *to be*. Indisputably, as the head of the Pentagon and the chief military adviser to the President of the United States, Powell shapes and influences policies that affect blacks and nonblacks on military and nonmilitary matters, like the defense budget, communication between the president and the military (in which a disproportionate number are African-American), and action plans for the mightiest military force in the history of the world.

Powell's significance as a symbol of the black struggle *to be* is better accepted if he is understood as part of a post-*Brown v. Board of Education* generation of black achievers, like RON BROWN [96] and CLARENCE THOMAS [97], who in becoming *whatever they wanted to be* as Americans represent a greater participation of African-Americans in American life. To many, their successes and triumphs have eradicated the American lie: a declaration of the equal rights of all people and the simultaneous denial of those rights to those of African descent. Arguably, Powell's success and that of others cited in this book evince "progress" in the black struggle *to be whatever* each black American chooses, whether nationalist or integrationist, Democrat or Republican, Baptist or Muslim, liberal or conservative, or any combination of these and other ideologies and lifestyles. However, regardless of these successes and triumphs, the masses of African-Americans are still "hanging on a rope in Alabama," disproportionately unemployed, impoverished, incarcerated, underpaid, and segregated in housing, employment, and education when compared to the nonblack majority of Americans in the 1990s.

Powell himself recognized these contradictions and the inveterate American lie when a "hanging rope in Alabama" took the lives of four black girls in a bombing of a Baptist Church in Birmingham, Alabama in

September 1963, during Dr. Martin Luther King, Jr.'s Birmingham civil rights campaign: "My family lived in Birmingham that terrible summer of 1963. My wife and infant son were living with her parents. I wasn't there. I was a young infantry captain in Vietnam. When I returned that Christmas, I was hit full force with what had happened in my absence. I was stunned, disheartened and angry. While I had been fighting in Vietnam alongside brave soldiers trying to preserve their freedom, in my own land a long-simmering conflict had turned into an open fight in our streets and cities—a fight that had to be won."

Colin Luther Powell was born on April 5, 1937, in Harlem, New York, to Luther Theophilus and Maud Ariel Powell, nearly two months before JOE LOUIS [71] won the heavyweight boxing title from James Braddock. Both his parents were born in Jamaica, and immigrated to the United States before he was born. His father was a shipping clerk in the New York garment district, and his mother worked as a seamstress.

Powell's family moved to a multiethnic section of the South Bronx when he was young. There he attended elementary and secondary schools, graduating from Morris High School in 1954. He attended City College of New York, graduating in 1958 with a B.S. in geology. While at City College, he joined the Reserve Officers Training Corps and received a commission as a second lieutenant upon graduation. His basic training was at Fort Benning, Georgia, where he was exposed to noxious forms of the American lie.

In 1963, he married Vivian Johnson, the daughter of a high school principal in Birmingham, Alabama. Shortly thereafter, he went to South Vietnam as a military adviser. In 1968–69, Powell served in Vietnam as a battalion executive officer and division operations officer. Upon his return to the states after two tours of duty, he entered George Washington University, graduating with an MBA in 1971. During that year he was also awarded a White House Fellowship, which exposed him to the body politic of Washington.

After a series of high-level and influential positions in and out of the military between 1972 and 1978, Powell served from 1979 to 1981 in the Carter administration as executive assistant to the secretary of energy and as senior military assistant to the deputy secretary of defense (1983–1986). Later, he was commanding general of the Fifth Corps in Frankfurt, Germany, then accepted the position of ranking assistant to the national security adviser of the National Security Council (NSC), Frank Carlucci. When Carlucci left the NSC to become secretary of defense, Powell was named national security adviser, the most important advisory position in the United States on matters affecting national security, such as the environment, trade and investment, the defense budget, and education.

In 1989, Powell reached the pinnacle of his profession when President George Bush named him chairman of the Joint Chiefs of Staff, the most powerful military position in the world. A palpable expression of Powell's authority and ability as chairman of the Joint Chiefs can be seen in his conduct of military actions involving an alliance of global powers in forcing the Iraqi military from Kuwait after the invasion in August 1990. Powell emerged as the key adviser to President Bush and as the architect of Operation Desert Shield, which was designed to move American and international forces and materials into the Middle East to execute the most intricate and high-tech military campaign in history: Operation Desert Storm. In March 1991, after less than a month of concerted action, the global alliance of forces had defeated the Iraqis, one of the largest military machines in the world.

In 1991, President Bush reappointed Powell chairman of the Joint Chiefs of Staff, continuing his role as "a voice in who's running this country" and as a symbol of the struggle of African-Americans *to be*. Powell has said on this point, "I am . . . mindful that the struggle is not over . . . [it will not be] until every American is able to find his or her own place in our society, limited only by his or her own ability and his or her own dream."

96

August Wilson

1945–

What I think is happening is that more of the young people
are self-generated... they don't bring baggage, they don't
bring history, they just bring an appetite—a raw appetite for
sensation. That can give you energy and color and rhythm and
a whole lot of exciting things. What it cannot give you is
depth, continuity and an understanding of the human
condition, which is what art should also be about... they're
highly unfortunate in that they have no sense of history.

OSSIE DAVIS

Unlike the work of the young, modern black media artists described above by OSSIE DAVIS [91] as having "no sense of history," August Wilson's plays have come to symbolize the rich, proud history of peoples of African descent who, through their struggle *to be*, represent the "depth, continuity, and understanding of the human condition"—the essence of art.

Wilson's "bringing the baggage" of the rich and beautiful history of peoples of African descent into all of his plays has illuminated the "who" of African Americans and the "where" of their having been in America. Wilson has challenged black Americans to use his works to:

> . . . re-examine their time spent here to see the choices that were made as a people. I'm not certain the right choices have always been made. That's part of my interest in history—to say "Let's look at this again and see where we've come from and how we've gotten where we are now." I think if you know that, it helps determine how to proceed with the future.

Using metaphors and images rooted in the blues, (the fountainhead that was recognized by DUKE ELLINGTON [67] as the "African pulse"), Wilson has sought to illustrate the continuous struggle of Africans in the American diaspora for full citizenship in a society that denies them equality because of their African ancestry.

Wilson has stated more pointedly and instructively that the blues:

> . . . is at the bedrock of everything I do, the foundation on which all my plays are based. The ideas and attitudes of the characters are ideas and attitudes that I discovered in the blues. Because I began to look at the blues as a cultural response of black Americans to the world that they found themselves in. It contains an entire system of philosophical thought that, in fact, teaches you how to live your life. Coming from the culture, which is part of an oral tradition, and the elements of the culture passed along orally, a lot of this is done in the blues. The music provides you with an emotional reference to the information, which is contained in the song.

Six of Wilson's plays: *Ma Rainey's Black Bottom* (1984), *Fences* (1985), *Joe Turner's Come and Gone* (1986), *The Piano Lesson* (1987), *Two Trains Running* (1990), and *Seven Guitars* (1995), have in part accomplished his goal of writing about the "depth, continuity, and understanding" of the African-American experience in each decade of the twentieth century.

With the chronology of *Joe Turner's Come and Gone*, set in a boarding house in Pittsburgh in 1911, to *Two Trains Running*, set in a Pittsburgh restaurant in 1969, Wilson says he was "...trying to focus on what I felt were the most important issues confronting black Americans for that decade, so ultimately they could stand as a record of black experience over the past hundred years presented in the form of dramatic literature....Collectively, they can read, certainly not as a total history, but as some historical moments."

Wilson has said that the cumulative effect of his work is to:

> ..."Place" the tradition of black American culture, to demonstrate its ability to sustain us. We have a ground that is specific, that is peculiarly ours, that we can stand on, which gives us a world view, to look at the world and to comment on it. I'm just trying to place the world of that culture on stage and to demonstrate its existence and maybe also indicate some direction toward which we as a people might possibly move.

The influence of Wilson's plays in shaping a consciousness and understanding among both black and non-black Americans of African-American history and culture is evinced by his being awarded Pulitzer Prizes for drama for *Fences* (1987) and *The Piano Lesson* (1990). He is only the seventh playwright to win at least two, and the only African American to ever do so.

Born Frederick August Kittel in a predominantly poor, black neighborhood in Pittsburgh in 1945, by the time August was in a mostly white high school in 1961 he had had many real-life experiences with racism directed at African Americans. He dropped out of the ninth grade at Gladstone High School when his black teacher accused him of plagiarizing a paper on Napoleon. By the late 1960s August would adopt his mother Daisy Wilson's last name and start forming black cultural consciousness–raising collaborations like the Black Horizons Theatre in Pittsburgh's Black Hill District, with his friend and teacher Rob Penny.

August Wilson has emerged as one of the most influential and controversial black culturalists in the tradition of W. E. B. DU BOIS's [4] Krigwa Players' Little Negro Theatre in Harlem, which encouraged black community theatre to be:

1. *About Us*. That is, they must have plots that reveal Negro life as it is. 2. *By Us*. That is, they must be written by Negro authors who understand from birth and continued association just what it means to be a Negro today. 3. *For Us*. That is, the Negro theatre must cater primarily to Negro audiences and be supported by their entertainment and approval. 4. *Near Us*. The theatre must be in a neighborhood near the mass of Negro people.

Wilson has added to this call for a separate black theatre by saying, "We need a theatre to recount a positive image of ourselves. We can no longer permit our talents to wither and die."

97

Clarence Thomas

1948–

As a child, I could not dare dream that I would ever see the Supreme Court, not to mention be nominated to it. In my view, only in America could this have been possible.

CLARENCE THOMAS

On July 1, 1991, President George Bush nominated a forty-three-old black man, Clarence Thomas—an ideological opposite of THURGOOD MARSHALL [22]—to succeed Marshall and become the one hundred and sixth justice (the second American of African descent) to sit on the United States Supreme Court. The nomination gave substance to Thomas's words that "only in America could this have been possible." In October 1991, after a series of wrenching Senate confirmation hearings in which Thomas was accused by a black law professor, Anita Hill, of sexual harassment and was also portrayed by his foes as a black reactionary who would turn back the clock on the progress made by African-Americans in their ongoing struggle for full rights and freedoms, he was confirmed by a 52–48 Senate vote.

Thomas's listing and ranking here is due to the fact that as a Supreme Court justice he will play a dominant role, possibly for as long as the next forty years, in interpreting laws and the Constitution on crucial matters that affect all Americans, such as affirmative action, racial quotas, abortion, prisoners' rights, desegregation, privacy, and disparities in public spending in education. Thomas's interpretations on these matters will determine whether the American lie—a declaration of equal rights for all Americans and the simultaneous denial of those rights to people of African descent—will be eradicated or strengthened.

Thomas is also included here because he represents the diversity of ideology, tactics, and strategies among African-Americans in their quest *to be*. Arguably, not since the late 1960s, when the ideology and tactics of BLACK POWER [99] as symbolized by Stokely Carmichael and others galvanized blacks, has anyone stirred up black and nonblack America as to what African-Americans want and how they are going to go about getting it, than Clarence Thomas. Thomas's views on the need for black self-help and nongovernmental solutions mirror in many respects those in the "boot straps" approach of BOOKER T. WASHINGTON [3]. For example, Thomas has said, "I emphasize black self-help, as opposed to racial quotas and other race-conscious legal devices that only further and deepen the original problem"; this strategy of self-help was used by many of the black 100 to overcome nearly three centuries of racism and discrimination in a color-conscious America.

Thomas's being named by a conservative Republican president to the court "proves" again, as it did for COLIN POWELL [95], that a few blacks in a post-*Brown v. Board of Education* era can be *whatever they choose to be*, i.e., Democrat or Republican, conservative or liberal, black nationalist or integrationist. However, this fact does not negate, as Clarence Thomas has done in words and actions, the fact that the masses of blacks are still disproportionately unemployed, impoverished, incarcerated, poorly educated, and economically and politically powerless when compared to a nonblack majority of Americans in the 1990s.

Thomas has portrayed himself as a latter-day, black Horatio Alger, refuting by his "successes" and his "only in America" rhetoric that the masses of blacks continue to represent KENNETH B. CLARK's [76] view of them as symbolizing the American "nuclear irony." Thomas has said on this point: "I was raised to survive under the totalitarianism of segregation, not only without the active assistance of government but with its active opposition. . . . We were raised to survive in spite of the dark oppressive cloud of governmentally sanctioned bigotry. Self-sufficiency and spiritual and emotional security were our tools to carve out and secure freedom."

Regardless of what one thinks of Thomas's views and tactics as a so-called black conservative, the fact remains that he sits on the United States Supreme Court and has become, like Booker T. Washington and others, a potent symbol of the diversity and differences that exist among African-Americans in their quest *to be*. Columnist Haynes Johnson has insightfully summarized the effects of Thomas's confirmation hearings on destroying stereotypes about a post-*Brown* v. *Board of Education* generation of black achievers in their struggle *to be*:

> To an extraordinary degree, the televised confirmation hearings were a welcome destroyer of stereotypes, especially black stereotypes. The lingering white stereotypes—or prejudice—about blacks being predictable members of an ideological, political monolith who march in lockstep conformity was shattered forever by the sight of so many tough, savvy and bright young black professionals, men and women, stating strongly opposing conservative and liberal positions memorably and effectively.

Clarence Thomas was born on June 23, 1948, in Pin Point, Georgia, to M. C. and Leola Thomas. His father abandoned the family when Clarence was an infant. When he was seven years old, he and his older brother were sent to live with his grandfather, Myers Anderson, in Savannah, Georgia. He attended an all-black Catholic elementary school, St. Benedict's, and served as an altar boy in its parent church. He and another boy were the first blacks to attend the all-white Catholic boarding school, St. John Vianney Minor Seminary, from which he graduated in 1967.

After graduating from high school, Thomas attended Immaculate Conception Seminary in Missouri, hoping to become a priest; but he dropped out after eight months because of racist attitudes and actions among fellow seminarians. After working at odd jobs, he enrolled in Holy Cross College in Massachusetts and after graduating was accepted at Yale Law School through an affirmative action program designed to include more blacks and other nonwhite groups.

After Yale, he worked for the state of Missouri for about three years, leaving for employment in the private sector, until he joined the staff of U.S. Senator John Danforth of Missouri in 1979. In 1981, after the election of Ronald Reagan, Thomas joined the Department of Education as an assistant secretary of civil rights. In 1982, President Reagan appointed him to the Equal Employment Opportunity Commission (EEOC), which oversees compliance with federal policies and laws against discrimination in the private sector. It was while at the EEOC (1982–1990) that Thomas built his reputation as a black conservative and as an opponent of governmental intrusions into civil rights matters. Reporter Juan Williams has observed that Thomas's views on these matters explain in large part the strong antipathy toward him by some black and nonblack groups and women:

> Above all—and perhaps this is the main reason why he is regarded with such disdain by so many blacks, and so many Hispanics and women as well—Thomas refuses to see civil rights as a matter of corporate struggle and *group equality.* Are blacks, Hispanics, and women, as groups, victims of discrimination on the job, as evidenced by group statistics on hiring, promotion, and pay? Thomas is not very much interested in this question. What about an *individual* who claims discrimination? Here, and here alone, a black or a woman might find Thomas to be a friend in court.

In 1990, Thomas was nominated by President George Bush and confirmed by the Senate to the United States Circuit Court of Appeals for the District of Columbia, one of the most influential courts in the country. In July of 1991, he was nominated by Bush to the United States Supreme Court.

In an open letter to Clarence Thomas on November 29, 1991, civil rights activist and chief judge emeritus of the United States Court of Appeals for the Third Circuit, A. Leon Higginbotham, Jr., felt compelled to remind Thomas of the black struggle *to be* and of Thomas's moral obligation as a justice to produce decisions that will help the masses of blacks and nonblacks and women who still suffer the effects of racism and sexism in American life:

> You... must try to remember that the fundamental problems of the disadvantaged, women, minorities, and the powerless have not been solved simply because you have "moved on up" from Pin Point, Georgia, to the Supreme Court....
>
> I have written to tell you that your life today, however, should be not far removed from the visions and struggle of Frederick Douglass, Sojourner Truth, Harriet Tubman, Charles Hamilton Houston, A. Philip Randolph, Mary McLeod Bethune, W. E. B. Du Bois, Roy Wilkins, Whitney Young, Martin Luther King, Judge William Henry Hastie, Justices Thurgood Marshall, Earl Warren, and William Brennan, as well as the thousands of others who dedicated much of their lives to create the America that made your opportunities possible. I hope you have the strength of character to exemplify those values so that the sacrifices of all these men and women will not have been in vain.

The reality is that after his first six months on the Supreme Court, Thomas, by siding with other conservatives on the Court on issues affecting abortion rights to criminal rights to desegregation laws to voting, appears to be "far removed from the vision and struggle" of the vast majority of those who make up this book and millions of others whose sacrifices have made it possible for Americans of African descent *to be*, including Clarence Thomas to succeed as a justice of the United States Supreme Court.

98

Arthur Ashe

1943–1993

...While blood was running freely in the streets of
Birmingham, Memphis and Biloxi, I was playing tennis....

...A long time ago, I made peace with the state of Virginia
and the South.... but segregation had achieved by that time
what it was intended to achieve: It left me a marked man,
forever aware of a shadow of contempt that lays across my
identity and my sense of self-esteem.... Racism ultimately
created the state in which defensiveness and hypocrisy are our
almost instinctive responses, and innocence and generosity are
invitations to trouble.

ARTHUR ASHE

Like the other mega symbols of athletic achievement in *The Black 100*—JACKIE ROBINSON [42], MUHAMMAD ALI [54], JESSE OWENS [56], JACK JOHNSON [63], JOE LOUIS [71], and HANK AARON [87]—Arthur Ashe, while "playing tennis" during the turbulent civil rights battles of the 1960s and the 1970s, used his celebrity in a color-conscious and racist society to counterattack the humiliating effects of being a "marked man" because he was black; at the same time, he often embraced controversial ideologies and tactics of "innocence and generosity" to make "trouble" in a society that continued to deny those of African descent full rights and freedoms.

Ashe's listing and ranking here acknowledge his singular impact as an athlete and activist in forcing both black and nonblack Americans during the 1960s through the early 1990s to consider what were the most effective ideologies, tactics, and agendas for liberating blacks and nonblacks in America and throughout the world from racism and discrimination. Ashe was often viewed superficially as too conservative or moderate by many blacks and nonblacks as the debate and struggle ensued over the choice of ideological and tactical weapons during this era.

Ashe, with poignancy, has expressed his feelings of regret and shame for not having been more involved in the direct, nonviolent tactics of this period:

> There were times, in fact, when I felt a burning sense of shame that I was not with other blacks—and whites—standing up to the fire hoses and the police dogs, the truncheons, bullets and bombs that cut down such martyrs as Chaney, Schwerner and Goodman, Viola Liuzzo, Martin Luther King, Jr., Medgar Evers and the little girls in that bombed church in Birmingham, Ala. As my fame increased, so did my anguish. I knew that many blacks were proud of my accomplishments on the tennis court. But I also knew that many others, especially many of my own age or younger, did not bother to hide their indifference to me and my trophies or even their disdain and contempt for me.

For more discussion on this era of the civil rights struggle, see REV. DR. MARTIN LUTHER KING, JR. [1], ROY WILKINS [33], LORRAINE HANSBERRY [77], and BLACK POWER [99].

By utilizing his accomplishments on the tennis court as the first prominent black male player, Ashe nonetheless came to symbolize the black athlete achiever as an advocate for freedom and equality *for all*, in America and throughout the world, especially as he brought attention to the evils of apartheid in South Africa, discrimination against Haitians by the United States government during the Bush administration (see KATHERINE DUNHAM [84]), and the lack of equal education opportunities for black athletes. In this regard, Ashe was much like athlete/activist/scholar/culturalist PAUL ROBESON [24].

Although not an ideological compatriot of CLARENCE THOMAS [97], Ashe also came to symbolize the diversity and differences that exist among African-Americans in their quest *to be whatever they choose to be*, i.e., Democrat or Republican, conservative or liberal, black nationalist or integrationist, radical or moderate, and so on. Like other post–*Brown v. Board of Education* achievers in *The Black 100*—Thomas, COLIN POWELL [95], OPRAH WINFREY [89], MARIAN WRIGHT EDELMAN [93], and AUGUST WILSON [96]—Ashe was a "marked" person because he was black. The accomplishments of these individuals do not negate the continuous effects of racism and discrimination in America in the 1990s, where blacks are still disproportionately unemployed, impoverished, incarcerated, poorly educated, and economically and politically powerless when compared to a nonblack majority.

Arthur Robert Ashe, Jr., was born July 10, 1943, to Mattie (Cunningham) and Arthur Robert Ashe, Sr., in Richmond, Virginia, a state that represented the cradle of slavery and racism in antebellum and post–Reconstruction America; and a state that personified the American lie: a declaration of the equal rights of all men (framed by a Virginian, Thomas Jefferson) and the simultaneous denial of those rights to people of African descent. (The reader is reminded that Virginia was the British colony in which blacks began their quest *to be* in English-speaking North America, in Jamestown in 1619, when "twenty and odd Negroes" were sold as indentured servants.)

Ashe's great-grandparents were slaves, and one of his paternal great-grandmothers was brought from West Africa to Yorktown, Virginia, by the slave ship *Doddington* in 1735, four years after the birth of BENJAMIN BANNEKER [16]. His mother died when he was six years old. Ashe attended segregated elementary and secondary schools in Richmond.

At the age of seven Ashe began playing tennis, a game which was introduced in the United States in about 1873, the same year P. B. S. PINCHBACK [20] was elected to the U.S. Senate. Exhibiting exceptional tennis skills early, Ashe honed his game under the tutelage of Dr.

Walter Johnson, a medical doctor from Lynchburg, Virginia, who had coached many up-and-coming black players, including Althea Gibson, the first black woman to win a major tennis championship, Wimbledon, in 1957 and 1958.

In 1960 and 1961, Ashe won the national junior indoor singles title, catapulting him into the inner circle of the world of amateur tennis dominated by white males. During his senior year of high school, Ashe was invited by the highly respected tennis coach Richard Hudlin of St. Louis, Missouri, to further develop his tennis skills under Hudlin's guidance. Ashe accepted and moved to St. Louis, where he finished secondary school at Sumner High School, the alma mater of DICK GREGORY [88].

After high school, Ashe accepted a tennis scholarship to the University of California at Los Angeles. While at UCLA he earned a spot on the U.S. Davis Cup team, won the U.S. Men's Hard Court Championship, and led UCLA to the National Collegiate Athletic Association (NCAA) national championship. Ashe graduated from UCLA in 1966 with a bachelor's degree in business administration.

Ashe then joined the U.S. Army as a second lieutenant in the Adjutant General's Corps. During his time in the service, he continued to play tennis, winning the U.S. Men's Clay Courts title in 1967, the U.S. Men's Singles title in 1968, and, that same year, he won the first U.S. Open title, becoming the number-one ranked player by the U.S. Lawn Tennis Association (USLTA). Thus, Ashe became the first black male to dominate white male bastions of tennis, debunking—much as Hank Aaron would do nearly six years later—another significant symbol of white male athletic prowess: "tennis champion," a symbol often used by white racists and elitists not only to justify the exclusion of blacks from the world of tennis but also from the benefits and freedoms of American life.

Sensitized by the black struggle and by black and nonblack ideologues and protesters during the 1950s and 1960s, Ashe participated in a demonstration against apartheid in South Africa before winning the U.S. Open. In 1969, he applied for a visa to play in the first South African Open and was denied it by the South African government. It was also during 1969 that Ashe turned professional and, through 1980, won numerous tennis titles, including Wimbledon and the World Championship of Tennis in 1975, earning him the number-one ranking in the world and placing him at the pinnacle of a sport predicated on the exclusion of blacks and the poor. (See MUHAMMAD ALI [54], for a discussion on how Ali's persona and views influenced the thoughts and actions of this period.)

In 1979, Ashe had to curtail his competitive tennis when he underwent quadruple bypass heart surgery. In 1980, he officially retired from competitive tennis; that same year, he was named captain of the U.S. Davis Cup team, which won titles under him in 1981 and 1982. In 1985, Ashe became the first black male named to the International Tennis Hall of Fame.

Other measures of Ashe's impact on the struggle of African-Americans *to be* were his pioneering efforts on behalf of black athletes whom he had come to symbolize and his landmark, three-volume book *A Hard Road to Glory* (1988), which documented for the first time the history and contributions of black athletes to American life. Ashe also supported Proposition 48, which sought to increase the academic requirements for all athletes at institutions involved in NCAA–sanctioned sports. Ashe believed that these requirements would give black athletes higher academic goals and begin to hold these institutions accountable for their success or failure. Ashe formed the African-American Athletic Association to facilitate these goals while "at the same time, without destroying kids dreams or taking away that motivating factor [athletics], . . . to make it clear that many of them won't make it in athletics, and get them to focus on other things."

Arthur Robert Ashe, Jr., died on February 6, 1993, within ten months of having announced that he had AIDS, which he contracted from tainted blood during a transfusion for his second bypass operation in 1983. During this ten-month period, Ashe founded the Arthur Ashe Foundation for the Defeat of AIDS, raising millions of dollars and increasing awareness about this equal opportunity killer of humankind, and finished a memoir, *Days of Grace*, forty-eight hours before his death.

One last measure of Ashe's impact was evinced by the thousands of Americans and persons from around the world who attended a memorial service in Richmond, Virginia, on February 17, 1993, after his body had lain in state in the executive mansion. Among those in attendance was Douglas Wilder, the first black governor of Virginia. Maybe, just maybe, "Virginia and the South" had made peace with Arthur Ashe and the people for and with whom he struggled.

99

Eldridge Cleaver   **H. "Rap" Brown**

Black Power

There are two Americas, black and white, and nothing has more
clearly revealed the divisions between them than the debate
currently raging around the slogan of "Black Power." Despite—
or perhaps because of—the fact that this slogan lacks any clear
definition, it has succeeded in galvanizing emotions on all
sides.... Black Power has touched off a major debate—the most
bitter the community has experienced since the days of Booker
T. Washington, and W. E. B. Du Bois, and one which threatens
to ravage the entire civil rights movement.

BAYARD RUSTIN

Stokely Carmichael addressing college students.

This is the only list in *The Black 100* that is not a person, but represents the immemorial spirit, ideology, and assertion of blacks in their struggle *to be*. The ranking of Black Power here is intended to show what Americans of African descent have always known, ever since their contacts with English-speaking colonists in Jamestown, Virginia in 1619, when "twenty and odd Negroes" were sold as indentured servants: that "there are two Americas, black and white."

Stokely Carmichael (who later changed his name to Kwame Ture) in the late sixties came to symbolize the advocacy of Black Power, which according to BAYARD RUSTIN [59] succeeded "in galvanizing emotions on all sides," among blacks and nonblacks, sparking debate characterized as "the most bitter the [black] community has ever experienced since the days of Booker T. Washington and W. E. B. Du Bois, and one which threatens to ravage the entire civil rights movement."

With his call for Black Power at the end of his speech in May 1966 at a demonstration in Jackson, Mississippi, Carmichael set in motion among blacks, during the turbulent 1960s and 1970s, a debate as to what were the most effective ideologies, tactics, and agendas for liberating blacks in America and throughout the world, from racism and discrimination. Among those leaders and organizations involved in this debate as to the efficacy and soundness of Black Power to the ongoing struggle of blacks *to be* were: Carmichael, James Forman, H. "Rap" Brown, and John Lewis of the Student Nonviolent Coordinating Committee (SNCC); Ron Karenga of US; James Farmer and Floyd McKissick of the Congress of Racial Equality (CORE); Huey Newton, Bobby Seale, and Eldridge Cleaver of the Black Panther Party for Self-Defense; Arthur Ashe, athlete and activist; Roy Wilkins of the National Association for the Advancement of Colored People (NAACP); Dr. Martin Luther King, Jr., of the Southern Christian Leadership Conference (SCLC); and Whitney Young of the National Urban League (NUL). These and tens of thousands of other blacks were debating what African-Americans had been fighting for over nearly 350 years: how best to empower those Americans of African descent—both psychologically and non-psychologically—to control their own destiny in a struggle *to be*.

An in-depth discussion of what Black Power means is beyond the scope of this book. What's important to understand about Black Power—with all of its different meanings and implied strategies as popularized in the 1960s by Carmichael and others—is that it represented a continuation of an ongoing dialogue among African-Americans in their choice of those strategies and tactics which would best destroy the "two Americas, black and white," separate and unequal, and the American lie: a declaration of the equal rights of all people and the simultaneous denial of those rights to those of African descent.

Black Power as a concept and tactic is as old as the debate among slaves like Denmark Vesey, Gabriel Prosser, and NAT TURNER [10], to revolt or not to revolt; as old as conflicts among black abolitionists like JAMES FORTEN [11], FREDERICK DOUGLASS [2], HENRY H. GARNET [14], HARRIET TUBMAN [12], MARTIN R. DELANY [13], and DAVID WALKER [9], whether to assimilate or to emigrate; as old as the debate over the need for a "white God" versus a "black God"; as old as the debate whether to separate or to integrate; as old as the conflicts over the efficacy of political power without economic power; as recent as the debate over "Black Power" versus nonviolent tactics and strategies; and as recent as black self-help, nongovernmental intrusion versus quotas and affirmative action. In other words, Black Power personifies the total quest of all those included in *The Black 100*, along with millions of others, over the history of blacks in America.

Black Power represents a struggle within the continuum of struggle of blacks *to be;* and as long as one American of African descent is not free *to be* whatever his or her talents, aspirations and dreams should permit him or her *to be,* then there will be a need for Black Power. It is precisely this continued denial of equal and full participation of the masses of blacks in America that, like during the eighties and nineties in which the two Americas, black and white, have become even more polarized and ghettoized, make the words spoken by KENNETH CLARK [76] nearly twenty-five years ago about the reality of Black Power still relevant:

> "Black Power" is a reality in the Negro ghettos of America, increasing in emotional intensity, if not in rational clarity. And we, if we are to be realistic, cannot afford to pretend that it does not exist. Even in its most irrational and illusory formulations ... "Black Power" is a powerful political reality, which cannot be ignored by realistic Negroes or white political officials.

100

Rosa Parks

1913–

God hath chosen the weak things of the world to confound the things which are mighty.

I CORINTHIANS 1:27

But when the fullness of time was come God sent forth. . . .

GALATIANS 4:4

The above two verses from the Bible appear elsewhere in this book: I Corinthians 1:27 was used to introduce HARRIET TUBMAN [12] as a symbol of the indomitable spirit of blacks in their quest *to be* against the pernicious institution of slavery; and Galatians 4:4 was used to introduce DR. MARTIN LUTHER KING, JR. [1] as the quintessential leader of the African-American unending quest for full economic, political, and social equality in America.

These verses now serve to introduce Rosa Parks, who like her spiritual soulmates HARRIET TUBMAN [12], SOJOURNER TRUTH [15], FANNIE LOU HAMER [75], and millions of other black women—who by their humble stations in life represented "the weak things of the world"—symbolize the "common black woman" as the spine of the ongoing black struggle for freedom and equality.

By refusing to give up her seat on a bus to a white man on December 1, 1955, in Montgomery, Alabama, Rosa Parks also came to represent the "fullness of time" on the continuum of the black struggle, "midwifing" a civil rights revolution against racism and discrimination led by Dr. King and others during the 1950s and 1960s. Parks's listing and ranking here acknowledge her as the spark that ignited blacks in their struggle over nearly four centuries in America. Parks's listing also shows the interrelatedness of all those in this book to the ongoing fight to make, in the words of A. Philip Randolph, "America a moral and spiritual arsenal of democracy."

Parks was born Rosa Louise McCauley on February 4, 1913, in Tuskegee, Alabama, to James and Leona McCauley, only a month before the death of Harriet Tubman. Her parents separated when she was two years old, and her mother moved the family to Pine Level, Alabama, to live with Parks's maternal grandparents. Her mother taught school and even taught her in some of her early elementary grades.

When Parks was eleven, her mother sent her to live with an aunt in Montgomery, where Rosa attended the Montgomery Industrial School for Girls, established and operated by Northern white women. Parks then entered Booker T. Washington High School in Montgomery but dropped out to attend to her mother's failing health. She briefly enrolled at Alabama State Teachers College. In 1932 she married Raymond Parks, a barber, in Montgomery.

During her marriage, Parks worked at assorted jobs, including that of a seamstress and a domestic. In the early forties, she became a member of the Montgomery Chapter of the NAACP and served as its secretary from 1943 to 1956. She also was involved in the early fifties with voter registration drives through her association with the Montgomery Voters League.

It was on a Thursday evening, December 1, 1955, while riding a bus home from work as a seamstress in a downtown department store that Rosa Parks refused to give up her seat to a white man. The giving up of seats was dictated by Jim Crow laws and customs that required blacks to do so whenever the "white" seats on the bus were filled. Blacks were forced to stand and give their seats in the "black section" to whites. Parks refused the white bus driver's "request" to give up her seat, even after four other blacks had obeyed. She was arrested and jailed after the driver called the police to enforce these seating laws that were designed to rob blacks of their dignity and essence as human beings.

Rosa Parks, with Dr. Martin Luther King, at a dinner in her honor during Southern Christian Leadership Conference, 1965.

After spending a few hours in jail, Parks was released on a bond paid by local civil rights leaders and given a trial date of December 5, 1955, to defend herself against these seating laws. By December 5, local black leaders had formed the Montgomery Improvement Association, with Dr. Martin Luther King, Jr., as president, to boycott the segregated busing system and other segregated public facilities in Montgomery. After 381 days, the boycott brought about the abolition of segregated busing and other segregated public facilities. Success launched King and a local civil-rights movement into a national one, as described by Lerone Bennett:

> King transformed a spontaneous local protest into a national passive resistance movement with a method and ideology. "Love your enemies," he said, and tens of thousands of blacks straightened their backs and sustained a year-long bus boycott which was, as King pointed out, "one of the greatest [movements] in the history of the nation." The movement brought together laborers, professionals and students. More importantly perhaps, it fired the imagination of blacks all over America....
>
> Skillfully utilizing the resources of television and mass journalism, King made Montgomery an international way station....

On December 20, 1956, the United States Supreme Court upheld a lower court ruling that Montgomery buses had to desegregate. This ruling represented the total vindication of a humble, "common" black woman, who, because she was in tune with the struggle of her people *to be*, "confound[ed] the things which were mighty" and ushered in the modern civil rights era.

SELECT BIBLIOGRAPHY

In addition to the numerous books and articles cited in the text, the following works have been selected to complement the reader's understandings and insights into *The Black 100*.

Aaron, Hank, with Lonnie Wheeler. *I Had a Hammer.* New York, 1991.

Aptheker, Herbert, ed. *A Documentary History of the Negro People in the United States*, 7 vols. New York, 1951–1994.

_____. *Afro-American History, the Modern Era.* New York, 1971.

Ashe, Arthur. *Days of Grace.* New York, 1993.

_____. *Hard Road to Glory*, 3 vols. New York, 1988.

Baker, Donald P. *Wilder: Hold Fast to Dreams.* Washington, D.C., 1989.

Bell, Derrick. *Faces at the Bottom of the Well.* New York, 1992.

Ben-Jochannan, Yosef. *Africa: Mother of Western Civilization.* Baltimore, 1988.

Bernard, Jacqueline. *Journey Toward Freedom: The Story of Sojourner Truth.* New York, 1967.

Berry, Faith. *Langston Hughes: Before and Beyond Harlem.* New York, 1992.

Bogle, Donald. *Toms, Coons, Mulattoes, Mammies, and Bucks.* New York, 1989.

_____. *Blacks in American Films and Television: An Encyclopedia.* New York, 1988.

Bradford, Sarah E. *Harriet Tubman: The Moses of Her People.* New York, 1961.

Brown, William Wells. *Clotel.* New York, 1989.

Butler, Addie Louise Joyner. *The Distinctive Black College—Talladega, Tuskegee and Morehouse.* Metuchen, N.J., 1977.

Carmichael, Stokely, and Hamilton, Charles V. *Black Power.* New York, 1967.

Christopher, Maurine. *Black Americans in Congress.* New York, 1971.

Clarke, John H. *Malcolm X, The Man and His Times.* Trenton, N.J., 1990.

_____. *Marcus Garvey and the Vision of Africa.* New York, 1974.

Clarke, John H., et al. *Black Titan: W. E. B. Du Bois.* Boston, 1970.

Cone, James H. *Martin and Malcolm and America: A Dream or a Nightmare.* New York, 1991.

Davis, David Brion. *Slavery and Human Progress.* New York, 1984.

Douglass, Frederick. *Life and Times of Frederick Douglass.* New York, 1983.

Foner, Philip S., ed. *The Voice of Black America.* New York, 1972.

_____. *Paul Robeson Speaks.* New York, 1978.

Franklin, John Hope. *Racial Equality in America.* Chicago, 1976.

Hansberry, William Leo. *Africa and Africans as Seen by Classical Writers.* Washington, D.C., 1977.

Hauser, Thomas. *Muhammad Ali: His Life and Times.* New York, 1991.

Hemenway, Robert E. *Zora Neale Hurston: A Literary Biography.* Chicago, 1977.

Higginbotham, A. Leon. *In the Matter of Color: Race and the American Legal Process, the Colonial Period.* New York, 1978.

Inge, M. Thomas, et al. *Black American Writers*, vol. 1. New York, 1978.

Jackson, John G. *Man, God and Civilization.* New York, 1972.

Johnson, Charles. *Middle Passage.* New York, 1990.

Kent, George E. *A Life of Gwendolyn Brooks.* Lexington, Ky., 1989.

King, Martin Luther, Jr. *Why We Can't Wait.* New York, 1964.

————. *Stride Toward Freedom.* New York, 1958.

Lerner, Gerda. *The Majority Finds Its Past, Placing Women in History.* New York, 1979.

Litwack, Leon F. *North of Slavery.* Chicago, 1961.

Logan, Rayford. *The Negro in American Life and Thought: The Nadir, 1877–1901.* New York, 1954.

McClester, Cedric. *Kwanzaa: Everything You Always Wanted to Know But Didn't Know Where to Ask.* New York, 1990.

McNeal, Genna Rae. *Groundwork: Charles Hamilton Houston and the Struggle for Civil Rights.* Philadelphia, 1983.

Mootry, Maria K., and Smith, Gary. *A Life Distilled, Gwendolyn Brooks, Her Poetry and Fiction.* Urbana, 1987.

Nichols, Charles H., ed. *Arna Bontemps, Langston Hughes, Letters 1925–1967.* New York, 1980.

Null, Gary. *Black Hollywood.* New York, 1990.

Ottley, Roi. *The American Negro: His History and Literature.* New York, 1968.

Panassié, Hugues. *Louis Armstrong.* New York, 1971.

Quarles, Benjamin. *Black Abolitionists.* New York, 1991.

Redding, Saunders. *The Lonesome Road.* New York, 1958.

Robinson, Donald L. *Slavery in the Structure of American Politics 1765–1820.* New York, 1971.

Rogers, Joel A. *Africa's Gift to America.* New York, 1961.

Roucek, Joseph S., and Kiernan, Thomas, ed. *The Negro Impact on Western Civilization.* New York, 1970.

Rustin, Bayard. *Down the Line.* Chicago, 1971.

Salley, Columbus, and Behm, Ronald. *What Color Is Your God? Black Consciousness and the Christian Faith.* New York, 1988.

Shaw, Arnold. *Belafonte: An Unauthorized Biography.* Philadelphia, 1960.

Stampp, Kenneth M. *The Peculiar Institution.* New York, 1956.

Southern, Eileen. *The Music of Black Americans: A History.* New York, 1971.

Sullivan, Leon. *Build Brother Build.* Philadelphia, 1969.

Tate, Claudia, ed. *Black Women Writers at Work.* New York, 1983.

Thorpe, Earl E. *Black Historians.* New York, 1971.

Toppin, Edgar A. *A Biographical History of Blacks in America Since 1528.* New York, 1971.

Washington, Booker T., and Du Bois, W. E. B. *The Negro in the South.* New York, 1970.

Washington, Booker T. *Up From Slavery.* New York, 1989.

Weatherby, W. J. *James Baldwin: Artist on Fire.* New York, 1989.

Weiss, Nancy J. *Whitney M. Young, Jr., and the Struggle for Civil Rights.* Princeton, N.J., 1989.

Wells, Ida B. *Crusader for Justice: The Autobiography of Ida B. Wells,* edited by Alfreda M. Duster. Chicago, 1970.

Woodson, Carter G., ed. *Negro Orators and Their Orations.* Washington, D.C., 1925.

Wright, Bruce. *Black Robes, White Justice.* New York, 1990.

Young, A. S. "Doc." *Negro Firsts in Sports.* Chicago, 1963.

PICTURE ACKNOWLEDGMENTS

All photographs and illustrations not otherwise credited below are reprinted with permission of the Schomburg Center for Research in Black Culture, The New York Public Library. The author thanks the following for permission to reprint:

Charles Houston, p. 23: Moorland Spingarn Research Center, Howard University

William M. Trotter, p. 111: William Monroe Trotter Institute, University of Massachusetts at Boston

James Forten, p. 45: The Historical Society of Pennsylvania, 1300 Locust Street, Philadelphia, Pennsylvania, 19107

Title page of Banneker's Almanac, p. 64: The Bettmann Archive

Martin Luther King, Jr., and Malcolm X, p. 93: UPI/Bettmann

Jackie Robinson, p. 156: UPI/Bettman

Jesse Jackson, p. 172: Reuters/Bettmann

Toni Morrison, p. 262: UPI/Bettmann

Lorraine Hansberry, p. 276: UPI/Bettmann

William Gray, p. 301: UPI/Bettmann

Hank Aaron, p. 316: UPI/Bettmann Newsphotos

Oprah Winfrey, p. 324: Photofest

Ron Karenga, p. 328: Karenga Photo

Marian Wright Edelman, p. 339: © Rick Reinhard, 1984, 1910 Park Road, N.W., Washington, D.C. 10010

August Wilson, p. 353: Corbis-Bettmann Archives

Clarence Thomas, p. 357: The Bettmann Archive

Rosa Parks, p. 371: UPI/Bettmann

Arthur Ashe, p. 362: Jeanne Moutoussamy-Ashe

INDEX